TOP ACCOUNTING ISSUES FOR 2011
CPE COURSE

CCH Editorial Staff Publication

Mixed Sources
Product group from well-managed
forests, controlled sources and
recycled wood or fiber
www.fsc.org Cert no. SCS-COC-00648
© 1996 Forest Stewardship Council

.CCH
a Wolters Kluwer business

Contributors

Editor.. Colleen Neuharth McClain, CPA
Contributing Editors.. David Alexander
Simon Archer
Steven C. Fustolo, CPA
Technical Review.. Sharon Brooks, CPA, MBA
Production Coordinator... Susan Haldiman
Production .... Lynn J. Brown
Layout and Design ....Laila Gaidulis

This publication is designed to provide accurate and authoritative information in regard to the subject matter covered. It is sold with the understanding that the publisher is not engaged in rendering legal, accounting, or other professional service. If legal advice or other expert assistance is required, the services of a competent professional person should be sought.

ISBN 978-0-8080-2435-4

Printed in the United States of America

Introduction

CCH's *Top Accounting Issues for 2011 CPE Course* helps CPAs stay abreast of the most significant new accounting standards and important projects. It does so by identifying the events of the past year that have developed into hot issues and reviewing the opportunities and pitfalls presented by these changes. The topics reviewed in this course were selected because of their impact on financial reporting and because of the role they play in understanding the accounting landscape in the year ahead.

Module 1 of this course reviews the authoritative literature on IFRS and is designed to assist accounting practitioners in putting these principles into practice.

Chapter 1 reviews the IASB and the basic authoritative literature of IFRS for preparing financial statements. The IASB's formal objectives are to develop and promote use of "a single set of high quality, understandable and enforceable global accounting standards" to help users of financial information obtain high-quality, transparent information with which to make economic decisions.

This chapter outlines the structure of the IASB and the work it does with national accounting standard-setters, discusses the IFRS framework, and details the elements of financial statements that IFRS requires.

Chapter 2 discusses the requirements for first-time adopters of IFRS. Recognizing that the wholesale adoption of International Standards, by switching from a national GAAP system, raised issues of a great magnitude, the IASB issued IFRS 1, "First-Time Adoption of International Reporting Standards," effective from January 1, 2004.

IFRS 1 has been regularly updated to take account of new standards as they appear. This increasingly created a disorganized standard. Accordingly, IASB completely redesigned and re-sequenced the material in IFRS 1. The new version was issued in November 2008, and became fully effective from July 1, 2009.

Module 2 of the course distills requirements of recent FASB literature into a concise analysis that is designed to assist accounting practitioners in putting these principles into practice.

Chapter 3 covers FAS 167 (now codified as part of FASB ASC Topic 810), which has as its primary goal to improve the application of certain provisions found in FIN 46R, including changes made to the Qualified Special Purpose Entity (QSPE) rules. The chapter discusses what characterizes a VIE, the tests that should be performed to determine whether an entity is a VIE, and other requirements related to VIEs.

Chapter 4 continues the analysis of FAS 167 (FASB ASC Topic 810) and looks at how to identify variable interests in a VIE, how to determine the primary beneficiary, what is required for consolidation, what constitutes a variable interest, and more.

Module 3 of the course distills requirements of recent FASB literature into a concise analysis that is designed to assist accounting practitioners in putting these principles into practice.

Chapter 5 discusses FASB No. 165 (now codified as part of ASC Topic 855), *Subsequent Events,* which strives to put U.S. GAAP more in line with international standards and in particular, IAS 10, *Events after the Reporting Period.*

Chapter 6 explains the changes made as a result of FAS 166 (now codified as ASC Topic 860) related to the accounting for the transfer of financial assets. It covers the background and scope of the statement, as well as the accounting and disclosures required by the statement for transfers of financial assets.

Chapter 7 discusses changes to the source of authoritative U.S. GAAP, the FASB Accounting Standards Codification™ (FASB Codification), which are communicated through an Accounting Standards Update (ASU).

Throughout this course you will find Examples and Observations to illustrate the topics covered and assist you with comprehension of the course material, as well as Study Questions to help you test your knowledge. Answers to the Study Questions, with feedback on both correct and incorrect responses, are provided in a special section beginning on page 219. To assist you in your later reference and research, a detailed topical index has been included for this course, beginning on page 241.

This course is divided into three Modules. Take your time and review each course Module. When you feel confident that you thoroughly understand the material, turn to the CPE Quizzer. Complete one or all Module Quizzers for Continuing Professional Education credit. You can complete and return the Quizzers to CCH for grading at an additional charge. If you receive a grade of 70 percent or higher on the Quizzers, you will receive CPE credit for the Modules graded. Further information is provided in the CPE Quizzer Instructions on page 249.

August 2010

COURSE OBJECTIVES

This course provides an overview of important accounting developments. At the completion of the course, the reader will be able to:

- Outline the objectives of the IASB
- Describe the IFRS Framework
- List the elements of financial statements according to IFRS
- Describe what is included in the definition of IFRS
- Point out the significance of cost in generating an entity's first IFRS financial statements
- List the requirements for an entity's opening IFRS balance sheet
- List the situations in which retrospective application is prohibited by IFRS and in which cases it is optional
- Describe how historical information should be presented under IFRS
- Describe what characterizes a VIE
- Explain the tests, both qualitative and quantitative, that are used to determine whether an entity is a VIE and who should perform those tests
- List the requirements under FIN 46R (now codified as part of FASB ASC Topic 810) that must be satisfied in order for one entity to consolidate an off-balance sheet entity
- State when a VIE should be recharacterized and at what value
- List examples of variable interests
- Determine whether an entity has an interest in a VIE
- Determine who is the primary beneficiary in a VIE
- List the disclosure requirements under FIN 46R (FASB ASC 810)
- Describe the scope, terms, and requirements of ASC Topic 855
- Explain the disclosure requirements of ASC Topic 855
- Describe the scope of FASB 166 (ASC Topic 860)
- List what is required in order for the transfer of a financial asset to be accounted for as a sale
- Identify what constitutes an entire financial asset
- Explain the accounting required for different situations described in ASC Topic 860
- Describe the objectives for the disclosure requirements of ASC Topic 860
- Explain how to determine whether to aggregate disclosures for multiple transfers of financial assets
- Describe the changes made to GAAP due to recently issued ASUs
- List the specific requirements of several selected ASUs in 2009 and 2010

CCH'S PLEDGE TO QUALITY

Thank you for choosing this CCH Continuing Education product. We will continue to produce high quality products that challenge your intellect and give you the best option for your Continuing Education requirements. Should you have a concern about this or any other CCH CPE product, please call our Customer Service Department at 1-800-248-3248.

NEW ONLINE GRADING gives you immediate 24/7 grading with instant results and no Express Grading Fee.

The **CCH Testing Center** website gives you and others in your firm easy, free access to CCH print Courses and allows you to complete your CPE Quizzers online for immediate results. Plus, the **My Courses** feature provides convenient storage for your CPE Course Certificates and completed Quizzers.

Go to **www.cchtestingcenter.com** to complete your Quizzer online.

One **complimentary copy** of this book is provided with certain CCH publications. Additional copies may be ordered for $37.00 each by calling 1-800-248-3248 (ask for product 0-0970-300). Grading fees are additional.

TOP ACCOUNTING ISSUES FOR 2011 CPE COURSE

Contents

MODULE 3: RECENT ASCs AND ASUs

MODULE 1: IFRS — CHAPTER 1

IFRS: Introduction to International Financial Reporting Standards

LEARNING OBJECTIVES

Upon completion of this chapter, the reader will be able to:

- Outline the objectives of the IASB
- Describe the IFRS Framework
- List the elements of financial statements according to IFRS

THE INTERNATIONAL ACCOUNTING STANDARDS BOARD

Introduction

The present International Accounting Standards Board (IASB) is a result of a comprehensive restructuring in 2001 of the former International Accounting Standards Committee (IASC):

> an independent, private sector body, formed in 1973 with the objective of harmonising the accounting principles which are used by businesses and other organisations for financial reporting around the world.

The IASB's formal objectives, as stated in its International Financial Reporting Standards (IFRS), are:

> (a) to develop, in the public interest, a single set of high quality, understandable and enforceable global accounting standards that require high quality, transparent and comparable information in financial statements and other financial reporting to help participants in the various capital markets of the world and other users of the information to make economic decisions;

> (b) to promote the use and rigorous application of those standards; and

> (c) to work actively with national standard-setters to bring about convergence of national accounting standards and IFRSs to high quality solutions.

Thus, the original objective of "harmonising accounting principles" has evolved into the objectives of "develop[ing] . . . a single set of *high quality . . . global accounting standards* . . . to help participants in *capital markets* and others make *decisions*," "promot[ing] the . . . *rigorous application* of those standards" and "bring[ing] about *convergence . . . [toward] high quality solutions.*"

This evolution of its objectives is associated with its collaboration with the International Organization of Securities Commissions since 1995, which led in 2000 to a comprehensive restructuring of the IASC, which took effect in 2001.

The New Structure

Like the FASB in 1972, and the U.K. Accounting Standards Board in 1990, which replaced the APB and the ASC, respectively, the new IASB differs from its predecessor by having a two-tier structure, based on an organ of governance not involved in standard-setting (the Trustees), and a standard-setting Board. According to Clause 3 of the IASC Constitution:

> The governance of IASC shall rest with the Trustees and the Board and such other governing organs as may be appointed by the Trustees or the Board in accordance with the provisions of this Constitution. The Trustees shall use their best endeavors to ensure that the requirements of this Constitution are observed; however, they are empowered to make minor variations [in the Constitution] in the interest of feasibility of operation if such variations are agreed by 75% of all the Trustees.

The new structure is broadly the one proposed in the Strategic Working Party's November 1999 report, "Recommendations on Shaping IASC for the Future." There are 22 Trustees of the IASC Foundation, of whom six should be from North America, six from Europe, six from the Asia/Pacific region, and four from any area, subject to establishing an "overall geographical balance." The new Board differs significantly from its predecessor (the Committee) by having 12 full-time members as well as two part-time members. Moreover, its members are to be chosen for their technical expertise and background experience and (in contrast to the Trustees) not on the basis of geographical representation. The original (2000) constitution contained tightly defined requirements concerning liaison responsibilities with national standard-setters and also as regards the professional backgrounds of the membership. These have now been relaxed (from 2005). Liaison with "national standard setters and other official bodies concerned with standard-setting" is to be maintained, and the IASB membership should provide "an appropriate mix of recent practical experience among auditors, preparers, users and academics" (Constitution, clauses 22 and 21). Each member has one vote and most decisions are to be made by a simple majority of members attending in person or by a telecommunications link, with a quorum being such attendance by "at least 60% of the members" and the Chairman having a casting vote. The publication of an exposure draft, final IFRS, or final interpretation of the IFRIC, which replaced the Standing Interpretations Committee (SIC), requires approval by at least nine members of the Board. This change to majority voting is significant, as the old IASC required a 75 percent majority.

Trustees

The trustees consist of 20 individuals with diverse geographic and functional backgrounds. Trustees will:
- Appoint the Members of the Board, the Standing Interpretations Committee, and the Standards Advisory Council
  - Monitor IASB's effectiveness
  - Raise its funds
  - Approve IASB's budget
- Have responsibility for constitutional change

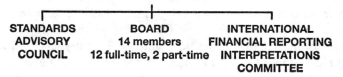

| | STANDARDS ADVISORY COUNCIL | BOARD 14 members 12 full-time, 2 part-time | INTERNATIONAL FINANCIAL REPORTING INTERPRETATIONS COMMITTEE |

The first Chairman of the IASC Foundation Trustees was Paul A. Volcker, former Chairman of the U.S. Federal Reserve Board. The first Chairman of the new Board was Sir David Tweedie, who moved from being Chairman of the U.K. Accounting Standards Board and was formerly U.K. technical partner for KPMG, after an academic career in Scotland.

The International Financial Reporting Interpretations Committee (IFRIC) has a role similar to that of its predecessor, the SIC. The IFRIC has 12 voting members and a non-voting Chairman, all appointed by the Trustees. An interpretation is approved if no more than three members have voted against it after considering public comments on the draft interpretation.

The Standards Advisory Council, with about 40 members, provides a forum for participation by organizations and individuals with an interest in international financial reporting and having diverse geographic and functional backgrounds, with the objective of giving advice to the Board on agenda decisions and priorities, informing the Board of the view of members of the Council on major standard-setting projects, and giving other advice to the Board or the Trustees. The Chairman of the Standards Advisory Council, from 2005, is appointed by the Trustees and is not to be a member of the IASB or a member of its staff. He or she is invited to attend and participate in the Trustees' meetings.

Despite the complicated appointments procedures, the original membership of the Board was widely felt to be excessively "Anglo-Saxon" in its orientation and, in particular, lacking in representation from developing and emerging economies, where the determination of fair value by reference to market prices, among other things required by IASB GAAP, may be particularly problematic. The Standards Advisory Council may have been designed to allow at least some input from such other directions. The IASB is in the process of revising both constitution and membership. The number of members is being raised to 16, and the proportion of "Anglo-Saxon" membership of the Board is being reduced.

The Current Positions

In the report of the Strategic Working Party, "Recommendations on Shaping IASC for the Future" it was stated that:

> The primary attributes [considered desirable to establish the legitimacy of a standard setting organization] identified were the representativeness of the decision making body, the independence of its members, and technical expertise. . . . The proposed structure . . . provides a balanced approach to legitimacy based upon representativeness among members of the Trustees, the Standing Interpretations Committee (SIC), and the Standards Advisory Council, and technical competence and independence among Board Members.

The restructured IASB is undoubtedly much better equipped than its predecessor in these respects, as well as being far better resourced. Yet, the key to the IASB's future as a global accounting standard-setter will be the acceptance of its standards for cross-border listings by securities markets worldwide, by all members of IOSCO, *including the SEC for foreign registrants in the United States,* without the need for reconciliations to national GAAP. One of the watchwords of the IASB is *convergence.* This is a two-way process: national sets of accounting standards are to converge toward one another, with IFRSs as the points of convergence, but IFRSs are also expected to converge toward certain national standards in some cases where the latter are recognized as conceptually or technically superior to existing IASs. On certain particularly important and difficult matters, such as financial instruments, the IASB may look, as it has done in the past, to joint working parties composed of experts from countries such as Australia/New Zealand, Canada, the United Kingdom, and the United States, who with the former IASC formed the so-called G4+1.

The SEC's decision, announced in November 2007, not to require foreign registrants that comply with all applicable IFRSs to file reconciliations to U.S. GAAP is a most important milestone for the IASB.

Of major significance also was the decision of the European Commission to make compliance with IASB GAAP mandatory by 2005 for the consolidated financial statements of all corporations listed on stock exchanges in the EU. In its communication dated June 2000, the Commission set out this policy, but also referred to the need for an "endorsement mechanism" at EU level, "because it would not delegate accounting standard setting unconditionally and irrevocably to a private organization [the IASB] over which the EU has no influence . . . [and] it is important to create legal certainty by identifying the standards which listed companies will have to apply in the future. . . . Because the endorsement mechanism will have an important pro-active role, it can be expected that the new standards adopted by [IASB] will also be acceptable in an EU environment." The reference to "an important pro-active role" suggests an intention to influence the "convergence process" in a "European" direction, as a counterweight to other influences, particularly from the United States and the other countries whose accounting standard-setters made up, with the IASC, the now defunct G4+1 (Australia/New Zealand, Canada, and the U.K.).

As well as pressure from the U.S., therefore, the IASB has to contend with this endorsement mechanism set up by the European Commission. In this connection, a new private sector body, the European Financial Reporting Advisory Group (EFRAG), has been set up, and EFRAG has formed a Technical Expert Group (TEG) to advise the European Commission on the appropriateness of IASB standards for use in the EU. The TEG is composed of representatives from the accounting profession, financial analysts, stock exchange regulators, accounting standard-setters and financial statement preparers. The final component of the endorsement mechanism is the Accounting Regulatory Committee (ARC), which makes the final decision on whether to endorse IASB standards for use in the EU. The ARC is composed of government representatives from all of the EU member states and chaired by a representative of the EC; in other words, it has a political character.

When the endorsement mechanism was first set up, the issue arose of whether it would serve merely to satisfy the considerable body of legal opinion in the EU that does not accept the legitimacy of private sector standard-setting and therefore content itself with performing a purely formal legitimization role, or whether it would seek actively to influence IASB standards and thus provide a forum for lobbying intended to influence them. The experience of the endorsement in November 2004 of the standards existing at that date throws some light on this issue. All of those standards were endorsed, with the exception of IAS 39, "Financial Instruments: Recognition and Measurement," which received only partial endorsement, largely as a result of lobbying by banks in four EU member states: Belgium, France, Germany, and Italy.

In fact, 95 percent of the text of IAS 39 was endorsed, but there were two significant "carve-outs" involving a number of paragraphs dealing with:

- The "fair-value option" insofar as it permits the designation of any financial liability as "at fair value through profit and loss"
- Certain restrictions in hedge accounting on portfolio hedges of interest rate risk (e.g., the prohibition of designating a non-derivative financial asset or liability as a hedging item for interest rate risk)

Without the first carve-out, the second would have been superfluous, since items accounted for at fair value can act as hedges or hedged items without any need for being so designated, thus making hedge accounting unnecessary. The first carve-out, regarding the fair value option, has now been reversed ("carved back in"). The original fair value option was revised by the IASB, and this revised version was fully endorsed by the EU mechanism, with its application backdated to January 1, 2005. The second carve-out, though of less significance for the reason noted, still remains. It would seem that legalistic objections to the fair-value option (on the grounds that it contravenes the prohibition in the EC Fourth Directive of the recognition of unrealized gains), were overcome by use of the "true and fair override" contained in the Directive.

This experience with IAS 39 both indicates that the operation of the endorsement mechanism can influence the IASB's standard-setting process (the amendments to the fair-value option being a case in point) and suggests that lobbying of the ARC will be part of the picture. It has to be said, however, that IAS 39 has been a particularly controversial standard with respect to its requirements on hedges and hedge accounting. Some future standards may also be controversial.

The endorsement process and, in particular, the phase that consists of approval by the European Parliament, can have the effect of delaying the implementation of an IFRS or an amendment for what appear to be purely "bureaucratic" reasons. Thus, while both the EFRAG and the ARC approved IFRS 8, "Operating Segments" (issued in November 2006), the IFRS did not receive final endorsement until November 2007 (with the effect that the right to early adoption of the IFRS by EU reporting entities was effectively removed). There are other examples. As the majority of the reporting entities expected to apply IFRSs are domiciled in the EU, these bureaucratic (or political) delays can be tiresome. However, they may turn out to be a price that is worth paying, insofar as the EFRAG brings to bear on the IASB's way of thinking, a well-informed and friendly but critical view, notably on such topics as "fair value measurement" (see, for example, the EFRAG's Comment Letter, dated May 29, 2007, on the IASB's November 2006 Discussion Paper, "Fair Value Measurements").

Nevertheless, there are tensions that result from the fact that the IASB's close cooperation with the FASB in the "convergence program" is quite understandably perceived in the EU to be at the expense of the EU "voice" at the critical stages of the development of a new IFRS or a major revision of an existing one. The EFRAG has a formal say only when a new or revised IFRS is published; and, although it is kept informed of the development of the work, it does not have the same involvement as that of the FASB. During 2008 and 2009 these tensions were manifested in increasing "anti-IASB" feelings in parts of Europe, noticeably France, and a number of highly critical comments were expressed in the European Parliament (which, compared with national parliaments, has little, but gradually increasing, power).

The banking and credit crisis during 2008–2009 has also impacted the work of the IASB, which had to be seen as "doing something" in the face of the crisis. The IASB issued a press release in September 2008 to announce "a range of projects that collectively address issues highlighted by the current dislocation in credit markets." This has opened the door to direct political interference in the IASB standard-setting process, especially regarding IAS 39 and the use of fair values, resulting in the accelerated issuance of Exposure Drafts "Derecognition" in April 2009 and "Fair Value Measurement" in May 2009, mirroring similar political interference in the work of the SEC/FASB in the United States. Moreover, in July 2009, in response to recommendations from the G20 leaders that the IASB should "take action by the end of 2009 to improve and simplify the accounting requirements for financial instruments," the IASB issued a further exposure draft, "Financial Instruments: Classification and Measurement," containing proposals that "would necessitate extensive consequential amendments to IAS 39 and other IFRS and to the guidance on those IFRS." The IASB has been planning for some time to replace IAS 39 by a new IFRS, but following the G20 recommendations the intent is to gain time by doing this in three phases, the first of which is represented by the July 2009 exposure draft. (The quotation marks above indicate text from the Introduction to the ED.) Other forces have called strongly for the technical independence of the IASB to be preserved and respected. Conflicting demands seem to be at work.

Likely Future Developments

As discussed above, from January 1, 2005, approximately 7,000 European listed companies were required to use full IASB GAAP in their consolidated financial statements. This now includes 12 member countries largely from Eastern Europe who joined the European Union in 2004-2007 and whose accountants and regulators generally lack experience in operating within a capitalist context.

It is crucial that everyone involved, whether in Europe or in any other relevant countries, such as Australia, is aware of the exact regulations that they are supposed to be trying to follow. In other words, a period of stability regarding the detailed content of IASB GAAP is extremely important. This has created a major problem for the IASB, which both wishes and needs to make many changes to the standards it inherited, if true global convergence around IASB GAAP is to be achievable. The approach it has adopted is to attempt to divide its work into two parts.

Thus, the Board made many changes through the end of 2004, mostly effective from January 1, 2005, and a number of further important changes as part of the "convergence process" in 2007–2008, to be effective from either January 1 or July 1, 2009.

However, two more general issues are worthy of mention. The first, although the timing is unclear, is the project on reporting financial performance. The original essence of this initiative was to replace the income statement with, to use the full jargon, a layered matrix structure. Information would be presented vertically analyzed (layered) under various subheadings as well as horizontally so as to separate out the effects of remeasurements (as opposed to transactions). An idea of this proposal, though not the precise final detail, is given in Table 1.1.

Table 1.1: The Possible Format for Presenting Information under the Reporting Financial Performance Project

		Total	Profit Before Remeasurements	Remeasurements
Business	Revenue	500	Revenue	-
	Cost of sales	(200)	Materials, labour etc	Inventory impairments
	Selling, general, admin expenses	(125)	Depreciation/amortisation Rental/other income	PPE/intangible impairment
			Provision – initial recognition Service cost	Provision – remeasurement Change in pension obligation cash flow assumptions
	Operating Profit	175		
	Disposal gain/loss	50	-	Disposal gain/loss
	PPE revaluation	75	-	PPE revaluation
	Goodwill	(50)	Negative goodwill	Goodwill impairment
	FX gain/loss on net investment	(25)	-	FX gain/loss on net investment
	Investment property		-	Investment property fair value change
	Other Business Profit	50		
	Income from associates	25	Income from associates	-
	Write-down of accounts receivable	(5)	-	Write-down of accounts receivable
	Equity investments	(30)	-	Return on equity investments
	Debt investments	10	Interest income	Fair value changes on debt investments
	Pension plan assets	(75)		Return on pension plan assets
	Financial Income	(75)		
	Business Profit	150		
Financing	Interest on liabilities	(40)	Interest expenses	Change in provision discount rate
	Pension financing expenses	(60)	Unwinding of discount rate	Change in pension obligation discount rate
	Financing expense	(100)		
Tax		(15)	-	-
Discontinuing activities		(5)	Net discontinuing	Net discontinuing
Cash flow hedges		25	-	Fair value changes in cash flow hedging instruments
	Profit	55		

It can easily be seen from Table 1.1 that this new type of analyzed combined statement would be ideally suited to allow transparent reporting of the effects of unrealized revaluation changes (i.e., of remeasurements at fair value). The illustration shows operating profit by function in the total column. Each of the desegregation columns illustrates

- The columns within which various components of expense would be presented
- That related items should be presented on the same line (e.g., depreciation and impairment.)

The use of "-" indicates a blank cell; for example, the tax charge is not required to be disaggregated between the columns.

The omission of a total at the bottom of the "Profit Before Remeasurements" column is deliberate. It contains the "realized" items and roughly corresponds to the current income statement. Because *all* the items are included in "Total Profit" for the year of their occurrence, the question of possible recycling automatically disappears. Such a format as illustrated here is thus ideally suited to embrace an increasing emphasis on the use of fair value accounting. At one stage, it looked as though some proposal vaguely on the lines described above would emerge fairly quickly. However, there is clearly some rethinking, and perhaps more fundamental criticism, at work. For more information, check out the IASB web site: **http://www.iasb.org.**

In September 2007, the IASB issued another revision to IAS 1, "Presentation of Financial Statements," mandatory from January 1, 2009. The major development is a significant expansion of the requirements for performance reporting (as opposed to a statement of position). Titles of several required statements have also been changed, though IAS 1 explicitly accepts that the previous, or indeed other, titles may be used. IAS 1 now requires:

- A statement of financial position as at the end of the period
- A statement of comprehensive income for the period (The components of profit or loss may be presented as a separate statement, or as part of this single statement of comprehensive income.)
- A statement of changes in equity for the period
- A statement of cash flows
- Notes
- An opening statement of financial position as at the *beginning* of the earliest comparative period presented

The effect of these changes, while not as radical as the proposals of Table 1.1, is to force a visible and transparent presentation of *all* changes in equity over the reporting period.

Other general issues that are being discussed more seriously concern the question of an increasing adoption of fair values. Much of the discussion is at a theoretical stage, and practical outcomes are hard to predict. Suffice to suggest here that:

- The IASB is broadly in favor of an extension of fair value usage
- Many preparers and regulators in a number of countries are much more cautious
- Use of the concept and practicalities of measurement are not yet effectively thought through

This is a very interesting and important time for the IASB. The outcome in terms of whether or not it achieves its "single set . . . of enforceable global accounting standards" is still unclear. In the short term, as explained above, it had to focus extensively on the 2005 deadline agreed to with the EU. Consequently, it had to divide a number of its projects into two parts, generally termed Phase 1 and Phase 2. Good examples are the revision of the Business Combinations requirements and accounting for Insurance Contracts. A number of changes had been made and were IASB GAAP requirements from January 1, 2005 (Phase 1). However, further significant developments took place in 2007-2008 or are firmly in development (Phase 2), and this split has sometimes led to obscurities and oddities in the interregnum.

A further issue still not entirely resolved concerns the level of detail that should be included in financial reporting standards. Convergence is being attempted, inter alia, between the U.S. system, which has become highly detailed and prescriptive in recent years, and the old IASC tradition of a more principles-based approach. The latest new IASB standards do seem to be significantly imbued with a sense that a considerable level of detailed regulation, and sometimes more explicit guidance, is necessary. This is especially true where convergence toward existing U.S. regulation is being pursued. Nevertheless, it is unclear that such a level of prescription will lead to more effective operationalization of the letter *and spirit* of IASB GAAP.

The IASB, partly in its own right, and also as part of its ongoing convergence project with the FASB, has a large number of projects that are continuing to lead to amendments, often significant ones, to existing Standard requirements. Experience suggests that indications regarding the direction of these changes cannot reliably be assumed to be retained through to the eventual formalization of new Standard requirements. Accordingly, it would be unhelpful to provide much detail, which may be erroneous and therefore confusing. It is worth pointing out that the IASB and the FASB are on record as intending complete convergence by 2014.

A final point much heard in Europe, perhaps partly related to the issue discussed in the previous paragraph, is that, at least in the short term, most users of IASB GAAP will be based in Europe, whilst a major influence on the contents of IASB GAAP is coming from the United States. Full U.S. acceptance of IASB GAAP without the need for an additional reconciliation to U.S. GAAP would remove the basis for such concerns. So far, a condition for such full acceptance by the SEC has been full convergence—a worthy objective, but not achievable in the short term.

On May 3, 2007, Conrad Hewitt, Chief Accountant of the Securities and Exchange Commission (SEC), gave a speech in which he made the following significant statements:

> The Commission anticipates issuing a Proposing Release [in] summer [2008] that will request comments on proposed changes to the Commission's rules which would allow the use of IFRS in financial reports filed by foreign private issuers that are registered with the Commission. In addition, the Commission plans a Concept Release relating to issues surrounding the possibility of treating U.S. and foreign issuers similarly in this respect by also providing U.S. issuers the alternative to use IFRS.

There is, of course, no firm commitment in these statements. Moreover, it is possible that with regard to the "quality of compliance" with IFRSs, the SEC will be more stringent in its requirements than the national regulators of some foreign issuers that use IFRSs. If so, such foreign issuers will have to satisfy the SEC's criteria in order to be treated "similarly to U.S. issuers." But, perhaps at last there are signs of a move toward real flexibility and compromise that will be revealed in time.

On the other hand, the dangers of political interference seem to be increasing. As already indicated, political attacks on the IASB from within Europe have increased in intensity, and indeed have directly caused changes in requirements. In the United States the new chairman of the SEC, Mary Schapiro, told Congress in February 2009, in relation to the proposal to produce common IASB and FASB standards by 2014, that the SEC could not work with a standard-setter that was subject to political interference. Irony of ironies, in March 2009 the SEC and FASB were forced by Congress to change U.S. GAAP on financial instruments in three weeks with, in the words of a respected commentator, "only the merest fig-leaf of due process" ! Multiple political interference is a sure way to destroy the effectiveness of global standards.

STUDY QUESTIONS

1. The IASB was created to replace which of the following?
   a. Financial Accounting Standards Board
   b. Standing Interpretations Committee
   c. International Accounting Standards Committee

2. Which of the following is an objective of the IASB?

   a. To develop American accounting standards that benefit auditors

   b. To converge other national accounting standards and IFRS

   c. To prevent the transparency of financial reporting

3. The members of the IASB Board are selected on the basis of geographical representation. *True or False?*

4. Where are the majority of the users of IASB GAAP located?

   a. Asia

   b. Europe

   c. North America

5. The IASB is very interested in eliminating the use of fair value measurement. *True or False?*

FRAMEWORK FOR THE PREPARATION AND PRESENTATION OF FINANCIAL STATEMENTS

Overview

The IASB's Framework belongs to the family of conceptual frameworks for financial reporting that has been developed by accounting standard-setters in a number of countries where accounting standard-setting is carried out by a private sector body. On one level, such conceptual frameworks may be considered attempts to assemble a body of accounting theory (or inter-related concepts) as a guide to standard-setting, so that standards are (as far as possible) formulated on a consistent basis and not in an *ad hoc* manner. On another but complementary level, they may be thought of as devices to confer legitimacy and authority on a private sector standard-setter that lacks the legal authority of a public body. The IASC, as a private sector standard-setter, shared these reasons for developing a conceptual framework.

Conceptual frameworks developed by accounting standard-setters are essentially based on identification of "good practice" from which principles are derived inductively. The criteria for identifying "good practice" are related to the assumed objectives of financial reporting. At the same time, attention is paid to conceptual coherence, and the development process typically involves "conceptual tidying up." Conceptual frameworks may be written in a prescriptive style or a descriptive style, or a mixture of the two. Whatever the style, they are essentially *normative,* since they seek to provide a set of principles as a guide to setting and interpreting accounting standards. Such guidance, however, does not necessarily preclude a standard being issued that, for compelling pragmatic reasons, departs from a principle set out in the applicable conceptual framework.

The IASB's Framework is written in a descriptive style (in fact, it is IASB policy to use the word "should" only in standards) and seeks to avoid being excessively prescriptive. A principal reason for this is that it needs to have broad international applicability. In the final paragraph of the Framework, the then IASC stated:

> This Framework is applicable to a range of accounting models and provides guidance on preparing and presenting the financial statements constructed under the chosen model. At the present time [1989], it is not the intention of the Board of IASC to prescribe a particular model other than in exceptional circumstances, such as . . . a hyperinflationary economy.

In common with other conceptual frameworks, notably the FASB's set of Statements of Financial Accounting Concepts, the IASB's Framework covers the following topics:

- **Objective of financial statements.** The Framework takes the position that, because investors are providers of risk capital to an entity, financial statements that meet investors' needs will also meet most of the needs of other users that financial statements can satisfy. On that basis, the objective of financial statements is to provide information about the financial position, performance, and changes in financial position of an entity that is useful to a wide range of users in making economic decisions, including assessment of the stewardship or accountability of management. The Framework states as "underlying assumptions" that, in order to meet their objectives, financial statements are prepared on the accrual basis of accounting and (normally) on the "going concern" basis.
- **Qualitative characteristics of financial statement information.** The Framework cites four main qualitative characteristics: understandability, relevance, reliability, and comparability. Materiality is mentioned as an aspect of relevance. "Faithful representation," "substance over form," "neutrality" (freedom from bias), "prudence" (subject to neutrality), and "completeness" (within the bounds of materiality and cost) are mentioned as aspects of reliability. The Framework does not deal directly with the concepts of "true and fair view" (TFV) or "fair presentation" (FP), but states that "the application of the principal qualitative characteristics and of appropriate accounting standards normally results in financial statements that convey what is generally understood as [a TFV or FP] of such information." However, IAS 1, "Presentation of Financial Statements," as revised in 1997, states fair presentation as a requirement (see below).

- **Elements of financial statements.** The Framework relates the elements to the measurement of financial position and performance. As elements of financial position, it provides definitions of assets, liabilities, and equity; and as elements of performance, it defines income (including revenue and gains) and expenses (including losses). The definitions given in the section on elements, and especially those of assets and liabilities, are the core of the Framework as a prescriptive basis for standard-setting.
- **Principles for recognition of the elements.** The Framework states that recognition is the process of recording in the financial statements (subject to materiality) an item that meets the definition of an element and satisfies the two criteria for recognition, namely, (a) it is *probable* that any future economic benefit associated with the item will flow to or from the entity; and (b) the item has a cost or value that can be measured with reliability. Assessments of the degree of probability of the flow of future economic benefits "are made when the financial statements are prepared."
- **Bases for measurement of the elements.** Unlike the section in which the elements of financial statements are defined, the treatment of measurement in the IASC's Framework avoids being prescriptive. It cites a number of different measurement bases and notes that the basis most commonly adopted is historical cost, usually combined with other bases.

The Framework also covers another topic, which is not necessarily dealt with specifically in other conceptual frameworks:

- **Concepts of capital and capital maintenance.** The treatment of capital maintenance in the Framework also avoids being prescriptive. It distinguishes between (a) *financial* capital maintenance, in two forms, nominal (i.e., monetary units) or real (units of constant purchasing power) and (b) *physical* capital maintenance or operating capability. It states that the physical capital maintenance concept requires the use of a particular measurement basis, namely current cost, whereas neither form of the financial capital maintenance concept requires any particular measurement basis. It also states the implications of each concept of capital maintenance for profit measurement.

The IASB's Framework is a succinct document of 36 pages. It is thus much briefer than the FASB's set of six "Statements of Accounting Concepts," each one of which is longer than the Framework. It is also shorter than the U.K. ASB's "Statement of Principles," which runs to some 130 pages. Succinctness is possible because of the limits that the then IASC placed on its prescriptive aims. The IASC also benefited from the trailblazing work of the FASB, thanks to which most of the issues dealt with in the Framework had already been publicized.

The IASB and FASB are jointly developing a common conceptual framework as part of the process of convergence between the two sets of GAAP. This project is divided into eight phases, A to H, as follows:

A. Objectives and qualitative characteristics
B. Elements, recognition, and measurement
C. Measurement
D. Reporting entity
E. Presentation and disclosure
F. Purpose and status
G. Application to not-for-profit entities
H. Finalization

Purpose and status. The Framework does not have the status of an IAS, does not override any specific IAS, and in case of conflict between the Framework and an IAS, the latter prevails (pars. 2–3). The purpose of the Framework is stated as follows (par. 1):

1. To assist the Board of IASC in the development of future IASs and in its review of existing IASs

2. To assist the Board of IASC in promoting harmonization of regulations, accounting standards and procedures relating to the presentation of financial statements by providing a basis for reducing the number of alternative accounting treatments permitted by IASs

3. To assist national standard-setting bodies in developing national standards

4. to assist preparers of financial statements in applying IASs and in dealing with topics that have yet to form the subject of an IAS

5. To assist auditors in forming an opinion as to whether financial statements conform with IASs

6. To assist users of financial statements in interpreting the information contained in financial statements prepared in conformity with IASs

7. To provide those who are interested in the work of the IASC with information about its approach to the formulation of accounting standards

Scope. Paragraph 5 of the Framework mentions the following as constituting its scope:
- Objectives of financial statements
- Qualitative characteristics that determine the usefulness of financial statement information
- Definition, recognition, and measurement of financial statement elements
- Concepts of capital and capital maintenance

The Framework is concerned with "general purpose financial statements," including consolidated financial statements. These are described as being prepared and presented at least annually and being directed toward the common information needs of a wide range of users. They do not include special purpose reports such as prospectuses and tax computations (par. 6).

The term *financial statements* is understood as comprising a balance sheet, an income statement, a statement of changes in financial position, and those notes and other statements and explanatory material that are an integral part of the financial statements. Supplementary schedules and information derived from, and expected to be read with, financial statements may also be included. Examples include segment reporting and information about the effects of changing prices. However, financial statements do not include such items as directors' reports, chairman's statements, management reports, and similar material that may be included in a financial or annual report (par. 7).

The Framework applies to the financial statements of all commercial, industrial, and business reporting entities, whether in the private or the public sectors (par. 8).

> **OBSERVATION**
>
> The wording of paragraph 7 reads oddly in parts. The reference to the statement of changes in financial position states that this "may be presented in a variety of ways, for example as a statement of cash flows or a statement of funds flows." However, IAS 7 (revised in 1992) clearly requires a statement of cash flows. Likewise, it is stated that financial statements "*may . . . include supplementary . . . information [such as] . . . financial information about industrial and geographical segments.*" Yet IAS 14 , originally issued in 1981, *requires* such information. Hence, these apparent discrepancies are only partly the result of the Framework not having been revised. It seems that paragraph 7 does not set out fully to reflect the implications of IASs as to what should be considered as making up "financial statements."

Users and Their Information Needs, the Objective of Financial Statements, and Underlying Assumptions

Users and their information needs. The Framework (par. 9) cites seven categories of "users" of financial statements, with comments on their needs. The seven categories are

- Investors
- Employees
- Lenders
- Suppliers and other trade creditors
- Customers
- Governments and their agencies
- The public.

The Framework argues that there are needs for financial statement information that are common to all users, and that, because investors are providers of risk capital to the entity, financial statements that meet their needs will also meet "most of the needs of other users that financial statements can satisfy" (par. 10).

OBSERVATION

This argument to the effect that, as investors provide risk capital, basing financial statements on their needs will satisfy (as far as is practicable) most of the needs of other users, is not obviously correct and begs some questions that are not addressed in the Framework. The FASB employed similar but not identical wording in SFAC 1 , referring to "investors and creditors" rather than just "investors." The FASB stated in support of its position that the information needs (or, at least, the decision models) of investors and creditors are reasonably well known, and better known than those of such other groups as customers and employees.

Objective of financial statements. The Framework states that the objective of financial statements is to provide information about the *financial position, performance,* and *changes in financial position* of an enterprise that is useful to a wide range of users in making economic decisions. It is acknowledged that financial statements do not provide all the information that users may need to make economic decisions, since they are largely oriented toward the *financial* effects of *past* events (pars. 12–13). Paragraph 14 mentions the use of financial statements for assessing the stewardship or accountability of management but sees such assessments as included within economic decisions.

Paragraphs 15–18 provide conventional explanations of the ways in which information about financial position, performance, and changes in financial position is useful. Information about financial position is primarily provided in a balance sheet, information about performance is primarily provided in an income statement, while information about changes in financial position is provided "by means of a separate statement" (par. 19). (As noted above, the Framework does not take a position as to what type of statement of changes in financial position is required.) Paragraph 20 draws attention to the interrelationships and complementarities of the three categories of financial statement, while paragraph 21 mentions notes and supplementary schedules as being part of the financial statements.

Underlying assumptions. Paragraphs 22 and 23 discuss the underlying assumptions of the "accrual basis" and "going concern." Paragraph 22 presents conventional arguments as to why financial statements prepared on the accrual basis (rather than on a cash basis) "provide the type of information about past transactions and other events that is most useful to users in making economic decisions." If the going concern assumption cannot be applied because "the enterprise has . . . an intention or need . . . to liquidate or curtail materially the scale of its operations, the financial statements may have to be prepared on a different basis and, if so, the basis used is disclosed" (par. 23).

Qualitative Characteristics of Financial Statements

The Framework (pars. 24–39) cites four main qualitative characteristics, understandability, relevance, reliability, and comparability. Materiality is mentioned as an aspect of relevance. "Faithful representation," "substance over form," "neutrality" (freedom from bias), "prudence" (subject to neutrality), and "completeness" (within the bounds of materiality and cost) are mentioned as aspects of reliability.

The subject of *understandability* is a difficult one, because of the notorious complexity of the financial statements of large multinational groups and of the accounting rules underlying them. The Framework states that "users are assumed to have a reasonable knowledge of business and economic activities, and accounting, and a willingness to study the information with reasonable diligence." Information about complex matters that is relevant should not be excluded just because it may be too difficult for some users to understand (par. 25). In this sense, relevance is more important than understandability.

On the subject of *relevance and materiality*, the Framework points out that in some cases the nature of an item of information is sufficient to determine its relevance, irrespective of materiality in the quantitative sense.

EXAMPLE

There is a pending lawsuit from which the possible financial penalties are not of material size but which might lead to significant reputational damage and its commercial consequences. For this reason, such a pending lawsuit should be mentioned in a note, since it is relevant to users' economic decisions about the entity.

More generally, the Framework states that "information is material if its omission or misstatement could influence the economic decisions of users taken on the basis of the financial statements . . . the size of the item or error [being] judged in the particular circumstances of its omission or misstatement" (par. 30). Thus, the key characteristic is relevance, and materiality should be interpreted as a guide to relevance, since it is relevant to users' economic decisions about the entity.

The Framework presents *faithful representation* as a necessary condition of reliability, and *"substance over form"* as a necessary condition of faithful representation. There is a risk that financial information may be "less than a faithful representation of that which it seeks to portray . . . not due to bias, but rather to inherent difficulties either in identifying the transaction and other events to be measured or in devising and applying [appropriate] measurement and presentation techniques." This type of difficulty is given as a reason why internally generated goodwill is not recognized (par. 34).

Neutrality is also presented as a necessary condition of reliability. The well-known tension between neutrality (or freedom from bias) and *prudence* is considered in paragraphs 36 and 37. Financial statements are not neutral if, by the selection and presentation of information, they influence the making of a decision or judgment in order to achieve a predetermined outcome. Prudence is "the inclusion of a degree of caution in the exercise of judgments needed in making the estimates required under conditions of uncertainty, such that assets or income are not overstated and liabilities or expenses are not understated." But the exercise of prudence, as defined in the Framework, does not permit, for example, the creation of hidden reserves or excessive provisions, the deliberate understatement of assets or income, or the deliberate overstatement of liabilities or expenses, because this would fail to meet the requirement for neutrality and hence that for reliability.

> **OBSERVATION**
>
> In fact, it is not obvious that neutrality or freedom from bias *as such* is a necessary condition of reliability, provided the bias is *known* to the user. Neutrality, as defined in the Framework, means the absence of the kind of bias that, by the selection or presentation of information, influences decisions or judgments in order to achieve a predetermined outcome (as in "creative accounting"). Hence, biases the effects of which can be reasonably assumed to be known to the user because they are part of IASB GAAP, such as the "prudently" asymmetric treatment of certain unrealized gains (unrecognized) and unrealized losses (recognized), do not imply lack of neutrality in the sense of the Framework.
>
> It should be noted, however, that in its last set of standards the IASC has shifted the balance between neutrality and prudence in favor of the former. It has done this by promoting both measurement on the basis of "fair values" and the recognition in income of the resultant unrealized gains and losses from remeasurement. An example is IAS 39, "Financial Instruments: Recognition and Measurement " . The result has been a substantial reduction in the extent of the asymmetric treatment of unrealized gains and losses in IASB GAAP.

Completeness (within the bounds of materiality and cost) is a necessary condition of reliability, since "an omission can cause information to be false or misleading and thus unreliable" (par. 38).

> **OBSERVATION**
>
> The Framework does not make it clear how a trade-off between completeness and cost would be made, in the case of an omission that would cause the information to be unreliable. Some guidance on this matter is given in the disclosure requirements of individual IASs, which are fairly detailed.

Comparability of financial statements, both over time and cross-sectionally, is important to users. Comparability over time is needed in order to identify trends in an entity's financial position and performance. Cross-sectional comparability is necessary so that the financial statements of different entities may be used to evaluate their relative financial positions, performances, and changes in financial position (pars. 39–42).

Comparability requires consistency in the measurement and disclosure of the financial effects of similar transactions and other events. One important implication is that users need to be informed of the entity's accounting policies, of any changes in these, and of the effects of such changes. However, comparability over time should not be given precedence over the introduction of improvements in financial reporting (pars. 40–41). On the other hand,

comparability over time makes the provision of corresponding prior-p
information important (par. 42).

There are trade-offs to be made between timeliness and reliability, bε
efits and costs, and between different qualitative characteristics. There i
moreover, a need for professional judgment in making such trade-offs, given
that "the overriding consideration is how best to meet . . . the objective of
financial statements, . . . [that is,] to satisfy the economic decision-making
needs of users" (pars. 43–45).

OBSERVATION

In commenting on the trade-off between benefits and costs, the Framework (par. 44) states that "the costs do not necessarily fall on those users who enjoy the benefits. Benefits may also be enjoyed by users other than those for whom the information is prepared." The latter sentence refers to the so-called "free rider" problem, but the formulation in the Framework seems to assume that the costs would be expected to be borne by those users for whom the information is prepared. In fact, costs are more usually considered to be borne by *preparers* of financial statements, whom the Framework seems to have left out of the equation. "Preparers," in this sense, are the entity's management and the common shareholders whom they represent, and it is the shareholders who effectively bear the costs.

There might seem to be a tacit assumption in the Framework that the users for whom the information is prepared can be identified with the preparers; in other words, those for whom the information is prepared (investors) are those on whose behalf management acts in preparing financial statements, and who end up bearing the cost. This identification would restrict the intended beneficiaries of the information to equity investors (common shareholders), to the exclusion of other investors.

However, the Framework gives as an example "the provision of further information to lenders [which] may reduce the borrowing costs of an enterprise." Yet, in that case, the lenders would not bear the cost of preparing such further information; it would be borne by the common shareholders (who would also benefit from the reduction in borrowing costs). One is forced to conclude that the comments on this issue in the Framework are somewhat confused.

The Framework does not deal directly with the concepts of "true and fair view" (TFV) or "fair presentation" (FP), but states that "the application of the principal qualitative characteristics and of appropriate accounting standards normally results in financial statements that convey what is generally understood as [a TFV or FP] of such information" (par. 46). As noted above, however, IAS 1, "Presentation of Financial Statements ," as revised in 1997, states fair presentation as a requirement.

STUDY QUESTIONS

> **6.** The IASB policy is to use which of the following words when developing its standards?
>
>   **a.** Can
>   **b.** Should
>   **c.** Must
>
> **7.** The IASB Framework takes the position that if financial statements meet the needs of which of the following users, it will also meet the needs of other users?
>
>   **a.** Employees
>   **b.** Investors
>   **c.** The public
>
> **8.** Regarding the qualitative characteristics of financial statements, the Framework states that which of the following is true?
>
>   **a.** Materiality is an aspect of understandability.
>   **b.** Substance over form is an aspect of comparability.
>   **c.** Completeness is an aspect of reliability.
>
> **9.** In regards to reporting information about complex matters, the Framework states that which of the following is more important than understanding?
>
>   **a.** Relevance
>   **b.** Substance over form
>   **c.** Faithful representation
>
> **10.** Which of the following is understood to be included when the term "financial statements" is used in the Framework?
>
>   **a.** Directors' reports
>   **b.** Supplementary schedules
>   **c.** A statement of changes in financial position

The Elements of Financial Statements

The section of the Framework concerning the elements of financial statements (pars. 47–80) consists essentially of definitions of the elements of financial statements as identified by the Framework.

OBSERVATION

The definitions given in this section, and especially those of assets and liabilities, are the core of the Framework as a prescriptive basis for standard-setting. The section on Recognition of Elements (pars. 82–98 , see below) acts to reinforce this core. In particular:

- The Framework defines income and expenses in terms of increases and decreases in economic benefits that are equated with changes in assets and liabilities;
- The latter are defined in terms of "resources controlled" and "present obligations" to exclude some of the types of items that have been previously recognized as assets or liabilities (accruals and deferrals) in the name of "matching" expenses and revenues; and
- The effect of these tighter definitions, together with those of the recognition criteria set out in the section on recognition, can be seen particularly in the implications of the definition of a liability for the recognition of provisions, and in the implications of the definition of an asset for the recognition of intangible items.

There is an overlap between definitions and recognition criteria, since satisfying the definition of an element is the principal criterion for recognition. The Framework, however, seeks to distinguish definition issues from recognition issues as far as possible.

The Framework relates the elements of financial statements to the measurement of financial position and performance. As elements of financial position (in the balance sheet), it provides definitions of assets, liabilities, and equity; and as elements of performance (in the income statement), it defines income, including revenue and gains, and expenses, including losses. As for the statement of changes in financial position, this "usually reflects income statement elements and changes in balance sheet elements," and so the Framework does not identify any elements associated uniquely with this statement (par. 47).

Financial position. The elements considered to be "directly related to the measurement of financial position" are assets, liabilities, and equity, which are defined as follows (par. 49):

1. An asset is a resource (a) controlled by the enterprise, (b) as a result of past events, and (c) from which future economic benefits are expected to flow to the enterprise. Recognition as an asset thus requires that the three components of the definition, (a), (b), and (c), be satisfied.

2. A liability is (a) a present obligation of the enterprise, (b) arising out of past events, (c) the settlement of which is expected to result in an outflow from the enterprise of resources embodying economic benefits. Recognition as a liability thus requires that the three components of the definition, (a), (b), and (c), be satisfied.

3. Equity is defined as the residual interest in the assets of the enterprise after deducting all its liabilities.

> **OBSERVATION**
>
> Financial position comprises a number of attributes, including liquidity, solvency, leverage, asset structure, reserves available to cover dividends, and so forth. While each of these attributes may be measured, it is not clear what is meant by "measurement" of financial position as such, which is the terminology used in paragraph 49. A term such as "evaluation of financial position" would be more usual.

Merely satisfying the above definitions does not entail recognition, since the recognition criteria in pars. 82–98 must also be satisfied, and also the principle of "substance over form" must be respected.

> **EXAMPLE**
>
> This principle requires fixed assets held under finance leases to be recognized by the lessee as fixed assets (with corresponding leasing liabilities), while the lessor recognizes a financial asset (pars. 50–51).

Balance sheets drawn up in accordance with "current" IASs may include items the treatment of which does not satisfy the *above* definitions, but the definitions will underlie "future" reviews of existing standards and the formulation of new ones (par. 52). As noted above, the IASC acted accordingly, and it would now be unusual to find an item whose treatment according to a current IAS would conflict with the definitions.

Assets. The "future economic benefit embodied in an asset" is defined as "the potential to contribute, directly or indirectly, to the flow of cash and cash equivalents to the enterprise," including "a capability to reduce cash outflows." In case that definition should leave the status of cash itself as an asset unclear, it is stated that cash satisfies this definition, because it "renders a service to the enterprise because of its command over other resources." Assets embody future economic benefits that may flow to the enterprise by having one or more of the following capabilities:

- Being exchanged for other assets
- Being used to settle a liability
- Being distributed to the enterprise's owners (three capabilities that cash conspicuously possesses)
- Being used singly or in combination with other assets in the production of goods and services to be sold by the enterprise (pars. 53–55)

Neither having physical form, nor being the object of a right of ownership, is an essential attribute of an asset. Intangible items such as patents and copyrights may satisfy the definition of an asset, as may a fixed asset held under a finance lease (by virtue of which it is a resource controlled though not owned by, and from which future benefits are expected to flow to, the entity). Moreover, knowledge obtained from development activity may meet the definition of an asset (capitalized development costs) even though neither physical form nor legal ownership is involved, provided there is *de facto* control such that, by keeping the knowledge secret, the enterprise controls the benefits that are expected to flow from it (pars. 56–57).

Assets may result from various types of past transactions and other past events. Normally, these are purchase transactions and the events associated with production; but they may include donation (for example, by way of a government grant) or discovery (as in the case of mineral deposits). Expected future transactions or events do not give rise to assets.

> ### EXAMPLE
> This principle requires fixed assets held under finance leases to be recognized by the lessee as fixed assets (with corresponding leasing liabilities), while the lessor recognizes a financial asset (pars. 50–51).

While expenditure is a common way to acquire or generate an asset, expenditure undertaken with a view to generating future economic benefits may fail to result in an asset, for example, if the intended economic benefits cannot be expected or are not controlled by the entity (pars. 58–59).

Liabilities. An essential characteristic of (or necessary condition for) a liability is that the entity should have a "present obligation." An obligation is "a duty or responsibility to act or perform in a certain way." The duty or responsibility may arise from the law, for example, the law of contract; or it may arise from normal business practice, which leads to legitimate expectations that the entity will act or perform in a certain way (that is, a constructive obligation). An example of the latter is a constructive obligation to extend the benefits of a warranty for some period beyond the contractual warranty period, because this is an established practice (par. 60).

A present obligation (in the relevant sense) is not the same as a future commitment. An entity may have a commitment to purchase an asset in the future at an agreed price; however, this does not entail a net outflow of resources. The commitment does not give rise to a liability, which arises only when the purchase has actually taken place and title in the asset has passed to the entity, leaving the latter with an obligation to pay for it. In the case of a cash transaction, no liability would arise (par. 61).

There are a number of ways in which a liability may be settled or discharged, which include replacement by another obligation, conversion into equity, and the creditor waiving or forfeiting its rights. There are also various types of "past transactions or past events" from which liabilities may result (pars. 62–63). If a provision involves a present obligation and satisfies the rest of the definition of a liability given in the Framework, it is a liability even if the amount has to be estimated (par. 64).

> **OBSERVATION**
>
> Paragraph 64 does not emphasize the equally important point that a provision that fails to satisfy the criterion of being an *obligation* arising from a past transaction or past event is not a liability. This point, however, was crucial in arriving at the requirements for recognition of provisions in IAS 22, "Business Combinations," and IAS 37, "Provisions, Contingent Liabilities, and Contingent Assets".

Equity. Paragraphs 65–68 are concerned with equity. The fact that equity is defined as a residual interest (assets minus liabilities) does not mean that it cannot be meaningfully divided into subclassifications that are shown separately in the balance sheet. Examples are the differences among the following:

- Paid-in capital (capital stock and paid-in surplus);
- Retained earnings
- Reserves representing appropriations of retained earnings
- Reserves representing the amounts required to be retained in order to maintain "real" capital, that is, either real financial capital or (real) physical capital (par. 65)

There are various legal, tax, and valuation considerations that affect equity, such as requirements for legal reserves, and whether or not the enterprise is incorporated. It is emphasized that transfers to legal, statutory, and tax reserves are appropriations of retained earnings and not expenses. (Likewise, releases from such reserves are credits to retained earnings and not income, but this is not spelled out.) The rather obvious point is made that the amount at which equity is shown in the balance sheet is not intended to be a measure of the market value of the entity, either as a going concern or in a piecemeal disposal. It is stated that the definition and treatment of equity in the Framework are appropriate for unincorporated enterprises, even if the legal considerations are different.

Performance. Paragraphs 69–81 contain the section of the Framework in which definitions of the financial statement elements relating to performance are given. "Profit is frequently used as a measure of performance or as the basis for other measures, such as return on investment and earnings per share" (par. 69). However, this section of the Framework does not discuss the relationship between the elements of performance and the profit measure, except to say that "the recognition and measurement of income and expenses, and hence profit, depends in part on the concepts of capital and capital maintenance used by the entity in preparing its financial statements." The determination of profit and related issues are discussed in a later section of the Framework (pars. 102–110).

The elements of income and expenses are defined as follows:

1. Income is increases in economic benefits during the accounting period in the form of inflows or enhancements of assets or decreases of liabilities that result in increases in equity, other than those relating to contributions from equity participants.

2. Expenses are decreases in economic benefits during the accounting period in the form of outflows or depletions of assets or incurrences of liabilities that result in decreases in equity, other than those relating to distributions to equity participants (par. 70).

These definitions identify the essential features of income and expenses but do not attempt to specify their recognition criteria (par. 71).

OBSERVATION

The definitions given above make it clear that the Framework's approach treats the definitions of assets and liabilities as *logically prior to* those of income and expenses. This is sometimes characterized as a "balance sheet approach" to the relationship between financial statements. This term is potentially misleading, however. The Framework's approach should certainly not be understood as implying the subordination of the income statement to the balance sheet from an *informational* perspective.

Income and expenses may be presented in different ways in the income statement in order to provide relevant information. An example given is the distinction between items of income or expense that arise in the course of the ordinary business activities of the particular entity and those that do not (a distinction required by IAS 1, "Presentation of Financial Statements." Combining items of income and expense in different ways also permits different measures of entity performance to be provided. Examples are the alternative income statement formats with different analyses of expenses, by nature and by function (pars. 72–73). (These different formats are discussed in IAS 1, pars. 80–82.

Income. The Framework's definition of income encompasses both revenue and gains. Revenue is described as arising in the course of the ordinary activities of an entity and includes sales, fees, interest, royalties, and rent. Gains may or may not arise in the course of ordinary activities. Gains may arise on the disposal of non-current assets and also include unrealized gains such as those arising on the revaluation of marketable securities and from increases in the carrying amount of long-term assets. Gains, when recognized in the income statement, are usually displayed separately because their economic significance tends to differ from that of revenue, and they are often reported net of related expenses (pars. 74–77).

The counterpart entry corresponding to a credit for income may be to various asset accounts (not only cash or receivables), or to a liability account such as when a loan is discharged by the provision of goods or services (par. 77).

Expenses. The Framework's definition of expenses encompasses losses as well as expenses that arise in the course of the ordinary activities of the enterprise. Examples given of expenses that arise in the course of ordinary activities are cost of sales, wages, and depreciation. They usually take the form (that is, are the accounting counterpart) of an outflow or depletion of assets such as cash and cash equivalents, inventory, property, or plant and equipment (par. 78).

Losses represent items that may or may not arise in the course of ordinary activities. They include those that result from such disasters as fire or flood, as well as those arising on the disposal of non-current assets, and also encompass unrealized losses, such as those arising from the effects of adverse currency exchange rate movements on financial assets or liabilities. Losses, when recognized in the income statement, are usually displayed separately because their economic significance tends to differ from that of other expenses, and they are often reported net of related income (pars. 79–80).

OBSERVATION

Paragraphs 76 and 80 contain the phrases "when gains are recognized in the income statement" and "when losses are recognized in the income statement." IASs require or allow certain unrealized gains to be included directly in equity (for example, certain revaluation surpluses on non-current assets and foreign exchange gains), or to have their recognition deferred until realization occurs. IASs also require or allow certain losses, such as revaluation losses and foreign exchange losses, to be included directly in equity. Thus, the issue of recognition in the income statement needs to be considered in the context of individual IASs.

It is stated in paragraph 77 that "various kinds of assets may be received or enhanced by income." Likewise, expenses are described in paragraph 78 as "usually tak[ing] the form of an outflow or depletion of assets. . . ." We believe that such points are made more clearly by using the accounting relationships, in virtue of which the income statement effect is the reflection or counterpart of (rather than merely consisting of) the related balance sheet movement. The importance of the accounting relationships in the context of recognition is mentioned in paragraph 84.

Capital maintenance adjustments. The effects on equity of revaluations or restatements of assets and liabilities meet the Framework's definitions of income and expenses, but their inclusion in the income statement depends on which concept of capital maintenance is being applied (par. 81). This matter is discussed further later in this chapter.

Recognition of the Elements of Financial Statements

Recognition issues are dealt with in paragraphs 82–98. Recognition is described as "the process of incorporating in the balance sheet or [the] income statement an item that meets the definition of an element and satisfies the criteria for recognition set out in paragraph 83." (The statement of changes in financial position is not mentioned because its elements consist of those that are also elements of financial position or performance.) Failure to recognize *in the main financial statements* items that satisfy the relevant definition and recognition criteria is not rectified by disclosure of the accounting policies used or by use of notes or other explanatory material.

The recognition criteria set out in paragraph 83 are that an item which meets the definition of an element should be recognized if:

- It is probable that any future economic benefit associated with the item will flow to or from the entity
- The item has a cost or value that can be measured with reliability

Recognition is subject to materiality. Accounting interrelationships are also significant, since recognition in the financial statements of an item that meets the definition and recognition criteria for a particular element, for example an asset, entails the recognition of another (counterpart) element, such as income or a liability (par. 84). (This refers, strictly speaking, to the initial recognition of an item. However, a similar point could be made about the implications of remeasurement or valuation adjustments.)

The probability of future economic benefit. The concept of *probability* is used in the recognition criteria "to refer to the degree of uncertainty [as to whether] the future economic benefits associated with the item will flow to or from the enterprise . . . in keeping with the uncertainty that characterizes the environment in which an enterprise operates." Assessments of such uncertainty are made on the basis of the evidence available when the financial statements are prepared. In regard to receivables, for example, for a large population of accounts, some statistical evidence will usually be available regarding collectibility (par. 85).

> **OBSERVATION**
>
> The Framework does not offer any guidance, beyond that mentioned above, on the interpretation of "probable." IAS 37, "Provisions, Contingent Assets and Contingent Liabilities ," contains an interpretation of "probable" as "more likely than not," that is, a probability in excess of 50 percent, but states that this interpretation is not intended to be applied in other contexts. Others have suggested an interpretation of "probable" in the present context as a probability of at least 75 percent. However, in the case of the receivables example mentioned above, the allowance to be made for probably uncollectible accounts would normally be based on past statistics, perhaps adjusted to take account of the current economic environment.

Reliability of measurement. Reliability, the second recognition criterion, was discussed in the section "Qualitative Characteristics of Financial Statements" above. If an item does not possess a cost or value that can be measured with reliability (so that the information has that qualitative characteristic), then it is not appropriate to recognize it. However, in many cases, cost or (more particularly) value must be estimated; indeed, the use of reasonable estimates is an essential part of the financial reporting process and need not undermine reliability. In cases where an item satisfies the definition of an element but not the recognition criteria, it will not be recognized in the financial statements themselves, but its relevance is likely to require its disclosure in the notes to the financial statements or in other supplementary disclosures. This applies when the item meets the probability criterion of recognition but not the reliability criterion, but may also apply to an item that meets the definition of an element when neither recognition criterion is met. The key issue here is whether the item is considered to be relevant to the evaluation of financial position, performance, or changes in financial position. An item that does not satisfy the recognition criteria for an asset or a liability at one time may do so later, if more information relevant to estimating its probability, cost, or value becomes available (pars. 86–88).

Recognition of assets. An asset is recognized in the balance sheet when it is probable that future economic benefits will flow to the entity (as a result of its control of the asset) and the asset's cost or value can be measured reliably. When expenditure has been incurred but it is not considered probable that economic benefits will flow to the entity beyond the current accounting period, this expenditure will be recognized as an expense, not as an asset. The intention of management in undertaking the expenditure is irrelevant (pars. 89–90).

Recognition of liabilities. A liability is recognized in the balance sheet when it is probable that an outflow of resources embodying economic benefits will result from the settlement of a present obligation and the amount of that settlement can be measured reliably. Obligations under executory contracts, that is, non-cancelable contracts that are equally proportionately unperformed (such as the amount that will be a liability when inventory ordered and awaiting delivery is received), are not generally recognized as liabilities in the balance sheet, nor are the related assets recognized in the balance sheet. In some cases, however, recognition may be required (par. 91).

> There may, however, be other types of executory contract (for example, involving financial instruments) in respect of which recognition of an asset (or expense) and a related liability (or income) may be the most appropriate treatment.

Recognition of income. Recognition of income occurs simultaneously with the recognition of increases in assets or decreases in liabilities (or a combination of the two). The normal recognition procedures used in practice are applications of the Framework's recognition criteria. An example is the requirement that revenue should be earned (that is, it should be associated with a simultaneous increase in assets or decrease in liabilities). These procedures are concerned with restricting the recognition of income to items that, in effect, meet the Framework's recognition criteria of *probability* (a sufficient degree of certainty that an economic benefit has flowed or will flow to the entity) and *reliability* of measurement (pars. 92–93).

Recognition of expenses. Recognition of expenses occurs simultaneously with the recognition of an increase in liabilities or a decrease in assets (or a combination of the two). Expenses are commonly recognized in the income statement on the basis of an association (matching) between the incurrence of costs and the earning of specific items of revenue, that result directly and jointly from the same transactions or other events. An example is the matching of the cost of goods sold with the associated sales revenue. However, the Framework does not permit the application of the matching procedure to result in the recognition of items in the balance sheet that do not meet the definition of assets or liabilities (pars. 94–95).

OBSERVATION

While the last sentence above is true of the Framework, individual IASs may require the recognition of balance sheet items that arguably do not meet the Framework's definitions. Examples include the deferral and amortization of government grants following the matching principle, required by IAS 20 ; and the similar treatment of gains on certain sale and leaseback transactions, required by IAS 17.

Depreciation and amortization are procedures for dealing with a situation in which a decrease in the future economic benefits embodied in an asset takes place over several accounting periods. It may not be feasible or cost-effective to relate such decreases directly to revenue. In such cases, the expense is recognized in the income statement on the basis of procedures that systematically and rationally allocate it over those accounting periods in which the economic benefits embodied in the asset may be considered to be consumed or to expire (par. 96).

An expense is recognized immediately in the income statement in the case of an expenditure that produces no future economic benefits that qualify for recognition as an asset in the balance sheet. An expense is also recognized in the income statement when a liability is incurred without an asset being recognized. An example is the recognition of a liability under a product warranty and of the associated warranty expense (pars. 97–98).

OBSERVATION

The paragraphs on the recognition of income and expenses use a terminology that we have avoided above. Income is described as being recognized in the income statement "when an increase in the future economic benefits related to an asset or a decrease of a liability has arisen that can be measured reliably." The description of the conditions for recognition of expenses is similar, with "decrease" being substituted for "increase" and vice versa. While logically correct in the Framework's terms, this terminology, with its reference to "future economic benefits," is rather cumbersome and is not essential to clarifying the criteria for recognition of income and expenses.

Measurement of the Elements of Financial Statements

Paragraphs 99-101 deal with measurement issues, insofar as these are covered in the Framework. The treatment here is descriptive and avoids being prescriptive. Measurement is described as "the process of determining the monetary amounts at which the elements of the financial statements are to be recognized and carried in the balance sheet and income statement." It involves the selection of a particular basis of measurement.

Four different measurement bases are specifically mentioned and described (without any claim to exhaustiveness): historical cost, current cost (of replacement or settlement), realizable or (for liabilities) settlement value, and present value. Historical cost is mentioned as the measurement basis most commonly adopted by entities in preparing their financial statements, usually in combination with other measurement bases. An example of the latter is the carrying of inventories at the lower of historical cost and net realizable value. Marketable securities may be carried at market value, and pension liabilities are carried at their present value. Current cost may be used as a means of taking account of the effects of changing prices of nonmonetary assets.

Concepts of Capital and Capital Maintenance

Concepts of capital. The Framework identifies two main concepts of capital: the financial concept and the physical concept. The financial concept of capital may take two forms: invested money (nominal financial) capital or invested purchasing power (real financial) capital. In either case, capital is identified with the equity of the entity (in either nominal or real financial terms) and with its net assets measured in those terms. The physical concept of capital is based on the notion of the productive capacity or operating capability of the entity, as embodied in its net assets. Most enterprises adopt a financial concept of capital, normally (in the absence of severe inflation) nominal financial capital (par. 102).

> **OBSERVATION**
>
> The Framework does not distinguish clearly between nominal and real financial capital; however, the two are quite distinct and will be treated accordingly below. Physical capital is also a form of "real" capital concept.

Capital maintenance and the determination of profit. Choice of a concept of capital is related to the concept of capital ma intenance that is most meaningful, given the implications of the choice for profit measurement and the needs of the users of the financial statements in that regard, as follows:

- **Maintenance of nominal financial capital.** Under this concept a profit is earned only if the money amount of the net assets at the end of the period exceeds the money amount of the net assets at the beginning of the period, after excluding any distributions to, and contributions from, equity owners during the period.
- **Maintenance of real financial capital.** Under this concept a profit is earned only if the money amount of the net assets at the end of the period exceeds the money amount of the net assets at the beginning of the period, restated in units of the same purchasing power, after excluding distributions to, and contributions from, owners. Normally, the units of purchasing power employed are those of the currency at the end of the period, into which the net assets at the beginning of the period are restated.
- **Maintenance of real physical capital.** Under this concept a profit is earned only if the operating capability embodied in the net assets at the end of the period exceeds the operating capability embodied in the net assets at the beginning of the period, after excluding distributions to, and contributions from, owners. Operating capability embodied in assets may, in principle, be measured by employing the current cost basis of measurement (pars. 103–106).

The main difference among the three concepts of capital maintenance is the treatment of the effects of changes in the carrying amounts of the entity's assets and liabilities. Under nominal financial capital maintenance, increases in the money-carrying amounts of assets held over the period (to the extent that they are recognized as gains) are part of profit.

Under real financial capital maintenance, such increases are part of profit only if they are "real" increases, that is, increases that remain after money-carrying amounts have been restated in units of the same purchasing power. The total amount of the restatement is known as a "capital maintenance adjustment" and is transferred to a capital maintenance reserve, which is part of equity (but not of retained profits). Real financial capital maintenance may be used in conjunction with historical cost as a measurement basis but would more normally be used in conjunction with the current cost basis.

Under real physical capital maintenance, changes in the money prices (current costs) of assets and liabilities held over the period are considered not to affect the amount of operating capability embodied in those items, and therefore the total amount of those changes is treated as a capital maintenance adjustment and excluded from profit.

EXAMPLE

Assume that a company begins with capital stock of $100 and cash of $100. At the beginning of the year, one item of inventory is bought for $100. The item of inventory is sold at the end of the year for $150; its replacement cost at that time is $120; and general inflation throughout the year is 10 percent. Profit measured using each of the capital maintenance concepts mentioned previously would be as shown below.

	Nominal Financial Capital Maintenance	Real Financial Capital Maintenance	Real Physical Capital Maintenance
Sales	$150	$150	$150
Less cost of sales	(100)	(100)	(120)
Operating profit	50	50	30
Less inflation adjustment	—	(10)	—
Total gain	$50	$40	$30
Capital maintenance adjustment	$0	$10	$20

Column 1 shows the gain after ensuring the maintenance of the stockholders' opening capital measured as a sum of money. Column 2 shows the gain after ensuring the maintenance of the stockholders' opening capital measured as a block of purchasing power. Both of these are concerned, under different definitions, with the maintenance of financial capital—in terms either of its money amount or of its general purchasing power. Column 3 shows the gain after ensuring the maintenance of the company's initial operating capacity and is therefore of a completely different nature.

Different combinations of measurement bases and capital maintenance concepts provide different accounting models, between which management should choose, taking into account relevance and reliability. The IASB does not "presently" intend to prescribe a particular model, other than in exceptional circumstances such as when reporting in the currency of a hyperinflationary economy (pars. 107–110).

> **OBSERVATION**
>
> IAS 29, "Financial Reporting in Hyperinflationary Economies " requires a choice between two different models: real financial capital, together with historical costs restated in units of the same purchasing power by use of a general price index; and real physical capital with adjustments for the purchasing power gain or loss on the net monetary position, together with current costs.

STUDY QUESTIONS

11. Which of the following does the IASB Framework define as "increases and decreases in economic benefits that are equated with changes in assets and liabilities?"

  a. Amortization
  b. Equity
  c. Income and expenses

12. Which of the following is an element of performance according to the Framework?

  a. Assets
  b. Liabilities
  c. Expenses

13. Which of the following is *not* one of the main concepts of capital according to the Framework?

  a. Financial concept
  b. Physical concept
  c. Maintenance concept

14. Which of the following do elements of financial statements relate to, according to the Framework?

  a. The measurement of probability
  b. The measurement of assessment
  c. The measurement of performance

15. For which of the following does the Framework *not* identify any elements?
- **a.** Income statement
- **b.** Balance sheet
- **c.** Statement of changes in financial position

IFRS: First-Time Adoption of International Financial Reporting Standards

LEARNING OBJECTIVES

Upon completion of this chapter, the reader will be able to:

- Describe what is included in the definition of IFRS
- Point out the significance of cost in generating an entity's first IFRS financial statements
- List the requirements for an entity's opening IFRS balance sheet
- List the situations in which retrospective application is prohibited by IFRS and in which cases it is optional
- Describe how historical information should be presented under IFRS

OVERVIEW

The reporting of changes in accounting policies, as well as the implications of such changes, is an important aspect of effective transparency. This has long been covered by IAS 8, "Accounting Policies, Changes in Accounting Estimates, and Errors". Recognizing that the wholesale adoption of International Standards, by switching from a national GAAP system, raised issues of a greater order of magnitude, IASB first issued an interpretation (SIC-8, "First-Time Application of IAS as the Primary Basis of Accounting") on this matter. However, with the importance of the mass adoptions foreseen in 2005 amongst European listed enterprises and elsewhere, a full-blown standard was deemed desirable, hence IFRS 1, "First-Time Adoption of International Reporting Standards " This standard became effective from January 1, 2004.

IFRS 1 was regularly updated (and is likely to continue to be regularly updated) to take account of new standards as they appear. This increasingly created a disorganized and apparently rather ad hoc standard. Accordingly, IASB has completely redesigned and re-sequenced the material in IFRS 1. The new version was issued in November 2008, and became fully effective from July 1, 2009, earlier application being permitted. The IASB specifically states that this "new version retains the substance of the previous version, but within a changed structure." This course uses the new version, but there should be no significant changes in the implications of the requirements compared with earlier versions.

The IFRS applies when an entity adopts IFRSs for the first time by an explicit and unreserved statement of compliance with IFRSs. In general, it requires an entity to comply with each IFRS effective at the reporting date for its first IFRS financial statements. In particular, the IFRS requires an entity to do the following in the opening IFRS balance sheet that it prepares as a starting point for its accounting under IFRSs:

- Recognize all assets and liabilities whose recognition is required by IFRSs.
- Not recognize items as assets or liabilities if IFRSs do not permit such recognition.
- Reclassify items that it recognized under previous GAAP as one type of asset, liability, or component of equity but that are a different type of asset, liability, or component of equity under IFRSs.
- Apply IFRSs in measuring all recognized assets and liabilities.

IFRS 1 grants limited exemptions from these requirements in specified areas where the cost of complying with them would be likely to exceed the benefits to users of financial statements. It also prohibits retrospective application of IFRSs in some areas, particularly where retrospective application would require judgments by management about past conditions after the outcome of a particular transaction is already known. IFRS 1 also requires disclosures that explain how the transition from previous GAAP to IFRSs affected the entity's reported financial position, financial performance, and cash flows.

OBSERVATION

Depending on the particular situation and industry involved, the effects on the reported results of an entity of the switch to IFRS could be highly significant. This implies that readers of published financial statements will need to be "educated" about the effects of these accounting changes (which are not "real" changes), in order to receive a realistic impression of the genuine underlying trend of performance. Interim reports issued *during* the year of the transition to IFRS GAAP will particularly require careful explanation by preparers, and careful interpretation by users.

STUDY QUESTION

> **1.** The new version of IFRS 1 became fully effective from:
> **a.** January 1, 2008
> **b.** December 31, 2008
> **c.** November 1, 2008
> **d.** July 1, 2009

BACKGROUND

As outlined above, a complete switch from one set of regulatory requirements to a different set raises important issues for the preservation of consistency and trend analysis. IFRS 1 represents a formalization and a tightening of the requirements of SIC-8. The objective of IFRS 1 is stated as follows (par. 1):

> The objective of this IFRS is to ensure that an entity's first IFRS financial statements, and its interim financial reports for part of the period covered by those financial statements, contain high quality information that:
>
> — Is transparent for users and comparable over all periods presented
> — Provides a suitable starting point for accounting under International Financial Reporting Standards (IFRSs)
> — Can be generated at a cost that does not exceed the benefits to users

STUDY QUESTION

> **2.** An entity's first IFRS financial statements should do all of the following **except:**
> **a.** Be transparent for users
> **b.** Provide a suitable starting point
> **c.** Be generated at a reasonable cost
> **d.** Be more complex than under previous U.S. GAAP

SCOPE AND DEFINITIONS

The required scope is that an entity should apply IFRS 1 (par. 2) in:
- Its first IFRS financial statements
- Each interim financial report, if any, that it presents under IAS 34, "Interim Financial Reporting," for part of the period covered by its first IFRS financial statements

In a departure from earlier practice, key definitions are given in an appendix (Appendix A), which is defined as an integral part of the IFRS. These definitions are given below.

Date of transition to IFRSs	The beginning of the earliest period for which an entity presents full comparative information under IFRSs in its first IFRS financial statements
Deemed cost	An amount used as a surrogate for cost or depreciated cost at a given date. Subsequent depreciation or amortization assumes that the entity had initially recognized the asset or liability at the given date and that its cost was equal to the deemed cost
Fair value	The amount for which an asset could be exchanged or a liability settled, between knowledgeable, willing parties in an arm's-length transaction
First IFRS financial statements	The first annual financial statements in which an entity adopts International Financial Reporting Standards, by an explicit and unreserved statement of compliance with IFRSs
First IFRS reporting period	The latest reporting period covered by an entity's first IFRS financial statements
First-time adopter	An entity that presents its first IFRS financial statements
International Financial Reporting Standards	Standards and Interpretations adopted by the IASB. They comprise: - International Financial Reporting Standards - International Accounting Standards - Interpretations originated by the International Financial Reporting Interpretations Committee (IFRIC) or the former Standing Interpretations Committee (SIC)
Opening IFRS statement of financial position	An entity's statement of financial position at the date of transition to IFRSs
Previous GAAP	The basis of accounting that a first-time adopter used immediately before adopting IFRSs

The IASB has had considerable anxiety about what exactly is meant by "first IFRS financial statements." Paragraph 3 gives the essential point:

> An entity's first IFRS financial statements are the first annual financial statements in which the entity adopts IFRSs, by an explicit and unreserved statement in those financial statements of compliance with IFRSs.

It follows from this that any earlier set of financial statements that did not include this explicit and unreserved statement of compliance with International Standards cannot have been the "first IFRS financial statements," *even if they did, in fact, fully comply with IAS requirements as at that time.*

It also follows, on the other hand, that a set of financial statements that makes the required statement of compliance, but does not in fact correctly so comply, *is* still the "first IFRS financial statements," in which case IAS 8 would apply to the process of correcting such errors in future years. Despite this surely successful attempt to avoid ambiguity, IFRS 1 gives a number of example situations in both directions in paragraphs 3-5.

STUDY QUESTIONS

3. Which of the following is required for an entity's financial statements to be considered its "first IFRS financial statements"?
    a. Fully complying with IFRS requirements
    b. Fully complying with IAS requirements
    c. An explicit and unreserved statement of compliance with International Standards
    d. A statement that the financial statements have always been reported in accordance with U.S. GAAP

4. Which of the following is defined in IFRS as the amount for which an asset could be exchanged or a liability settled, between knowledgeable, willing parties in an arm's-length transaction?
    a. Purchase price
    b. Fair value
    c. Deemed cost

RECOGNITION AND MEASUREMENT

Taking as an example an enterprise that has a financial year-end on December 31 and is required to produce its first IFRS financial statements for a reporting date of December 31, 2009, a number of implications arise. First, it will already have produced and published its financial statements for the reporting date of December 31, 2008, under its previous GAAP. Second, when the enterprise eventually publishes its first IFRS financial statements with a reporting date of December 31, 2009, it will need to produce complete comparative figures for the previous year that are fully comparable and consistent with the 2009 data. It will therefore need to prepare a complete restatement of its 2008 report under IFRS requirements, as part of the 2009 reporting package. It follows from this that, third, the enterprise will need to prepare an opening balance sheet as at the opening of business on January 1, 2008, under IFRS GAAP, in order that the correct changes and adjustments required for the 2008 IFRS financial statements can be calculated. With effect from January 1, 2009, under the revised version of IAS 1, "Presentation of Financial Statements", this opening balance sheet (statement of financial position) is required to be published.

There is obviously the theoretical possibility that the content of IASB requirements will have altered over the two or more years dealt with in the first IFRS financial statements. Indeed, given the state of considerable flux and development attending IFRS GAAP, this is extremely likely. The general rule under IFRS 1 for dealing with this problem is very clear (pars. 7 and 8):

> An entity shall use the same accounting policies in its opening IFRS statement of financial position and throughout all periods presented in its first IFRS financial statements. Those accounting policies shall comply with each IFRS effective at the end of its first IFRS reporting period, except as specified in paragraphs 13-19 and Appendices B-E.

> An entity shall not apply different versions of IFRSs that were effective at earlier dates. An entity may apply a new IFRS that is not yet mandatory if it permits early application.

Thus, in the earlier example of a reporting date of December 31, 2009, the opening IFRS balance sheet as at January 1, 2008, and *all* the published (IFRS) comparatives for 2008, should as a general rule be prepared under International Standards effective on December 31, 2009. The purpose and advantage of this, of course, is to maximize consistency and comparability within the 2009 financial statements considered as a whole. The necessary adjustments to the opening IFRS balance sheet as compared with the version published earlier under the previous GAAP should be recognized directly in equity, usually in retained earnings (par. 11).

It follows from paragraphs 7 and 8 that, subject to the exceptions referred to in the paragraph 7 and discussed below, an entity's opening IFRS balance sheet will (par. 10):

- Recognize all assets and liabilities whose recognition is required by IFRSs as at the reporting date
- Not recognize items as assets or liabilities if IFRSs do not permit such recognition

- Reclassify items that it recognized under previous GAAP as one type of asset, liability, or component of equity but that are a different type of asset, liability, or component of equity under IFRSs
- Apply IFRSs in measuring all recognized assets and liabilities

It is clear from the "Basis of Conclusions" document that Board members have deliberated long and hard about arguments for and against the desirability of the above principle, and about possible exceptions to it. It should be noted that in the case, for example, of an asset that has been held for many years but not recognized as an asset under previous GAAP and that now needs to be recognized and measured under IFRSs, it may be necessary to go back in the accounting records for many years to properly meet the requirements for the opening IFRS balance sheet.

The result of all these deliberations is that the IFRS establishes two categories of exceptions to the principle that an entity's opening IFRS balance sheet shall comply with each IFRS:

- Appendices C–E grant exemptions from some requirements of other IFRSs
- Appendix B prohibits retrospective application of some aspects of other IFRSs

IFRS 1 allows (but does not require) certain limited exemptions from the general principle of paragraphs 7 and 10, summarized and delimited as follows:

- Business combinations (App. C)
- Share-based payment transactions (pars. D2 and D3)
- Insurance contracts (par. D4)
- Fair value or revaluation as deemed cost (pars. D5-D8)
- Leases (par. D9)
- Employee benefits (pars. D10 and D11)
- Cumulative translation differences (pars. D12 and D13)
- Investments in subsidiaries, jointly controlled entities, and associates (pars. D14 and D15)
- Assets and liabilities of subsidiaries, associates, and joint ventures (pars. D16 and D17)
- Compound financial instruments (par. D18)
- Designation of previously recognized financial instruments (par. D19)
- Fair value measurement of financial assets or financial liabilities at initial recognition (par. D20)
- Decommissioning liabilities included in the cost of property, plant, and equipment (par. D21)
- Financial assets or intangible assets accounted for in accordance with IFRIC 12, "Service Concession Arrangements" (par. D22)

- Borrowing costs (par. D23)
- Two further exemptions were granted on July 23, 2009. These amendments:
  - Exempt entities using the full cost method from retrospective application of IFRS for oil and gas assets
  - Exempt entities with existing leasing contracts from reassessing the classification of those contracts in accordance with IFRIC 4, *Determining Whether an Arrangement Contains a Lease*, when the application of their national accounting requirements produced the same result

The rationale behind allowing these optional exemptions is that the Board felt the costs incurred by enterprises if these limited exemptions were not available might well outweigh the informational benefits to users. These optional exemptions are discussed briefly below. There is little point in repeating every nuance of the IFRS 1 details, and reference should be made to the standard if such exemptions are being used in practice.

Business Combinations

A first-time adopter may elect not to apply IFRS 3, "Business Combinations," retrospectively to past business combinations (business combinations that occurred before the date of transition to IFRSs). However, if a first-time adopter restates any business combination to comply with IFRS 3, it shall restate all later business combinations.

For example, if a first-time adopter elects to restate a business combination that occurred on June 30, 2006, it shall restate all business combinations that occurred between June 30, 2006, and the date of transition to IFRSs.

If a first-time adopter does not apply IFRS 3 retrospectively to a past business combination, a number of specified consequences follow (par. C4). Major points include:

- The first-time adopter shall keep the same classification (as an acquisition by the legal acquirer, a reverse acquisition by the legal acquiree, or a uniting of interests) as in its previous GAAP financial statements.
- The first-time adopter shall recognize all its assets and liabilities at the date of transition to IFRSs that were acquired or assumed in a past business combination, other than:
  - Assets, including goodwill, and liabilities that were not recognized in the acquirer's consolidated balance sheet under previous GAAP and also would not qualify for recognition under IFRSs in the separate balance sheet of the acquiree.
  - Some financial assets and financial liabilities derecognized under previous GAAP. This is because a first-time adopter shall apply the derecognition requirements in IAS 39, "Financial Instruments Recognition and Measurement," prospectively from the effective date of IAS 39. In other words, if a first-time adopter derecognized financial

assets or financial liabilities under its previous GAAP in a financial year beginning before January 1, 2004, it shall not recognize those assets and liabilities under IFRSs (unless they qualify for recognition as a result of a later transaction or event). However, notwithstanding the above, an entity may apply the derecognition requirements of IAS 39 retrospectively from a date of its own choosing, provided that the information needed to apply IAS 39 to financial items derecognized as a result of past transactions was obtained at the time of initially accounting for those transactions (pars. B2 and B3).

- The first-time adopter shall exclude from its opening IFRS balance sheet any item recognized under previous GAAP that does not qualify for recognition as an asset or liability under IFRSs.
- If an asset acquired, or liability assumed, in a past business combination was not recognized under previous GAAP, it does not have a deemed cost of zero in the opening IFRS balance sheet. Instead, the acquirer shall recognize and measure it in its consolidated balance sheet on the basis that IFRSs would require in the separate balance sheet of the acquiree. To illustrate, if the acquirer had not, under its previous GAAP, capitalized finance leases acquired in a past business combination, it shall capitalize those leases in its consolidated financial statements, as IAS 17, "Leases," would require the acquiree to do in its separate IFRS balance sheet.
- Regardless of whether there is any indication that the goodwill may be impaired, the first-time adopter shall apply IAS 36, "Impairment of Assets," in testing the goodwill for impairment at the date of transition to IFRSs and in recognizing any resulting impairment loss in retained earnings (or, if so required by IAS 36, in revaluation surplus). The impairment test shall be based on conditions at the date of transition to IFRSs.

Share-Based Payment Transactions

A first-time adopter is encouraged, but not required, to apply IFRS 2, "Share-Based Payment," to:

- Equity instruments granted on or before November 7, 2002
- Equity instruments granted after November 7, 2002, that vested before the later of the date of transition to IFRSs or January 1, 2005
- Liabilities arising from share-based payment transactions that were settled before the date of transition to IFRSs
- Liabilities that were settled before January 1, 2005

Certain further detailed conditions apply (pars. D2 and D3).

Insurance Contracts

A first-time adopter may apply the transitional provisions of IFRS 4, "Insurance Contracts".

Fair Value or Revaluation as Deemed Cost

An entity may elect to measure an item of property, plant, and equipment at the date of transition to IFRSs at its fair value and use that fair value as its deemed cost at that date. A first-time adopter may elect to use a previous GAAP revaluation of an item of property, plant, and equipment at, or before, the date of transition to IFRSs as deemed cost at the date of the revaluation, if the revaluation was, at the date of the revaluation, broadly comparable to either of the following:

- Fair value
- Cost or depreciated cost under IFRSs, adjusted to reflect, for example, changes in a general or specific price index

These elections are also available for investment property, if an entity elects to use the cost basis in IAS 40, "Investment Property ," and for intangible assets that meet the recognition and revaluation criteria set out in IAS 38, "Intangible Assets." It should be noted that any such fair values should reflect conditions that existed at the date for which the fair values were actually determined (rather than conditions existing at the date the determination was carried out).

If the measurement date is after the date of transition to IFRS but during the period covered by the first IFRS financial statements, the event-driven fair value measurements may be used as deemed cost when the event occurs. An entity shall recognize the resulting adjustments directly in retained earnings (or if appropriate, another category of equity) at the measurement date. At the date of transition to IFRS, the entity shall either establish the deemed cost by applying the criteria in paragraphs D5–D7 or measure assets and liabilities in accordance with the other requirements in this IFRS. [paragraph D8 (b)]

Leases

A first-time adopter may apply the transitional provisions in IFRIC 4, "Determining Whether an Arrangement Contains a Lease". This means that the determination may be based on the facts and circumstances at the date of transition, not the earlier date of the arrangement.

Employee Benefits

A strict application of the "corridor" approach allowed by IAS 19, "Employee Benefits," by a first-time adopter would require retrospective analysis of cumulative actuarial gains and losses from the date of the inception of the plan. To avoid this necessity, a first-time IFRS adopter may recognize (i.e., take immediately to the income statement) all cumulative actuarial gains and losses at the date of transition to IFRS, even if it uses the corridor approach for later actuarial gains and losses. If a first-time adopter uses this election, it shall apply it to all plans.

Cumulative Translation Differences

IAS 21, "The Effects of Changes in Foreign Exchange Rates," requires an entity to classify some cumulative translation differences (CTDs) relating to a net investment in a foreign operation as a separate component of equity. The entity transfers the CTDs to the income statement on subsequent disposal of the foreign operation. A first-time adopter need not identify the CTDs at the date of transition to IFRSs. The first-time adopter need not show that identifying the CTDs would involve undue cost or effort.

Investments in Subsidiaries, Jointly Controlled Entities and Associates

When an entity prepares separate financial statements, IAS 27, "Consolidated and Separate Financial Statements," requires it to account for its investments in subsidiaries, jointly controlled entities, and associates either:

- At cost, or
- In accordance with IAS 39, "Financial Instruments: Recognition and Measurement."

If a first-time adopter measures such an investment at cost, it shall measure that investment at one of the following amounts in its separate opening IFRS statement of financial position:

- Cost determined in accordance with IAS 27, or
- Deemed cost. The deemed cost of such an investment shall be its:
  - Fair value (determined in accordance with IAS 39) at the entity's date of transition to IFRSs in its separate financial statements, or
  - Previous GAAP carrying amount at that date.

A first-time adopter may choose either fair value or the carrying amount to measure its investment in each subsidiary, jointly controlled entity, or associate that it elects to measure using a deemed cost.

Assets and Liabilities of Subsidiaries, Associates, and Joint Ventures

Potential problems arise if a subsidiary becomes a first-time IFRS adopter later, or earlier, than its parent, as the same items could have two different dates of first-time adoption, one for each "level" of the reporting process. Hence, under IFRS 1, if a subsidiary adopts IFRSs later than the parent (in the subsidiary's own published financial statements), the subsidiary may choose to measure its assets and liabilities at either:

- The carrying amounts that would be included in the parent's consolidated financial statements, based on the parent's date of transition to IFRSs, if no adjustments were made for consolidation procedures and for the effects of the business combination in which the parent acquired the subsidiary or

- The carrying amounts required by the rest of the IFRS, based on the subsidiary's date of transition to IFRSs

A similar election is available to an associate or joint venture that becomes a first-time adopter later than an entity that has significant influence or joint control over it.

However, if an entity becomes a first-time adopter later than its subsidiary (or associate or joint venture) the entity shall, in its consolidated financial statements, measure the assets and liabilities of the subsidiary (or associate or joint venture) at the same carrying amounts as in the separate financial statements of the subsidiary (or associate or joint venture), after adjusting for consolidation and equity accounting adjustments and for the effects of the business combination in which the entity acquired the subsidiary.

Compound Financial Instruments

A detailed exemption exists (par. D18) where the original liability component is no longer outstanding.

Designation of Previous Recognized Financial Instruments

IAS 39 permits the designation of a financial instrument on initial recognition as a financial asset or liability at fair value through profit or loss, or as available for sale. Such designation is, however, alternatively permitted at the date of transition to IFRSs.

Fair Value Measurement of Financial Assets or Financial Liabilities at Initial Recognition

A detailed specific exemption applies (see par. D20).

Decommissioning Liabilities Included in the Cost of Property, Plant, and Equipment

A first-time adopter need not comply with the requirements of IFRIC 1, "Changes in Existing Decommissioning, Restoration, and Similar Liabilities," in respect of changes in such liabilities that occurred before the date of transition to IFRSs. Conditions apply if the exemption is used, as specified in paragraph D21.

Financial Assets or Intangible Assets Accounted for in Accordance with IFRIC 12

A first-time adopter may apply the transitional provisions of IFRIC 12, "Service Concession Arrangements."

Borrowing Costs

A first-time adopter may apply the transitional provisions of IAS 23, "Borrowing Costs," as revised for mandatory application from January 1, 2009.

Prohibition of Retrospective Application

There are four situations in which the IASB *prohibits* retrospective application (in contrast to the *option* not to apply retrospective application in the circumstances discussed above). These relate to:

- Derecognition of financial assets and financial liabilities (par. B2 and B3)
- Hedge accounting (pars. B4-B6)
- Estimates (pars. 14-17)
- Some aspects of accounting for non-controlling interests

As regards the first of these, in general a first-time adopter shall apply the derecognition requirements in IAS 39, "Financial Instruments: Recognition and Measurement," prospectively for transactions occurring on or after January 1, 2004. In other words, if a first-time adopter derecognized non-derivative financial assets or non-derivative financial liabilities in accordance with its previous GAAP as a result of a transaction that occurred before January 1, 2004, it shall not recognize those assets and liabilities in accordance with IFRSs (unless they qualify for recognition as a result of a later transaction or event).

However, an entity may apply the derecognition requirements in IAS 39 retrospectively from a date of the entity's choosing, provided that the information needed to apply IAS 39 to financial assets and financial liabilities derecognized as a result of past transactions was obtained at the time of initially accounting for those transactions.

As regards hedging, the Board confirms that the transitional provisions of IAS 39 shall apply to all hedging relationships that existed at the date of transition to IFRS, except that an entity shall not reflect in its opening IFRS balance sheet a hedging relationship of a type that does not qualify for hedge accounting under IAS 39 (e.g., many hedging relationships in which the hedging instrument is a cash instrument or written option, the hedged item is a net position, or the hedge covers interest risk in a held-to-maturity investment). However, if an entity designated a net position as a hedged item under previous GAAP, it may designate an individual item within that net position as a hedged item under IFRSs, provided that it does so no later than the date of transition to IFRSs.

As regards estimates, because the date of transition to IFRSs is later than when the original estimates were made, more recent evidence that has become available may suggest (or as an adjusting event under IAS 10 would require) revision of the estimate. IFRS 1 prohibits the treatment of such additional evidence as an adjusting event (par. 14):

> An entity's estimates under IFRSs at the date of transition to IFRSs shall be consistent with estimates made for the same date in accordance with previous GAAP (after adjustments to reflect any difference in accounting policies), unless there is objective evidence that those estimates were in error.

The implication of this is that an entity shall not reflect such new information in its opening IFRS balance sheet (unless the estimates need adjustment for any differences in accounting policies or there is objective evidence that the estimates were in error). Instead, the entity shall reflect that new information in profit or loss (or, if appropriate, other comprehensive income) for the year in which the information becomes available.

For non-controlling interests, with effect from July 1, 2009, or on earlier adoption of IAS 27, "Consolidated and Separate Financial Statements," as amended in 2008, a first-time adopter shall apply the following requirements of IAS 27, "Consolidated and Separate Financial Statements" (as amended in 2008), prospectively from the date of transition to IFRSs:

- The requirement in paragraph 28 that total comprehensive income is attributed to the owners of the parent and to the non-controlling interests even if this results in the non-controlling interests having a deficit balance
- The requirements in paragraphs 30 and 31 for accounting for changes in the parent's ownership interest in a subsidiary that do not result in a loss of control
- The requirements in paragraphs 34–37 for accounting for a loss of control over a subsidiary, and the related requirements of paragraph 8A of IFRS 5

However, if a first-time adopter elects to apply IFRS 3 (as revised in 2008) retrospectively to past business combinations, it also shall apply IAS 27 (as amended in 2008) from that same date.

STUDY QUESTIONS

> **5.** For first-time IFRS adoption with a reporting date of December 31, 2009, the opening IFRS balance sheet as at January 1, 2008, and all the published (IFRS) comparatives for 2008, should as a general rule be prepared under International Standards effective on which of the following dates?
>
> **a.** December 31, 2007
> **b.** December 31, 2008
> **c.** December 31, 2009

---

6. If a first-time adopter elects to restate a business combination that occurred on June 30, 2002, and its date of transition to IFRS is January 1, 2009, it must restate all business combinations that occurred between which of the following dates?
   a. June 30, 2001 and June 30, 2002
   b. January 1, 2002 and December 31, 2002
   c. June 30, 2002 and January 1, 2009

7. A first-time IFRS adopter may recognize all cumulative actuarial gains and losses at the date of transition to IFRS, even if it uses the corridor approach for later actuarial gains and losses. If a first-time adopter uses this election:
   a. It may choose to do so on a plan by plan basis.
   b. It shall apply it to all plans.
   c. It shall require retrospective analysis of cumulative actuarial gains and losses.

8. There are four situations in which the IASB prohibits retrospective application (rather than providing the option not to apply retrospective application). Which of the following is **not** one of those situations?
   a. Hedge accounting
   b. Estimates
   c. Insurance contracts

PRESENTATION AND DISCLOSURE

The first point to emphasize is that all presentation and disclosure requirements of all IFRSs must be followed in full. This includes at least three statements of financial position, two statements of comprehensive income, two separate income statements (if presented), two statements of cash flows, and two statements of changes in equity and related notes, including comparative information.

The Board notes that many entities choose, or are required by other regulations, to provide either full comparatives for two or more years or historical summaries of selected data for a number of years. In any such event, consistency with IFRS beyond the one-year requirement is not necessary. However, in any financial statements containing historical summaries or comparative information under previous GAAP, an entity shall:

- Label the previous GAAP information prominently as not being prepared under IFRSs; and
- Disclose the nature of the main adjustments that would make it comply with IFRS. The entity need not quantify those adjustments.

As a general tenet (par. 23), an entity shall explain how the transition from previous GAAP to IFRSs affected its reported financial position, financial performance, and cash flows. The implications of this are spelled out by IFRS 1 in detail and, for completeness, this detail is repeated here.

Reconciliations

To comply with paragraph 23, an entity's first IFRS financial statements shall include (par. 24):

- Reconciliations of its equity reported under previous GAAP to its equity under IFRSs for both of the following dates:
  - The date of transition to IFRSs
  - The end of the latest period presented in the entity's most recent annual financial statements under previous GAAP
- A reconciliation to its total comprehensive income under IFRSs for the latest period in the entity's most recent annual financial statements. The starting point for that reconciliation shall be total comprehensive income under previous GAAP for the same period or, if an entity did not report such a total, profit or loss under previous GAAP.
- If the entity recognized or reversed any impairment losses for the first time in preparing its opening IFRS statement of financial position, the disclosures that IAS 36, "Impairment of Assets," would have required if the entity had recognized those impairment losses or reversals in the period beginning with the date of transition to IFRSs.

The reconciliations required by paragraph 24 shall give sufficient detail to enable users to understand the material adjustments to the statement of financial position and statement of comprehensive income. If an entity presented a statement of cash flows under its previous GAAP, it shall also explain the material adjustments to the cash flow statement (par. 25).

If any entity becomes aware of errors made under previous GAAP, the reconciliations required by paragraph 39 shall distinguish the correction of those errors from changes in accounting policies (par. 26).

IAS 8 does not apply to the changes in accounting policies an entity makes when it adopts IFRSs or to changes in those policies until after it presents its first IFRS financial statements. Therefore, IAS 8's requirements about changes in accounting policies do not apply in an entity's first IFRS financial statements.

If an entity did not present financial statements for previous periods, its first IFRS financial statements shall disclose that fact.

Designation of Financial Assets or Financial Liabilities (Par. 29)

An entity is permitted to designate a previously recognized financial asset or financial liability as a financial asset or financial liability at fair value through profit or loss or a financial asset as available-for-sale in accordance with paragraph D19. The entity shall disclose the fair value of financial assets or financial liabilities designated into each category at the date of designation and their classification and carrying amount in the previous financial statements.

Use of Fair Value as Deemed Cost

If an entity uses fair value in its opening IFRS statement of financial position as deemed cost for an item of (1) property, plant, and equipment, (2) an investment property, or (3) an intangible asset, the entity's first IFRS financial statements shall disclose, for each line item in the opening IFRS statement of financial position:
- The aggregate of those fair values
- The aggregate adjustment to the carrying amounts reported under previous GAAP

Similarly, if an entity uses a deemed cost in its opening IFRS statement of financial position for an investment in a subsidiary, jointly controlled entity, or associate in its separate financial statements (see paragraph 23B), the entity's first IFRS separate financial statements shall disclose:
- The aggregate deemed cost of those investments for which deemed cost is their previous GAAP carrying amount
- The aggregate deemed cost of those investments for which deemed cost is fair value
- The aggregate adjustment to the carrying amounts reported under previous GAAP

Interim Financial Reports

To comply with paragraph 23, if an entity presents an interim financial report under IAS 24, "Related Party Disclosures," for part of the period covered by its first IFRS financial statements, the entity shall satisfy the following requirements in addition to the requirements of IAS 34:
- Each such interim financial report shall, if the entity presented an interim financial report for the comparable interim period of the immediately preceding financial year, include:
  - A reconciliation of its equity under previous GAAP at the end of that comparable interim period to its equity under IFRSs at that date
  - A reconciliation to its total comprehensive income under IFRSs for that comparable interim period (current and year-to-date). The starting point for that reconciliation shall be total comprehensive income under previous GAAP for that period or, if an entity did not report such a total, profit or loss under previous GAAP.
- In addition to the reconciliations required by the first item above, an entity's first interim financial report under IAS 34 for part of the period

covered by its first IFRS financial statements shall include the reconciliations described in paragraph 24 (supplemented by the details required by paragraphs 25 and 26) or a cross-reference to another published document that includes these reconciliations.

- If an entity changes its accounting policies or its use of the exemptions contained in this IFRS, it shall explain the changes in each such interim financial report in accordance with paragraph 23 and update the reconciliations required by the items above.

IAS 34 requires minimum disclosures, which are based on the assumption that users of the interim financial report also have access to the most recent annual financial statements. However, IAS 34 also requires an entity to disclose "any events or transactions that are material to an understanding of the current interim period." Therefore, if a first-time adopter did not, in its most recent annual financial statements under previous GAAP, disclose information material to an understanding of the current interim period, its interim financial report shall disclose that information or include a cross-reference to another published document that includes it.

> **OBSERVATION**
>
> The basic principle of IFRS 1 is simple and sensible; that is, that the first set of full IFRS financial statements should present information over the two (or more) years involved on a fully consistent basis. To do this in full would require some very complex calculations, sometimes based on information from many years earlier, and IASB has granted a range of detailed exemptions. Unfortunately, the specification of these exemptions, designed to reduce complexity for preparers, has significantly increased the complexity of the Standard itself.

STUDY QUESTIONS

9. Which of the following is a first-time adopter of IFRS required to present in its financial statements?

   a. Three statements of comprehensive income
   b. Three statements of financial position
   c. Three statements of cash flow

10. To comply with paragraph 23, an entity's first IFRS financial statements is *not* required to include which of the following reconciliations?

  a. Reconciliation of its past five years income reported under previous GAAP to its income under IFRSs

  b. A reconciliation to its total comprehensive income under IFRSs for the latest period in the entity's most recent annual financial statements.

  c. If the entity recognized any impairment losses for the first time in preparing its opening IFRS statement of financial position, the disclosures that IAS 36 would have required if the entity had recognized those impairment losses in the period beginning with the date of transition to IFRSs.

CPE NOTE: When you have completed your study and review of chapters 1-2, which comprise Module 1, you may wish to take the Quizzer for this Module.

For your convenience, you can also take this Quizzer online at **www. cchtestingcenter.com.**

Determining Whether An Entity is a VIE: FASB ASC Topic 810

LEARNING OBJECTIVES

Upon completion of this chapter, the reader will be able to:

- Define a VIE
- Describe what characterizes a VIE
- Explain the tests, both qualitative and quantitative, that are used to determine whether an entity is a VIE and who should perform those tests
- List the requirements under FIN 46R (now codified as part of FASB ASC Topic 810) that must be satisfied in order for one entity to consolidate an off-balance sheet entity
- State when a VIE should be recharacterized and at what value
- List examples of variable interests

INTRODUCTION

FASB Interpretation No. 46R (FIN 46R) (now codified as part of ASC Topic 810) was issued in December 2003 and replaces the original Interpretation No. 46 that was issued in January 2003. FIN 46R, as revised, addresses the consolidation rules found in ARB No. 51, *Consolidated Financial Statements*, and FAS 94, *Consolidation of All Majority-Owned Subsidiaries*, as they relate to off-balance sheet entities, referred to as variable interest entities (VIEs).

In June 2009, the FASB issued FAS 167, *Amendments to FASB Interpretation No. 46R*, which has as its primary goal to improve the application of certain provisions found in FIN 46R including changes made to the Qualified Special Purpose Entity (QSPE) rules.

The general rule for consolidation of entities found in ARB No. 51, *Consolidated Financial Statements* (ASC Topic 810) is that consolidation occurs when one entity directly or indirectly has a controlling financial interest in another entity. A controlling financial interest is deemed to occur when one entity (the parent) owns more than 50 percent of the voting shares of another entity (the subsidiary.) Prior to FIN 46R, with respect to an enterprise that controlled, but did not own another entity, the rules had been scattered among a series of FASB Emerging Issues Task Force opinions. In most cases, an enterprise that controlled another (through contract, support, or otherwise), but did not own the majority of its voting equity, was not required to consolidate with that entity provided certain criteria were met. Thus, the concept of "off-balance sheet" entities (that is, unconsolidated entities), has evolved over the years.

FIN 46R, as amended, addresses those so called "off-balance sheet" entities (referred to as variable interest entities or VIEs) and establishes rules as to when one entity must consolidate another entity that it effectively controls, even though there may be no controlling ownership between the two entities.

FIN 46R replaces the previously used term "special purpose entity" or "SPE" with the term "variable interest entity" or "VIE," to identify those entities that now may have to be consolidated.

Consolidated Statements

The rules for consolidations are found in Accounting Research Bulletin (ARB) 51, *Consolidated Financial Statements*, as amended by Financial Accounting Standards Board (FASB) Statement No. 94, *Consolidation of All Majority-Owned Subsidiaries (ASC Topic 810, Consolidation*, in the Accounting Standards Codification).

ARB No. 51 states, "There is a presumption that consolidated statements are more meaningful than separate statements…"

In general, ARB No. 51 and FAS 94 require the consolidation of all majority-owned subsidiaries; that is, a situation in which one entity has a controlling financial interest (through ownership of more than 50 percent voting shares) in another entity.

> **NOTE**
>
> Previously, there were several exceptions to the consolidation requirement whereby an entity was not required to consolidate another even though ownership exceeded the 50 percent threshold. Those exceptions included situations involving non-homogeneous operations, foreign ownership, or where control was temporary or did not rest with the majority owner. FAS 94 and FAS 145 eliminated these exceptions. Now, an entity that owns more than 50 percent of the voting shares of another entity is required to consolidate that entity's financial statements with its own.

The Variable Interest Entity (VIE) Rules: FIN 46R

An exception to the more-than-50 percent-ownership rule for consolidation is where there is an off-balance entity that is categorized as a variable interest entity (VIE) as discussed in FASB Interpretation No. 46R, *Consolidation of Variable Interest Entities—An Interpretation of ARB No. 51*, as amended by FAS 167.

FIN 46R was issued in December 2003, and was amended by FAS 167, *Amendments to FASB Interpretation No. 46R*, in June 2009.

A discussion of FIN 46R takes up the remainder of this chapter. The terms "FIN 46R," "Interpretation FIN 46R," and "the Interpretation" are used interchangeably throughout this chapter.

Part of the challenge in dealing with FIN 46R is that, in writing the final document, the FASB chose to limit the guidance and examples that illustrate its application. Although not formerly identified as such, FIN 46R represents the FASB's first attempt at applying principles-based accounting under which broad concepts and principles are given with few rules to illustrate the application of those principles. The result is that the profession is left with a document that is difficult to understand and implement. A validation of this fact is that, subsequent to the issuance of the original Interpretation No. 46 in January 2003, the FASB Staff had issued six FASB Staff Positions (FSPs) essentially "interpreting FIN 46R," and had proposed five additional FSPs. Ultimately, it had to issue a revised Interpretation in December 2003.

Later, the FASB issued FAS 167 to make further changes to FIN 46R but added little additional guidance on how to implement it except that it expanded the number of examples within its appendix.

Even with the issuance of a revised Interpretation, as amended by FAS 167, there is little doubt that the FASB Staff will be required to issue more guidance in the future. Consequently, in this document the author has incorporated his own views on how to apply FIN 46R based on unofficial discussions with the FASB Staff and others.

In addition to amending FIN 46R, FAS 167 either rescinded or amended several FASB Staff Positions related to FIN 46R, as follows.

Changes Made to FSPs by FAS 167

FASB Staff Position Number and Title		Impact of FAS 167
FSP FIN46(R)-3	*Evaluating Whether, as a Group, the Holders of the Equity Investment at Risk Lack the Direct or Indirect Ability to Make Decisions about an Entity's Activities through Voting Rights or Similar Rights under FASB Interpretation No. 46 (revised December 2003)*	Rescinded the FSP
FSP FIN46(R)-4 and FIN 46(R)-8	*Disclosures by Public Entities (Reporting entities) about Transfers of Financial Assets and Interests in Variable Interest Entities*	Rescinded the FSP
FSP FIN46(R)-5	*Implicit Variable Interests under FASB Interpretation No. 46 (revised December 2003)*	Amended the FSP
FSP FIN 46(R)-6	*Determining the Variability to Be Considered in Applying FASB Interpretation No. 46(R)*	Amended the FSP

Key Changes Made to FIN 46R by FAS 167

FAS 167 was issued to amend FIN 46R to address concerns made by parties that key provisions had to be modified. In general, FAS 167 makes the following changes to FIN 46R:

- Adds qualifying special-purpose entities (QSPEs) to the scope of entities subject to FIN 46R
- Changes the concept of a primary beneficiary which may be required to consolidate a variable interest entity:
  - The definition of a primary beneficiary is changed.
  - Use of a quantitative method to determine whether an entity is the primary beneficiary has been eliminated and is replaced by sole use of a qualitative approach.
- Requires a variable interest holder to perform ongoing reassessments of a VIE to determine whether the variable interest holder is the primary beneficiary required to consolidate the VIE. Previously FIN 46R required that a reassessment be performed only if certain triggering events occurred.
- Amends the definition of a variable interest entity
- Adds an additional reconsideration event for determining whether an entity is a variable interest entity when certain facts and circumstances occur
- Enhances the disclosures required

Although most of the changes appear to be made for the better, FIN 46R, as amended, is still a highly complex and difficult standard to apply in practice.

The changes made by FAS 167 are effective as of the beginning of each reporting enterprise's first annual reporting period that begins after November 15, 2009, for interim periods within that first annual reporting period, and for interim and annual reporting periods thereafter. Early application is prohibited.

In 2010, the FASB issued an Accounting Standards Update (ASU) to ASC 810, *Consolidation*, entitled, *Amendments to Statement 167 for Certain Investment Funds*. The ASU defers the effective date of FAS 167 indefinitely for a reporting enterprise's (investment manager's) interest in an entity that either has the attributes of an investment company, or for which it is industry practice to apply measurement principles for financial reporting purposes that are consistent with those followed by investment companies.

What is a variable interest entity (VIE)? A variable interest entity (VIE) is nothing more than an off-balance sheet entity that now may be required to be consolidated by another entity from which it receives financial support.

A VIE is not self-supportive in that it cannot finance its activities without financial support from another entity or individual.

Example

A company is not able to obtain bank financing without an affiliate guaranteeing its bank loan. FIN 46R states that because the company must receive additional financial support from others (e.g., in this example, in the form of another entity guaranteeing its loan), it is not self-supportive. Thus, it is a VIE. If certain other criteria are met, the VIE must be consolidated with the reporting enterprise that has a controlling financial interest through other than ownership in equity.

Not all off-balance sheet entities are VIEs, and those that are not should not be consolidated under FIN 46R. In fact, many off-balance-sheet entities are not VIEs because they are self-supportive and can easily finance their activities without additional financial support from another entity or individual. A non-VIE is never consolidated under FIN 46R and is only consolidated if another entity owns more than 50 percent of its voting stock, as required by ARB No. 51.

The following chart summarizes the way in which the reader should look at the term VIE as used throughout the remainder of this chapter.

Off-Balance Sheet Entities

Type of Off-Balance Sheet Entity	General Description	Rules: Interpretation 46R
Variable interest entity (VIE)	Is not self-supportive—cannot finance its activities without additional subordinated financial support from others (e.g., guarantees, subordinated loans, etc.)	May have to be consolidated under FIN 46R if certain other criteria are met
Non-variable interest entity (Non-VIE)	Self-supportive—can finance its activities without additional subordinated financial support from others.	Not required to be consolidated under FIN 46R Consolidated only based on the traditional consolidation rules (more than 50 percent ownership in voting equity)

General Rules of FIN 46R

The term special-purpose entity (SPE) is superseded by the term "variable interest entity (VIE)." Typically, VIEs are involved in:

- Leasing arrangements, including sales with leasebacks (referred to as synthetic leases)
- Financing arrangements with third party financial institutions to fund acquisitions of certain assets or businesses
- Management of certain receivables or investments
- Research and development and other project development activities
- Hedge activities to manage risk
- Management services
- Distribution services

The rules apply to all entities (except as otherwise noted in below) and include any type of entity that is a legal structure used to conduct activities or to hold assets such as corporations, partnerships, limited liability companies, grantor and other types of trusts.

> **NOTE**
>
> The rules apply to all entities including one-member LLCs. Although a one-member LLC is a "non-entity" for income tax purposes, it is a legal entity to which FIN 46R applies. If a one-member LLC is a VIE, it is conceivable that it will be consolidated by another entity.

FIN 46R does not apply to:
- Not-for-profit organizations as defined in paragraph 168 of FAS 117, *Financial Statements of Not-for-Profit Organizations* (ASC 958).
  - The definition of a not-for-profit organization, found in Paragraph 168 of FAS 117 includes an entity that possesses the following characteristics:
    - Contributions of significant amounts of resources from resource providers who do not expect commensurate proportionate pecuniary return
    - Operating purposes other than to provide goods or services for profit
    - Absence of ownership interests like those of business reporting enterprises
  - Entities that fall outside the definition of a not-for-profit organization include all investor-owned companies, and entities that provide dividends, lower costs, or other economic benefits directly and proportionately to their owners, members, or participants. Examples of entities that do not meet the definition of not-for-profit organizations include mutual insurance companies, credit unions, farm and rural electric cooperatives, and employee benefit plans.

> **NOTE**
>
> Following are exceptions to the not-for profit organizations:
>
> - If a not-for-profit entity is used by a business reporting enterprise in a manner similar to a VIE in an effort to circumvent the provisions of FIN 46R, the not-for-profit entity is subject to FIN 46R.
> - A not-for-profit organization may be considered a related party for purposes of applying the related party rules found in FIN 46R.

> **NOTE**
>
> Upon the issuance of the original interpretation, it was not clear as to whether health care organizations were subject to FIN 46R. In a subsequently issued FSP, the FASB concluded that all not-for-profit organizations were excluded from the requirements of FIN 46R, including health care organizations subject to the Audit Guide. The revised Interpretation reaffirms that all not-for-profit organizations are excluded from the application of FIN 46R unless they are used by a for-profit organization to circumvent the rules of FIN 46R.

- An employee benefit plan subject to the provisions of FAS 87, Employers' Accounting for Pensions, FAS 106, Employers' Accounting for Postretirement Benefits Other Than Pensions (ASC 715), and FAS 112, Employers' Accounting for Postemployment Benefits (ASC 712). An example would be where a company is not required to consolidate with its pension plan even though the company may control that plan.
- Investments accounted for at fair value in accordance with the specialized accounting guidance in the AICPA Audit and Accounting Guide, Investment Companies (amended per FSP FIN 46(R)-7. Previously, the exemption applied to a reporting enterprise that was subject to SEC Regulation S-X, Rule 6-03(c.)(1))
- Separate accounts of life insurance entities as described in AICPA Audit and Accounting Guide, Life and Health Insurance Entities
- Special exemptions from FIN 46R for:
  - Non-substantive terms, transactions, and arrangements
  - Variable interest holders who have difficulty obtaining information
  - Certain entities that are businesses
- Certain governmental organizations: an entity shall not consolidate a governmental organization and shall not consolidate a financing entity established by a governmental organization unless the financing entity is not a governmental organization and is used by the business entity in a manner similar to a VIE in an effort to circumvent the provisions of FIN 46R.
- Property held individually: real estate or other assets held individually is not subject to consolidation under FIN 46R. Thus, determination as to whether real estate or other assets is consolidated differs based on how title is held to the real estate or other assets. Consider the following two examples.

Do the rules apply to an individual who is the primary beneficiary of a VIE?
An individual may be required to issue personal financial statements to a bank or other third party. That individual may have a controlling financial interest in a VIE (through ownership or non-ownership such as guarantees, or other forms of financial support). In such a case, the consolidation rules of FIN 46R do not apply. FIN 46R only applies to a legal entity and not to an individual.

What about qualifying SPEs? Prior to the issuance of FAS 167, FIN 46R excluded two entities from the application of FIN 46R:

- A transferor of financial assets or its affiliates to a special-purpose entity (SPE) or a formerly qualifying SPE as described in FAS 140, *Accounting for Transfers and Servicing of Financial Assets and Extinguishments of Liabilities*
- A reporting enterprise that holds variable interests in a qualifying SPE or a formerly qualifying SPE as described in FAS 140, *Accounting for Transfers and Servicing of Financial Assets and Extinguishments of Liabilities*

With the issuance of FAS 166, *Accounting for Transfers of Financial Assets* (ASC 860), the FASB eliminated the concept of a qualifying special-purpose entity (QSPE) that was previously covered in FAS 140. Consequently, in FAS 167, the FASB eliminated the exemption in FIN 46R related to QSPEs. Thus, QSPEs are included within the scope of FIN 46R.

STUDY QUESTIONS

1. The general rule for consolidation of entities found in ARB No. 51, *Consolidated Financial statements* (ASC 810), is that consolidation occurs when:

   a. An entity owns at least 75 percent of the operations of another entity.

   b. One entity directly or indirectly has a controlling financial interest in another entity.

   c. One entity owns less than 50 percent of the voting shares of another entity.

   d. There is an off-balance sheet entity.

2. Under FAS 94 (ASC 810) and FAS 145 (ASC 205), which of the following is an exception to the consolidation rules?

   a. Situations involving foreign ownership

   b. Situations involving non-homogeneous operations

   c. Situations where control was temporary

   d. There are no exceptions.

3. Under FIN 46R, a non-variable interest entity (non-VIE) is:

   a. Consolidated based only on the traditional consolidation rules

   b. Unable to finance its activities without additional subordinated financial support

   c. Not self-supportive

   d. Required to be consolidated

---

4. Which of the following is correct with respect to how qualifying SPEs should be accounted for under FIN 46R?

   a. QSPEs are excluded from FIN 46R's scope.
   b. QSPEs are included within FIN 46R's scope.
   c. QSPEs are not addressed by FIN 46R.

5. Which of the following replaced the term "special purpose entity (SPE)" with the issuance of FAS 167?

   a. Variable interest entity
   b. Non issuer
   c. Subsidiary

6. Consolidated financial statements generally provide which of the following?

   a. More meaningful financial statements
   b. More confusing financial statements
   c. More incentive to use the fair value option

RULES OF FIN 46R

The general rule for consolidation found in ARB No. 51 is that one reporting enterprise (parent) consolidates another other entity (subsidiary) if the parent owns more than 50 percent of the voting shares of the subsidiary. ARB No. 51 assumes that a parent that owns more than 50 percent of the voting shares of subsidiary has a controlling financial interest in that entity.

Interpretation 46R deals with instances in which one reporting enterprise does not own the majority of the voting shares of another. Yet, if certain conditions are satisfied, that reporting enterprise still may have a controlling financing interest through other than ownership.

Specifically, FIN 46R requires that one reporting enterprise (the primary beneficiary) consolidate an entity (the VIE) if the primary beneficiary has a controlling financial interest in the VIE that is not based on ownership.

A controlling financial interest is achieved by other than ownership if two criteria are satisfied:

- First, the primary beneficiary must have the power to direct the VIE's most significant activities.
- Secondly, the primary beneficiary is obligated to absorb the losses of the VIE and has the right to receive the benefits of the VIE.

Ownership of the VIE is not necessary for a reporting enterprise to be the primary beneficiary that consolidates a VIE.

Thus, FIN 46R expands the consolidation rules model found in ARB No. 51 (based on more-than-50 percent ownership) with one that requires consolidation based on a reporting enterprise (primary beneficiary) having the attributes of power and the economic risks and benefits, of that VIE, without having any ownership in that VIE.

FIN 46R is built on the premise that a reporting enterprise (the primary beneficiary) that has power and access to the economic risks and rewards of a VIE has a controlling financial interest in the VIE, thereby acting as a de facto owner even if that primary beneficiary has no ownership in the VIE. Therefore, in substance, the reporting enterprise should consolidate the VIE as if it were the majority owner of the VIE's equity.

FIN 46R uses the following terms:

- **Variable interest entity (VIE).** An entity that is not self-supportive in that it cannot finance its activities without receiving additional subordinated financial support from another entity or individual.
- **Variable interest (VI).** A form of financial support given by one entity or individual to a VIE in the form of a guarantee, loan, certain lease payments, certain management fees, etc.
- **Primary beneficiary (PB).** The entity or individual that has a controlling financial interest in a VIE by having the power to direct the VIE's significant activities, and the obligation to absorb the VIE's losses and right to receive the VIE's benefits that are significant to the VIE. If the primary beneficiary is an entity, it consolidates the VIE, while if it is an individual, it does not consolidate the VIE.

Flowchart 3.1

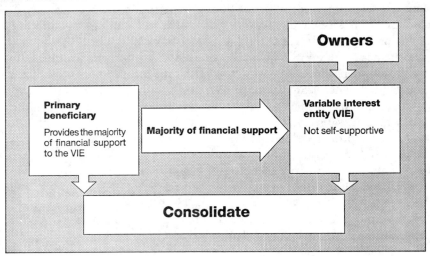

Basic Rules for Consolidation- Three Requirements

In order for one reporting enterprise to consolidate an off-balance sheet entity under FIN 46R, there are three requirements that must exist:

- **Requirement 1.** There must be a VIE (off-balance sheet entity that is not self-supportive).
- **Requirement 2.** Reporting entities and/or individuals must have variable interests in the VIE (e.g., provide subordinated financial support to the VIE through equity, loans, guarantees, etc.).
- **Requirement 3.** A reporting enterprise must be the primary beneficiary of the VIE by having a controlling financial interest in that VIE through other than majority ownership.

If all three requirements are met and if a reporting enterprise is the primary beneficiary, it must consolidate the VIE.

- If an individual (rather than a reporting enterprise) is the primary beneficiary, there is no consolidation required of the VIE.
- If all three requirements are not satisfied, no consolidation of the VIE is required.
- If a reporting enterprise has a variable interest in a VIE, but the reporting enterprise is not the primary beneficiary, consolidation is not required but certain disclosures must be made.

The three requirements must be met in order for one entity to consolidate another. The following chart illustrates the interrelation of the three requirements.

Three Requirements for Consolidation of a VIE

Three Requirements for Consolidation				
Is the entity a VIE? (not self-supportive)	Does a reporting enterprise have a VI in the VIE? (a form of financial support)	Is the enterprise the primary beneficiary lof the VIE? (controlling financial interest from other than ownership of the VIE's majority equity)	Consolidate?	Disclose?
Yes	Yes	Yes	Yes*	Yes
Yes	Yes	No	No- Consolidate based only on ARB No. 51 (more than 50 percent ownership).	Disclose if variable interest is significant (but not the primary beneficiary of the VIE).
Yes	No	No	No- Consolidate based only on ARB No. 51 (more than 50 percent ownership).	No- Must have a variable interest in a VIE to disclose.
No	Yes	Yes	No- Consolidate based only on ARB No. 51 (more than 50 percent ownership).	No – Must be a VIE to require disclosure.

* If the primary beneficiary is an individual, no consolidation of the VIE is required.

The following flowchart illustrates the logic used to apply the FIN 46R requirements.

Flowchart 3.2: Flowchart to Consolidation – FIN 46R

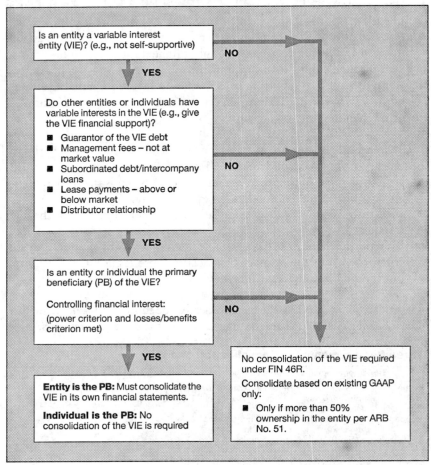

REQUIREMENT 1 FOR CONSOLIDATION OF A VIE

In order for an off-balance sheet entity to be consolidated, it must be a variable interest entity (VIE). A variable interest entity (VIE) is an entity that is not self-supportive by having one or both of the following conditions:

- It has an insufficient amount of equity for it to finance its activities, without receiving additional subordinated financial support from other parties or individuals.
- Its equity owners lack the typical power, risks and rights of equity owners.

An entity that either has an insufficient amount of equity to finance its activities or has equity owners that do not have the typical power, risks and rights of ownership is not self-supportive and is a VIE in that it needs additional sources of financial support to survive.

Because a VIE lacks financial support to survive, it must obtain such financial support from other individuals and reporting enterprises. That financial support is referred to as variable interests. If certain criteria are met, one of the reporting enterprises or individuals who gives the VIE financial support (a variable interest) may be considered the VIE's de facto parent, otherwise called the primary beneficiary who may consolidate the VIE.

Definition of a VIE

FIN 46R provides a formal definition of a VIE. An entity is considered a VIE if it has one or both of the following two conditions by design (FIN 46R states that the phrase "by design" refers to entities that meet the conditions of being a VIE because of the way they are structured. For example, an entity under the control of its equity holders that originally was not a VIE does not become one because of operating losses.).

Condition 1 to be a VIE. The total equity investment at risk is not sufficient to permit it to finance its activities without obtaining additional subordinated financial support provided by any parties (e.g., individual or entity), including equity holders.

Examples include situations in which:
- The entity does not have enough equity to fund its expected losses without additional financial support.
- The entity is unable to obtain outside financing from an independent third party (such as a bank or other lender), without additional financial support from other parties.

Such additional subordinated financial support (referred to as variable interests) may come in the form of any of the following:
- Guarantees of the entity's loans from lenders
- Management fees that are not at market value
- Above-market lease payments
- Subordinated (intercompany) loans
- Distribution of the entity's products by contract or other agreement
- Management or other services that are not at market value

Condition 2 to be a VIE. As a group, the holders of equity investments at risk lack any one of the following three characteristics:
- They lack the power through voting rights or similar rights to direct the entity's activities that most significantly impact the entity's economic

performance. Investors do not have the power if no owners hold voting rights or similar rights that are similar to those of a common shareholder in a corporation or a general partner in a partnership.

- They lack the obligation to absorb the expected losses of the entity. Investors do not have the obligation to absorb losses if they are directly or indirectly protected from the expected losses or are guaranteed a return by the entity itself or by other parties involved with the entity.
- They lack the right to receive expected residual returns of the entity. Investors do not have the right if their return is capped by the entity's governing documents or arrangements with other variable interest holders or the entity. The return is not considered to be capped by the existence of outstanding stock options, convertible debt, or similar interests because if the options are exercised, the holders will become additional equity investors.

The total equity investment at risk excludes:
- Equity interests that the entity issued in exchange for subordinated interests in other variable interest entities

> **NOTE**
>
> The FASB included this anti-abuse provision to preclude two entities from issuing excess equity capitalized with the same investment.

- Amounts provided to the equity investor directly or indirectly by the entity or by other parties involved with the entity (e.g., by fees, contributions, or other payments), unless the provider is a parent, subsidiary, or affiliate of the investor that is required to be included in the same set of consolidated financial statements as the investor.
- Amounts financed for the equity investor (such as by loans or guarantees of loans) directly by the entity or by other parties involved with the entity, unless that party is a parent, subsidiary, or affiliate of the investor that is required to be included in the same set of consolidated financial statements as the investor.

Impact of kick-out and participating rights on the power to direct activities. FAS 167 amends FIN 46R to address the impact of equity holders having kick-out rights or participating rights on whether other parties have power to direct activities.

Exceptions include:
- A single equity holder (including related parties and de facto agents) that has the unilateral ability to exercise such kick-out or participating rights does in fact, negate another party's power to direct activities.

- If interests other than those of equity holders hold such kick-out or participating rights, those rights do not prevent the equity holders from having such power unless one single party has the unilateral ability to exercise those rights.

What about protective rights? Protective rights are rights designed to protect the interests of the party holding those rights, without giving that party a controlling financial interest in the entity to which they relate. Protective rights held by other parties do not prevent a reporting enterprise from having the power to direct the activities of a VIE.

Flowchart 3.3

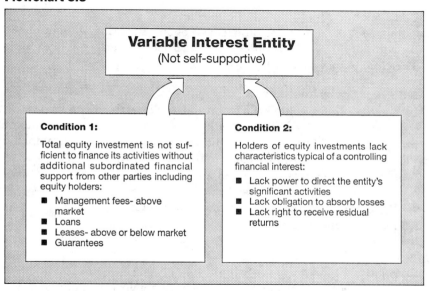

What if an entity is not a VIE? Is consolidation ever required? If an entity is not a VIE, there is no consolidation required of the entity under FIN 46R. By not being a VIE, the entity has demonstrated that it is self-supportive. Therefore, if an entity is not a VIE, it is not consolidated under FIN 46R. The only way it would be consolidated is under the existing consolidation rules; that is, if another entity owns more than 50 percent of the entity's voting stock.

Analysis of the Two Conditions to Being a VIE

Condition 1 to being a VIE is that the total equity investment at risk is not sufficient to permit it to finance its activities without obtaining additional subordinated financial support provided by any parties (e.g., individual or entity), including equity holders.

One way in which an entity is a VIE is if the total equity investment at risk is not sufficient for it to finance its activities without obtaining additional subordinated financial support from other parties, whether an individual or entity.

Example

Company A owns real estate and leases it to Company B. Company A seeks bank financing but is unable to obtain it because it does not have enough equity in the value of its real estate to satisfy the bank's underwriting requirements. Therefore, the bank requires that A obtain a guarantor of its note. B agrees to guarantee the note for A.

Conclusion

Company A's equity is not sufficient to obtain financing without obtaining additional financial support from other parties, such as B's guarantee. Therefore, A may be a VIE.

Sufficient Equity Investment

If an entity's equity is not sufficient to finance its activities on its own, the entity is considered a VIE because it is assumed it must rely on another party (entity or individual) for additional financial support. Examples of such additional support may come in the form of:

- Guarantees or cross-collateral of loans
- Management fees- not at market value
- Lease payments that are above or below market
- Distribution services
- Loans

Example

In order to receive a bank loan, an entity must obtain a guarantee of its loan from its shareholder or an affiliate.

Conclusion

The entity's equity is not sufficient because it must obtain additional financial support (e.g., guarantees) in order to obtain the outside bank financing. Thus, the entity is a VIE.

Example

An entity's equity is not sufficient to absorb its expected losses.

Conclusion

Because the entity's equity cannot absorb any expected losses, it is not sufficient to finance its activities. Therefore, the entity is a VIE.

> **NOTE**
>
> The term "finance activities" is not defined in FIN 46R. The FASB has indicated that one way an entity is able to "finance its activities" is if it can obtain non-recourse financing from an unrelated party (such as in the case of obtaining bank or other independent financing) without receiving additional subordinated financial support in the form of a guarantee or a subordinated loan. Additionally, an entity is able to "finance its activities" if it has enough equity to fund any expected losses (e.g., it has enough equity to fund a worst-case scenario of expected losses).

Determining whether an entity has sufficient equity investment to finance its activities without additional subordinated financial support is a matter of facts and circumstances.

FIN 46R provides several methods by which any entity can demonstrate it has sufficient equity to finance its own activities without additional financial support. There is also a 10-percent presumption rule that is discussed below.

Methods to Demonstrate Sufficiency of Equity: Condition 1

The revised Interpretation provides a series of methods to demonstrate that an entity has sufficient equity to finance its activities without additional subordinated financial support from other parties, including equity holders. The methods include both qualitative and quantitative analyses, as well as an overall 10-percent equity rule, summarized as follows:

- Overall rule- 10 percent presumption rule
- Methods to demonstrate sufficiency of equity
- Qualitative methods:
    - **Non-recourse financing method,** The entity has demonstrated that it can obtain non-recourse, investment-grade financing from an unrelated party, without additional subordinated financial support.
    - **Similar entity method.** The entity has at least as much equity as a similar entity that finances its operations with no additional subordinated financial support.
    - **Other facts and circumstances method.** Based on other facts and circumstances, the entity demonstrates that it can finance its activities without additional subordinated financial support.
- Quantitative Methods:
    - **Expected losses method.** The entity's equity is greater than its expected losses.

The demonstration that equity is sufficient may be based on either qualitative or quantitative analysis, or both, based on the following guidance:

- **Qualitative methods.** Use of qualitative methods will, in some cases, be conclusive to determine that the entity's equity at risk is sufficient.
- **Quantitative method.** The use of a quantitative method should be used if, after diligent effort, a reasonable conclusion about the sufficiency of the entity's equity at risk cannot be reached based solely on use of qualitative methods.
- **Both Qualitative and Quantitative Methods.** If neither a qualitative nor a quantitative method, taken alone, is conclusive, the combination of both qualitative and quantitative methods should be used to determine whether the equity at risk is sufficient.

If an entity can satisfy any one of the above methods (either qualitative, quantitative, or both), its equity is considered sufficient to finance its activities without additional subordinated financial support, resulting in the entity being self-supportive. Therefore, the entity is not a VIE based on Condition 1 (sufficiency of equity). Yet, it still could be categorized as a VIE based on Condition 2 (its shareholders lack one of certain characteristics:

- Power to direct significant activities
- Obligation to absorb expected losses
- Right to receive residual returns.

10 Percent Presumption Rule

FIN 46R provides a 10 percent equity rule that can be used as a benchmark as to whether an entity might have enough equity to finance its operations without additional subordinated financial support. The 10-percent equity presumption rule works as follows.

Less than 10 percent equity investment at risk. There is a presumption that an equity investment of less than 10 percent of the entity's total assets is not sufficient for the entity to finance its activities without additional subordinated financial support.

For purposes of the 10-percent test, both equity and total assets are measured at fair value, rather than book value.

$$\frac{\text{Fair value of equity}}{\text{Total assets at fair value}} = \% \text{ equity}$$

10 percent or more equity. It is not presumed that equity is sufficient at 10 percent or more equity. Therefore, an entity is not relieved of the responsibility to demonstrate that its equity is sufficient even if its equity is 10 percent or more. 10 percent or more equity is not a safe harbor threshold. Additional tests must be performed even when the equity is 10 percent or more of total assets.

Qualitative Methods for Determining the Sufficiency of Equity

As previously outlined, an entity should first consider qualitative methods to determine whether the entity has enough equity to finance its activities without additional subordinated financial support. If the entity can satisfy one of the qualitative methods (or the quantitative method- expected losses method), it is deemed to have sufficient equity and is not considered a VIE. If it is not a VIE, it will not be consolidated under the rules of FIN 46R.

The three qualitative methods include:

- **Non-recourse financing method.** The entity has demonstrated that it can obtain non-recourse, investment-grade financing from an unrelated party, without additional subordinated financial support.
- **Similar entity method.** The entity has at least as much equity as a similar entity that finances its operations with no additional subordinated financial support.
- **Other facts and circumstances method.** Based on other facts and circumstances, the entity demonstrates that it can finance its activities without additional subordinated financial support.

Qualitative Method 1: Non-Recourse Financing Method

In Qualitative Method 1, an entity's equity is sufficient if the entity

Has demonstrated that it can obtain non-recourse, investment grade financing from an unrelated party without additional subordinated financial support (loan guarantees, etc.) from other entities or individuals, including equity holders.

If an entity has demonstrated that it can obtain non-recourse, investment-grade financing, it satisfies Method 1 and its equity is considered sufficient to finance its activities without additional subordinated financial support. Because the entity is self-supportive, it is not a VIE.

If, instead, the entity has not demonstrated that it can obtain non-recourse, investment-grade financing, it fails Method 1. Thus, the only way to avoid categorizing the entity as a VIE is to use Qualitative Method 2 or 3 (similar entity method or other facts and circumstances method) or the Quantitative Method 1 (expected losses method).

OBSERVATION

The non-recourse financing method is found in Paragraph 9 of FIN 46R, which has been codified as FASB ASC 810-10-25-45. Specifically, the Paragraph states that an entity is not a VIE if it "has demonstrated that it can finance its activities without additional subordinated financial support." There is no specific mention of the requirement to demonstrate the ability to obtain non-recourse, investment-grade financing. The FASB Staff has stated that Paragraph 9(a) is satisfied if an entity has demonstrated that it can obtain "non-recourse, investment-grade financing" without additional subordinated financial support. That is, non-recourse investment-grade financing without receiving guarantees from others, loans, or other additional financial support that allows the entity to obtain that non-recourse financing.

Example

Company X has demonstrated that it can obtain a non-recourse, investment grade loan from a local bank. The loan does not require any guarantees from X's shareholders or affiliates. Further, X does not need an additional subordinated loan from another party (e.g., second mortgage or unsecured loan) in order to obtain the non-recourse bank financing.

Conclusion

X has demonstrated that it can obtain non-recourse, investment grade financing from an unrelated party (e.g., a bank) without additional subordinated financial support (loan guarantees, additional loans, etc.) from other entities or individuals. Therefore, X has satisfied the non-recourse financing method (Qualitative Method 1) and is considered to have equity sufficient to finance its activities without additional subordinated financial support. X is not a VIE.

Change the Facts

The Bank requires X's shareholder and affiliate to guarantee X's loan.

Conclusion

X has not demonstrated that it can obtain non-recourse, investment-grade financing without additional subordinated financial support, in that guarantees are required by other parties. The guarantee is a form of additional support. Thus, X fails Method 1 and must use one of the other two methods to demonstrate that it is not a VIE.

What is additional subordinated financial support? Additional subordinated financial support is referred to as an additional variable interest that will absorb some or all of an entity's expected losses, if they occur. Examples of variable interests include one entity supporting the other by means of paying management fees, lease payments, guarantees, or making subordinated or senior loans. In fact, a bank loan is also a variable interest in that the bank provides a form of financial support to the entity. Although, as a first lien holder, rarely will a bank be considered the primary beneficiary as it usually does not have enough risk or return to provide the majority of support to the VIE.

Further, additional subordinated financial support can come from all parties including the equity holders. Thus, for example, an equity shareholder that makes a loan to an entity in which it holds an equity investment is a form of additional subordinated financial support.

As it relates to the non-recourse financing method (Qualitative Method 1) and the ability to obtain non-recourse financing, additional subordinated financial support is usually in the form of any of the following variable interests:

- Guarantees of the entity's loan by its owners or other affiliated entities
- Additional loans (subordinated to the bank financing such as a second mortgage or intercompany loan) made to the entity to enable it to obtain bank financing
- Additional collateral for a loan
- Above-market lease payments, management or service contract fees paid to the VIE at the time the entity demonstrates it can obtain non-recourse, investment-grade financing
- Additional loans from the equity holders
- Additional equity infused by equity holders where the additional equity is not at risk.

FIN 46R does not address whether the entity actually has to obtain non-recourse investment-grade financing to demonstrate that it "could" obtain non-recourse financing. FASB ASC 810-10-25-45 (formerly Paragraph 9 of FIN 46R) uses the term "has demonstrated" as it relates to an entity's ability to satisfy non-recourse financing method (Qualitative Method 1).

At present, there are differing opinions as to the meaning of "has demonstrated." Following is a fact pattern to use as a basis of discussion of the issue.

Facts

Company X presently has a recourse loan outstanding with No Loan Bank secured by a commercial building. The loan was obtained 10 years ago when X had little equity in the real estate. At the time the loan was obtained (10 years ago), the loan-to-value was 75 percent, requiring a guarantee from both X's shareholder and Company Y, an affiliate that leases the building from X.

Now, 10 years later, the value of the real estate has increased significantly and the loan principal has been paid down, resulting in the existing loan-to-value of 45 percent. X does not wish to refinance the loan because of the transaction costs associated with such a refinancing.

However, X has contacted a mortgage broker who has confirmed that, based on X's existing equity, X could easily obtain a non-recourse bank loan at 45-percent loan-to-value, with no required guarantees or other subordinated financial support from others. X has received a letter from the mortgage broker, confirming X's ability to obtain such non-recourse financing.

Has X demonstrated that it can obtain non-recourse, investment-grade financing, thereby satisfying Method1? FIN 46R (ASC 810-10-25-45) does not address the meaning of "has demonstrated" thereby leaving the issue wide open.

The author believes that X has demonstrated it can obtain non-recourse, investment-grade financing. The term "has demonstrated" does not necessarily mean that the entity must actually obtain non-recourse financing. The intent of the non-recourse financing method (Qualitative Method 1) is to test the ability of an entity to be self-supportive at a particular point in time, thereby not being reliant on additional financial support from others. Provided an entity can demonstrate that it has the ability to obtain non-recourse financing, the author believes the entity has demonstrated that it "can" obtain such non-recourse financing, even though it chooses not to act on the financing at the present time.

Demonstrating the ability to obtain non-recourse, investment-grade financing? In satisfying the "has demonstrated" criterion, the author takes a position that is less conservative than certain other firms. His view is that in certain situations, an entity should be able to satisfy the "has demonstrated" criterion merely by being able to prove that it "can" obtain non-recourse financing, even though it chooses not to do so.

To demonstrate that an entity can obtain non-recourse financing, a comparison should be made of the entity's existing financial attributes to those benchmarks required by a lender to underwrite a non-recourse loan. The author believes that a specific lender should be identified and contacted and that its underwriting requirements be obtained in writing.

Examples of specific attributes of an entity that should be compared with those required to underwrite a non-recourse loan include:

- Amount of financing the entity would need
- Loan-to-value ratio
- Cash flow coverage ratio
- Whether the entity's industry is attractive to a non-recourse lender

Assuming an entity's attributes satisfy those required by a specific lender, it would appear that the entity has demonstrated that it can obtain non-recourse, investment-grade financing.

Of course, facts and circumstances of each situation must be considered. For example, an entity that barely meets the minimum underwriting criteria for obtaining non-recourse financing may not provide a sufficient margin for error to assert that it has demonstrated it can obtain non-recourse, investment grade financing. Conversely, an entity that easily satisfies such underwriting criteria is more likely to justify that it "has demonstrated" that it can obtain non-recourse, investment-grade financing.

Example

Company X is a real estate LLC that leases real estate to an affiliate. X has an existing recourse loan that has a balance at 68 percent loan-to-value.

Based on information obtained from several local banks in the area, certain lenders are willing to give a non-recourse loan at 70 percent loan-to-value. Based on a comparison of the entity's attributes to the underwriting standards for non-recourse financing, the entity might be able to satisfy the criteria, but approval may be difficult to obtain.

Conclusion

Although the entity might be able to satisfy the underwriting criteria to obtain non-recourse financing, the entity has not demonstrated that it can obtain such financing. The entity's financial criteria are too close to the minimum requirements needed to obtain non-recourse financing.

Thus, the entity probably has not satisfied the non-recourse financing method (Qualitative Method 1) in that it has not demonstrated that it can obtain non-recourse, investment-grade financing.

Change the Facts

The entity's loan-to-value is 30 percent and all evidence suggests that the entity could easily replace the 30 percent loan with a non-recourse loan at an investment-grade interest rate (prime rate).

Conclusion

The entity probably has satisfied Method 1 in that it has demonstrated that it can obtain non-recourse, investment-grade financing.

What is the definition of "investment-grade" financing? FIN 46R does not actually address the issue of investment-grade financing. The FASB Staff has indicated that it is assumed that any non-recourse financing must be investment-grade; that is, financing typically obtained from a bank or other lender at rates customarily offered to the lender's best customers.

- If an investment-grade threshold were not required, an entity could satisfy non-recourse financing method (Qualitative Method 1) by obtaining non-investment-grade, non-recourse financing from a lender that would accept a lower-equity threshold, by charging a higher interest rate.

> **NOTE**
>
> It would appear that an entity has demonstrated its ability to obtain non-recourse financing if it can obtain non-recourse financing at the same loan-to-value as its existing debt outstanding. For example, an entity that presently has a 70-percent loan-to-value recourse loan outstanding can demonstrate that it can replace a 70-percent recourse loan with a 70-percent non-recourse loan.

Example 1

Company S owns commercial real estate that it leases to Company P, an affiliate. John Smith is the 100 percent shareholder of Company S. Company S's financial information follows.

Total assets, primarily real estate (at fair value)	$5,000,000
Existing loan- bank	2,500,000
Equity (fair value)	2,500,000
Loan-to-value ratio	50%

P, as a variable interest holder, is testing S to determine if it is a VIE.

P has confirmed with a local bank that S can refinance its real estate with a non-recourse loan for the 50 percent loan-to-value, with no guarantees from S's shareholder, John Smith, or from P. Further, P has reviewed the bank's underwriting criteria and believes that S can easily satisfy its lending requirements for non-recourse financing.

Conclusion

Based solely on the information provided, Company S has demonstrated that it can obtain non-recourse financing, thereby satisfying non-recourse financing method (Qualitative Method 1).

S has demonstrated that it can obtain financing by the bank agreeing to offer non-recourse financing at the present 70-percent loan-to-value. Therefore, S satisfies the non-recourse financing method (Qualitative Method 1) and is deemed to have sufficient equity to finance its activities without additional subordinated financial support from others. Thus, S is not a VIE.

Example 2

Assume the same facts as in Example 1 except that the bank, as matter of policy, requires personal guarantees from both John Smith, its shareholder, and Company P, its affiliate. S has checked with several other banks that also require, at a minimum, personal guarantees from the shareholder(s) if the loan-to-value is 70 percent or greater.

Conclusion

Based solely on the information provided, Company S has not demonstrated that it can obtain non-recourse financing, in order to satisfy the non-recourse financing method (Qualitative Method 1).

In this Example, S determines that the bank requires more than 30 percent equity in order to obtain non-recourse financing. Consequently, S can only obtain recourse financing, thereby requiring additional subordinated financial support in the form of guarantees from others (P and John Smith).

The conclusion is that at its present loan-to-value, S cannot obtain non-recourse financing. Therefore, S fails non-recourse financing method (Qualitative Method 1), but can still use the other two qualitative methods (similar entity method or other facts and circumstances method), or use a quantitative method (expected losses method), to avoid being categorized as a VIE.

Example 3

Assume the same facts as in Example 2 except that the bank is willing to give S a 60-percent loan on a non-recourse basis without guarantees. S obtains the additional 10 percent from Joey "the Knuckles," a second-mortgage broker at prime plus eight percent.

Conclusion

Although S is able to obtain 60-percent non-recourse financing, it requires additional subordinated financial support in the form of a 10-percent second mortgage note. The second mortgage is additional subordinated financial support regardless of the fact that it is not investment grade (e.g., prime plus eight percent.) Thus, because S is required to obtain additional subordinated financial support to obtain 60-percent non-recourse bank financing, S fails the non-recourse financing method (Qualitative Method 1).

Qualitative Method 2: Similar Entity Method

The second qualitative method that can be used to determine whether an entity has sufficient equity to avoid being considered a VIE is to demonstrate that the entity has at least as much equity as a similar entity that finances its operations with no additional subordinated financial support.

Although FIN 46R does not give any guidance as to how this method should be applied, it appears that its use is limited to specialized industries. For example, certain industries, such as telecommunications, are able to obtain special financing terms due to government regulation.

Example

Company X is a telephone company and has only five-percent equity. Telephone companies are able to obtain 100-percent non-recourse financing under a special government program. Other telephone companies of similar size, assets and profitability have recently received such financing with similar equity levels (e.g., equity level of five percent or less).

Conclusion

Because X can demonstrate that it has at least as much equity as a similar entity that finances its operations with no additional subordinated financial support, X is considered self-supportive and not a VIE.

OBSERVATION

The similar entity method has very limited use in that it applies primarily to specialized industries that might offer favorable financing terms. If one entity in the industry is able to obtain non-recourse financing at particularly low equity levels, it would be reasonable for another entity, with a similar equity structure, to be able to obtain the same or similar financing.

Qualitative Method 3: Other Facts and Circumstances Method

The third qualitative method is to consider other facts and circumstances that may lead to the conclusion that an entity has sufficient equity to finance its activities without additional subordinated financial support. Here, no one single factor will be conclusive and the determination as to whether the entity has sufficient equity is based on the evidence as a whole. Further, some of the qualitative facts and circumstances may overlap with those found in Qualitative Methods 1 and 2.

Quantitative Method for Determining the Sufficiency of Equity

To recap, FIN 46R states that both qualitative and quantitative analyses should be considered in determining whether an entity has sufficient equity to finance its activities without obtaining additional subordinated financial support. Although the Board suggests that qualitative methods should be applied before using a quantitative method, the two categories, qualitative and quantitative, appear to be mutually exclusive.

The previous section discussed the three qualitative methods that can be used, including the non-recourse financing method, similar entity method, and the other facts and circumstances method. In many cases, the use of the qualitative methods will not provide the evidence to support that the entity's equity is sufficient. Consequently, use of a quantitative method is the last chance to otherwise avoid categorizing an entity as a VIE. The one quantitative method provided by FIN 46R is the expected losses method.

Quantitative Method 1: Expected losses method

One prime benchmark used by FIN 46R to determine whether an entity has sufficient equity investment to finance its activities without additional financial support from others, is to use the expected losses method. The expected loss concept is confusing, subject to a high degree of judgment, and very difficult to apply. Because qualitative methods may be futile to supporting a case that an entity's equity is sufficient, in most cases, the expected losses method may be the only method available to prove an off-balance sheet entity is not a VIE.

The basis of the expected losses method: FASB Concept Statement No. 7.

The basis for the expected loss method is the expected cash flows approach found in FASB Concept Statement No. 7, *Using Cash Flow Information and Present Value in Accounting Measurements.*

Using Statement No. 7's expected cash flows approach, multiple estimated cash flows are developed based on several scenarios. For each scenario, estimated cash flows are first discounted to present value using a risk-free interest rate. Then, the discounted cash flows are probability weighted to arrive at a series of expected cash flows that, in the aggregate, equal the fair value of the underlying asset. Concept Statement No. 7 applies the following rules on using the expected cash flows approach. Cash flows should reflect two components:

- Present value
- The range of possible estimated cash flows and their possible outcomes:
  - The sum of probability-weighted discounted cash flows is reflective of a series of possible outcomes.
  - Probability weighting of cash flows helps incorporate uncertainties in estimated cash flows.

In applying present value to cash flows, a risk-free interest rate should be used.

- Risk is already reflected in the probability weighting.
- Risk-free interest rate is the rate of a U. S. Treasury instrument for the period of time for which the cash flows relate.

The expected cash flows approach is more reflective of the range of possible outcomes than the traditional approach (e.g., a single estimated cash flow is discounted using a single credit-adjusted interest rate). Concept Statement No. 7's expected cash flow formula works as follows.

Facts

Assume that an entity is purchasing an asset that will generate estimated cash flows (including ultimate disposition of the asset) of between $100,000 and $300,000 one year from the date of purchase. The risk-free rate of return is five percent.

What is the fair value of the asset based on the expected cash flow approach?

Scenario	Possible Estimated Cash Flows	Probability of Occurrence	Expected Cash Flow	Present Value of Expected Cash Flows (5%, 1 Year)
1	$100,000	20%	$20,000	$19,048
2	200,000	30%	60,000	57,143
3	300,000	50%	150,000	142,857
		100%		$219,048

Using the expected cash flow approach, the asset's fair value is $219,048. If the entity purchases the asset for $219,048, based on its probability-weighted cash flows, it will generate a return of five percent one year from the date of purchase.

> **NOTE**
>
> Concept Statement No. 7's expected cash flows approach is certainly not without critics. Many believe that the approach is simply too arbitrary and dependent on too many variables. For example, a successful result is based on the entity being able to properly compute two variables: cash flows and probability-weighted cash flows.
>
> In comparison, the traditional cash-flow method (e.g., discount one cash flow at an interest rate commensurate with the risk), is less susceptible to the risk that assumptions have been misapplied.

The expected losses method computation. The expected losses method is based on the assumption that if an entity's equity is greater than its expected losses, it has demonstrated that it has enough equity to finance its activities without additional financial support. That is, if the worst case scenario occurs (e.g., expected losses exist), the entity still has enough equity to fund those losses without seeking additional outside financial support from others.

Moreover, the FASB selected expected losses as a benchmark because it indicates the amount of equity that an entity must have to induce lenders or investors to provide funds needed by the entity to conduct its activities.

Generally, for example, a lender looks at a borrower to satisfy certain profitability or cash-flow coverage ratios to demonstrate that it can support its debt service with its earnings and cash flow.

The expected losses formula looks like this.

| Equity | GREATER THAN | Expected losses | = | Entity *is not* a VIE (self-supportive) |
| Equity | LESS THAN | Expected losses | = | Entity *is* a VIE (not self-supportive) |

Definition of expected losses. For purposes of determining if an entity has an equity investment sufficient to finance its activities without obtaining financial support from other entities, an entity's equity investment is compared with its expected losses. Expected losses include the expected negative variability in the fair value of the entity's net assets, exclusive of variable interests. Expected variability in the fair value of net assets includes expected variability resulting from the operating results of the entity, which are usually the expected cash flows of the entity.

Expected cash flows exclude:

- Fees paid to a decision maker and service providers, such as management and other fees, that are considered variable interests.

> **NOTE**
>
> If such fees are not considered a variable interest, the fees are not excluded from the expected cash flows.

- Cash inflow and outflow related to variable interests such as:
  - Difference between actual rental income and market value rental income related to an above- or below-market lease (Rental income related to a market-value lease is included in the net cash flow computation.)
  - Principal and interest payments on debt
  - Fees and other expenses paid to variable interest holders
  - Fees paid to guarantors
  - Dividends and distributions to holders of equity investments that are at risk

The concept of expected losses found in FIN 46R is not based on expected cash flows but rather on the variability of the cash flows that create expected losses and residual returns (gains).

The methodology is based on Concept Statement No. 7's expected cash flows method under which expected cash flows are discounted and then converted to present value to arrive at the probability-weighted present value of cash flows, which should be the fair value of the asset.

Further, the computation of expected losses is made individually by each variable interest holder in determining whether an entity is a VIE. In theory, each variable interest holder, based on use of imperfect information, could reach a different conclusion as to whether an entity is a VIE.

Following is a simple example illustrating how the expected loss computation is made.

Example 1

Assume an entity makes an investment of $1,000 that is expected to generate total cash flows ranging from $0 to $1,100, one year from the investment date. Assume the risk free discount rate is five percent (e.g., the interest rate on a one-year Treasury instrument). All cash flows are expected to occur in one year or not at all. Expected cash flows would be determined as follows.

Scenario	Estimated Cash Flows	Present Value of Estimated Cash Flows (5%, 1 Year)	Probability of Occurrence	Present Value of Expected Cash Flows (5%, 1 year)
1	$ 0	$ 0	10%	$ 0
2	500	476	20%	95
3	900	857	30%	257
4	1,100	1,048	40%	419
			100%	
			Fair value of investment	$771

The fair value of the investment is $771. That is, if the entity purchases the investment for $771, based on probability weighting, it is expected to generate a five percent return within one year. There is a 10-percent probability that it will receive $0 from the investment (Scenario 1); that is, the investment becomes defunct. There is a 20-percent probability that Scenario 2 will occur and the entity will receive a total of $500 in one year. There is a 30-percent probability that it will receive $900, and a 40-percent probability that it will receive $1,100.

When the four weighted probabilities are factored into the formula along with a five percent discount, the fair value of the investment is $771.

Continuing with the example, if any one of the four scenarios above were to occur, the cash flow would not be exactly $771. Instead, it would be higher or lower than $771 resulting in a variance (gain or loss). For example, if Scenario 4 were to occur, there would be a variance between the present value of the estimated cash flows ($1,048) and the expected cash flow (fair value of $771), resulting in a positive expected variance of $277 (expected gain). Conversely, if Scenario 1 were to occur, there would be a negative variance between the present value of estimated cash flow received ($0) and the expected (fair value of $771), resulting in a expected loss of $771.

The following table illustrates the mechanics that follow to compute expected losses and gains.

Scenario	Present Value of Estimated Cash Flows	Expected Cash Flows (Fair Value)	Variance Difference (Loss or Gain)	Probability of Occurrence	Expected Losses	Expected Residual Return (Gain)
1	$ 0	$771	$(771)	10%	$ (77)	
2	476	771	(295)	20%	(59)	
3	857	771	86	30%		$ 25
4	1,048	771	277	40%		111
				100%	$(136)	$ 136

Based on each scenario, the expected cash flows (fair value of $771) are compared with the present value of estimated cash flows to compute a gain or loss. Expected losses are accumulated on one column, while expected gains are accumulated in another column.

The result is that in the worst case, on a present-value basis, total expected losses from the investment would be $(136) and expected returns (gains) would be $136. If the entity has expected losses of $(136), it must have at least $136 of equity to fund those expected losses. If the entity cannot fund those losses with its equity, some other entity or individual must fund those losses by providing additional financial support.

Assuming the entity above only has $100 of equity (at fair value), it would not be able to pay for the expected losses of $(136) if they were to occur. Consequently, the entity would have to call on another entity or individual for additional financial support to pay for the expected losses. In such a case, the entity would not be self-supportive, and would fail Quantitative Method 1. In order not to be categorized as a VIE, one of the qualitative methods would have to be satisfied.

Thus, the expected losses formula looks like this.

Equity	LESS THAN	Expected losses	=	Entity is a VIE (not self-supportive)
$100	<	($136)	=	Entity is a VIE (not self-supportive)

NOTE

Notice in the above example that on the other side, expected residual gains would be $136 and would be received by either the entity or another entity or individual. With few exceptions, expected losses of $(136) must equal expected residual gains of $136 because both are computed from the mean value which is fair value of $771.

Timing of Determining Whether an Entity is a VIE

The initial determination of whether an entity is a VIE is made on the date at which the variable interest holder first becomes involved with the VIE. The date at which the variable interest holder first becomes involved with the VIE is the date on which the entity consummates ownership, contractual or other pecuniary interests with the VIE.

Example

Company P makes a new loan to S on June 1, 20X3. P has no other variable interests in S.

Conclusion

On June 1, 20X3 (the date on which P first becomes involved with S), P should test S to determine if S is a VIE, using one of the three methods. The initial test is based on the fair value of S's equity on June 1, 20X3. The determination should be based on the circumstances on that date including future changes that are required in existing governing documents and existing contractual arrangements.

Who performs the VIE test? Each variable interest holder should perform the test of the VIE on the date the holder first becomes involved with the VIE. Therefore, if there are several variable interest holders, each would perform a separate test of the VIE and, presumably, each could arrive at a different conclusion as to whether the entity is a VIE and whether the holder is the primary beneficiary that should consolidate that VIE.

Example

Company X is an entity that receives financial support (variable interests) from several entities as follows.

Variable Interest Holder	Type of Variable Interest	First Date Involved with X
Company Y	Guarantees X's bank loan	February 5, 20X4
Company Z	Made loan to X	July 7, 20X4
Company C	Lease with X- above market	August 6, 20X4

Conclusion

Each variable interest holder tests Company X on the date that it first becomes involved with X. In this example, Y should test X on February 5, 20X4. Z should test X on July 7, 20X4, and C should test X on August 6, 20X4.

On each of the above dates, each variable interest holder separately tests X to determine whether X is a VIE using one of the three qualitative methods (non-recourse financing, similar entity, or other facts and circumstances methods) or the one quantitative method (expected losses method). If a variable interest holder determines that the entity is a VIE, the holder also tests to determine whether it is the primary beneficiary that should consolidate the VIE. If a variable interest holder determines that an entity is a VIE and that it is the primary beneficiary, it consolidates the VIE as of the date of the test (e.g., the date on which the variable interest holder first becomes involved with the VIE).

Because each variable interest holder performs its own independent test, there is the possibility that more than one variable interest holder reaches the conclusion that it is the primary beneficiary and consolidates the same VIE.

Reconsideration of VIE Status

An entity that previously was not subject to FIN 46R shall not become subject to it simply because of losses in excess of expected losses that reduce the equity investment.

Once an initial test is done to determine if an entity is a VIE, an update test is not done on a regular basis (e.g., no annual or periodic update date is performed). Specifically, a variable interest holder does not reconsider (retest) the VIE unless a triggering event occurs.

The initial determination of whether an entity is a VIE is reconsidered (retested) only if one or more of the following triggering events occurs:

- The VIE's governing documents or contractual arrangements are changed in a manner that changes the characteristics or adequacy of the entity's equity investment at risk.
- The VIE's equity investment, or some part thereof, is returned to the equity investors, and other parties become exposed to expected losses.
- The VIE undertakes additional activities or acquires additional assets, (beyond those that were anticipated at the later of the inception of the entity or the latest reconsideration event), that increase the entity's expected losses.
- The VIE receives an additional equity investment that is at risk, or the entity curtails or modifies its activities in a way that decreases expected losses.
- Changes in facts and circumstances occur such that the holders of the equity investment at risk, as a group, lose the power from voting rights or similar rights of those investments to direct the activities of the entity that most significantly impact the entity's economic performance.

NOTE

FAS 167 added the fifth provision triggering event noted above.

The reconsideration should be done at fair value of equity and total assets at the date on which the reconsideration is performed.

An entity that previously was not a VIE shall not become a VIE simply because subsequent losses reduce the equity investment to an insufficient level to obtain financing.

> **NOTE**
>
> Previously, FIN 46R stated that a troubled debt restructuring (as defined by FAS 15, *Accounting by Debtors and Creditors for Troubled Debt Restructurings*), was not a triggering event that requires reconsideration of whether the entity involved is a VIE. With the issuance of FAS 167, the troubled-debt exception was eliminated so that a troubled-debt restructuring may be considered a triggering event. On its face, a troubled debt restructuring typically results in the VIE's governing documents and/or contractual arrangements changing in a manner that may change the characteristics or adequacy of the entity's equity.

Discussion of Condition 2 to be a VIE

Following is a brief review the rules that determine whether an entity is a VIE. An entity can be categorized as a VIE based on having one of two conditions.

Condition 1. The total equity investment at risk is not sufficient to permit the entity to finance its activities without obtaining additional subordinated financial support provided by any party, including equity holders.

Condition 2. As a group, the holders of equity investments at risk lack any one of the following three characteristics:

- The power through voting rights or similar rights to direct the entity's activities that most significantly impact the entity's economic performance.
- The obligation to absorb the expected losses of the entity.
- The right to receive the expected residual returns of the entity.

Previously, this chapter discussed the approach performed to test whether an entity was a VIE because of Condition 1. Under Condition 1, FIN 46R provides three qualitative methods and one quantitative method under which an entity can demonstrate that its equity is sufficient for it to finance its activities without additional subordinated financial support. Those qualitative methods are Method 1: non-recourse financing method; Method 2: other facts and circumstances method; Method 3: similar entity method. The sole quantitative method is the expected losses method. If an entity satisfies any one of the three qualitative methods or the sole quantitative method, it is considered to be self-supportive and is not a VIE.

If an entity is not a VIE under Condition 1 (e.g., it can demonstrate that its equity is sufficient to finance its activities without additional subordinated financial support), it still may be considered a VIE based on meeting Condition 2.

In Condition 2, an entity is a VIE if its equity owners do not have the typical risks and rights of ownership.

OBSERVATION

An entity is a VIE if the holders of its equity investments lack any of the three characteristics that are typical of controlling equity interests; the power to direct the activities, absorb an entity losses, and receive an entity residual returns. If any one of these three characteristics is lacking, this means the equity owners do not engage in the entity's decisions nor give it financial support. Therefore, if the equity owners lack any of these three characteristics, some other entity or individual must have the power to direct the entity's activities, absorb the entity's losses and receive its residual gains.

STUDY QUESTIONS

7. What is a primary beneficiary in regards to a VIE?

   a. A form of financial support given by one entity or individual to a VIE

   b. An entity or individual that has a controlling financial interest in a VIE

   c. An entity that is not self-supportive

8. What condition characterizes a VIE?

   a. It has a sufficient amount of equity for it to finance its activities.

   b. It is either an individual or entity.

   c. Its owners do not hold the typical power, risks and rights of equity owners.

9. An entity is considered a VIE by design if, as a group, the holders of equity investments at risk have:

   a. An obligation to absorb the expected losses of the entity

   b. No right to receive the expected residual returns of the entity

   c. The direct ability to make decisions about the entity's activities that have a significant effect on the success of the entity

94 TOP ACCOUNTING ISSUES FOR 2011 CPE COURSE

10. The FASB has indicated that one way an entity is able to "finance its activities" without additional subordinated financial support is if it can obtain:

a. A guarantee from another party
b. A subordinated loan from another party
c. Above-market lease payments from a lessee
d. Non-recourse financing from an unrelated party

11. What method does FIN 46R suggest should be used first to determine if an entity is a VIE?

a. Combination of qualitative and quantitative
b. Expected losses
c. Qualitative
d. Quantitative

12. Which of the following methods to determine if an entity is a VIE is considered a quantitative method?

a. Similar entity method
b. Expected losses method
c. 10-percent equity threshold rule
d. Non-recourse financing exception

13. Company X makes a loan to Company Y on June 30, 20X1 and is a variable interest holder. On what date should Company X first perform the VIE test for the VIE?

a. Whenever certain triggering events occur
b. On June 30, 20X1
c. On June 30, 20X2

14. If an entity is reconsidering it's VIE status, such reconsideration should be done at:

a. Carrying value of equity and total assets at the date on which the reconsideration is performed
b. Fair value of equity and total assets at the beginning of the year of reconsideration
c. Fair value of equity and total assets at the date on which the reconsideration is performed

15. Which of the following is an entity considered to be if it satisfies any one of the three qualitative methods or the one quantitative method?

a. Self-supportive
b. A variable interest entity
c. In possession of at least 80 percent of its voting rights

Identifying Variable Interests in a VIE and Determining the Primary Beneficiary: FASB ASC Topic 810

LEARNING OBJECTIVES

Upon completion of this chapter, the reader will be able to:

- Define a variable interest
- Determine whether an entity has an interest in a VIE
- Describe the primary beneficiary of a VIE
- Determine who is the primary beneficiary in a VIE
- List the disclosure requirements under FIN 46R (FASB ASC 810)
- Note the effective date and transition requirements of FIN 46R (FASB ASC 810)

REQUIREMENT 2 FOR CONSOLIDATION

In order for one reporting enterprise to consolidate an off-balance sheet entity under FIN 46R (FASB ASC Topic 810), there are three requirements that must be met:

- **Requirement 1.** There must be a *variable interest entity (VIE)* (off-balance sheet entity that is not self-supportive).
- **Requirement 2.** Reporting entities and/or individuals must have *variable interests* in the VIE (e.g., provide subordinated financial support to the VIE through equity, loans, guarantees, etc.).
- **Requirement 3.** A reporting enterprise must be the *primary beneficiary* of the VIE by having a controlling financial interest in that VIE through other than majority ownership.

If all three requirements are met and if a reporting enterprise is the primary beneficiary, it must consolidate the VIE.

If, in Requirement 1, it is determined that an entity is not a VIE, there is no need to continue because the entity shall not be consolidated under FIN 46R (FASB ASC Topic 810). Instead, the only way it will be consolidated is based on majority ownership (more than 50 percent ownership).

Assume, instead, that in Requirement 1, the entity is deemed to be a VIE in that either it does not have sufficient equity or its owners do not have the typical power, risks or rewards of ownership. If so, Requirement 2 is to identify those parties that hold variable interests in the VIE (variable interest holders); that is, the enterprises or individuals that provide financial support to the VIE. Only a variable interest holder can consolidate with a VIE. The variable interest holder that ultimately consolidates the VIE is called the primary beneficiary. The concept of a primary beneficiary is discussed later in this chapter.

Definition of a Variable Interest

A variable interest is defined as a contractual, ownership, or other pecuniary interest in a VIE that changes with changes in the fair value of the VIE's net assets, exclusive of variable interests. A variable interest is a means through which one enterprise (or individual) provides financial support to a VIE that could result in the providing enterprise (or individual):

- Absorbing a portion of the VIE's expected losses or
- Receiving a portion of the VIE's expected residual returns.

The labeling of an item as an asset, liability, equity or as a contractual arrangement does not determine whether it is a variable interest. Instead, it is the role of the item, which is to absorb or receive the entity's variability due to the change in its net assets that determines if it is a variable interest.

> **NOTE**
>
> The best way to look at the variable interest is that it is a form of financial support provided by an entity or individual to a VIE that has a variable component to it that acts like an equity investment. The result is that the entity (or individual) that provides the financial support (variable interest) may receive upside (portion of expected residual returns) or downside (absorb a portion of expected losses) through its variable interest.

A variable interest can be in the form of ownership (ownership of voting or non-voting equity) or no ownership (guarantees, certain lease arrangements, debt, management and other service fees contracts in limited cases). The key point is that the variable interest holder (provider) acts like an equity owner even if it may not have formal ownership. Through its variable interest (support), the variable interest holder is exposed to the risk of absorbing a portion of the VIE's expected losses (absorbs a portion of the downside), or receives a portion of the VIE's expected residual gains (receives a portion of the upside). Examples of variable interests include:

- **Equity investments.** Equity investments in a VIE are variable interests to the extent that they are at risk. An equity interest that is not at risk still may be a variable interest provided it absorbs or receives some of the entity's variability.

■ **Liabilities, recorded or not recorded.** These can include:
  − Guarantees
  − Written put options on the assets of the VIE
  − Obligations that protect holders of senior interests from suffering
  − Subordinated beneficial interest
  − Subordinated debt due from the VIE such as unsecured loans
  − Senior debt including bank loans
  − Forward contracts to sell assets that are owned by the VIE
  − Derivatives

> **NOTE**
>
> Beneficial interests are rights to receive all or portions of specified cash inflows to a trust or other entity, including senior and subordinated shares of interest, principal, or other cash inflows to be passed-through or paid-through, premiums due to guarantors, commercial paper obligations, and residual interests, whether in the form of debt or equity.

■ **Certain contracts with the VIE .** These can include:
  − Leases:
    − Leases that have terms that are above or below market for similar property in the same geographic location.
    − Leases that have residual value guarantees, an option to acquire leased assets at a fixed or predetermined price or a lease renewal option at a fixed or predetermined lease rate.

> **NOTE**
>
> A lease that has a market rate and terms and has none of the above embedded features is not a variable interest.

  − Contracts for fees paid to a decision maker or service providers (e.g., management contracts) that are not at not arms length and do not satisfy six conditions. (See discussion below.)
  − Distribution contracts that have variable payments linked to an entity's performance.
  − Royalty, license and other contracts that have variable payments linked to an entity's performance.

A variable interest excludes:

- **Most assets of a VIE.** Most assets that create variability (e.g., create the change in fair value of assets)

> **NOTE**
>
> In general, assets are not variable interests because they create the variability (the gains or losses). However, assets of an entity that take the form of derivatives, guarantees, or other similar contracts may be variable interests.

- **Equity investments.** Equity investments in a VIE that are not at risk or do not absorb or receive some of the entity's variability.
- **Certain contracts.** These can include:
  - Contracts for fees paid to a decision maker or service providers (e.g., management contracts) that satisfy six conditions (see discussion below).
  - Leases at a market rate and terms and that have no residual value guarantee, no option to purchase the leased property at a fixed or predetermined price, or no renewal option at a fixed or predetermined lease rate.
  - Trade receivables and payables in the normal course of business
  - Casual purchases and sales at market value

Most liabilities and equity of a VIE are variable interests while most assets are not. Most assets of a VIE create variability; that is, they create the increase or decrease in the net fair value of the VIE. On the other side, most liabilities and equity absorb that variability in that they absorb the losses (decreases in fair value) and receives the residual gains (increases in fair value).

Both the equity and debt represent variable interests in that both either absorb a portion of expected losses or receive a portion of residual returns due to changes in the fair value of net assets.

A quick way to remember how variable interests work is that most assets create the change in fair value (e.g., create variability), while most liabilities and equity absorb the change in fair value (e.g., absorb the variability).

Fees Paid to Decision Makers or Service Providers

Contracts related to fees paid to a decision maker or service provider, such as management or service fees, are generally not variable interests if the contracts satisfy all of the following six conditions:

- The fees are compensation for services provided and are commensurate with the level of effort required to provide those services (e.g., the fees are at an arms-length rate).

- Substantially all of the fees are at or above the same level of seniority as other operating liabilities of the entity that arise in the normal course of the entity's activities, such as trade payables.
- The decision maker or service provider and its related parties, if any, do not hold other interests in the VIE that individually, or in the aggregate, would absorb more than an insignificant amount of the entity's expected losses or receive more than an insignificant amount of the entity's expected residual returns.

> **NOTE**
>
> Relates parties do not include employees of the decision maker or service provider, unless the employees are used in an effort to circumvent the provisions of FIN 46R.

- The service arrangement includes only terms, conditions, or amounts that are customarily present in arrangements for similar services negotiated at arm's length (e.g., the fees are at market value).
- The total amount of anticipated fees are insignificant relative to the total amount of the VIE's anticipated economic performance.
- The anticipated fees are expected to absorb an insignificant amount of the variability associated with the entity's anticipated economic performance.

Fees paid to decision makers or service providers that meet all of the above conditions are not considered variable interests.

Conversely, if fees paid to decision makers or service providers that do not meet all of the above conditions, the fees contract is considered a variable interest.

Leases

Leases represent one of the most significant transactions that must be addressed under FIN 46R. Confusion exists as to whether a lease is a variable interest, and whether embedded features such as residual value guarantees, options to purchase the leased property, or lease renewal options are variable interests.

In general, from the lessee's perspective, a lease that has lease terms that are at market terms of similar property in the same geographic location, is not a variable interest in the lessor (VIE).

If, instead, the lease terms are either above- or below-market value, the lease is a variable interest because the lessee may absorb some of the variability of the lessor. If the lease is above market value, the lessee absorbs some of the losses of the lessor by paying higher lease payments. Conversely, if the lease is below market value, the lessee receives some of the residual returns of the lessor through making lease payments that are below what the market bears.

Embedded features in a lease. If a lease has an embedded feature that absorbs the variability of the underlying leased asset, the lease is a variable interest, regardless of whether or not the lease is at market value. Embedded features that absorb variability include:

- Residual value guarantee
- Option to acquire leased assets at a fixed or predetermined price
- Lease renewal option at a fixed or predetermined lease rate for a period beyond the base lease term.

Residual value guarantee. It is common for a lease agreement to require the lessee to guarantee that the leased property is worth a certain value at the end of the lease, referred to as a residual value guarantee. A residual value guarantee is a variable interest in the VIE because the lessee absorbs some of the losses of the leased asset that would otherwise be absorbed by the equity holders.

Option to purchase the leased asset at a fixed or predetermined price. If a lease allows the lessee the option to purchase the leased property at a fixed or predetermined purchase price, the lease option is a variable interest. The reason is because the lessee has the option to purchase the leased asset at a price that is less than the fair value of the asset, pulling residual returns away from the equity owners. Through the option the lessee is receiving some of the residual returns of the VIE that would otherwise belong to the equity holders.

Lease renewal option at a fixed or predetermined lease rate. Most leases not involving related parties have renewal options at lease rates that are fixed or predetermined and may not be at market rates. A lease that has a renewal option at a fixed or predetermined lease rate for a period that is beyond the original term of the underlying lease, is a variable interest. The reason is because the renewal option allows the lessee to benefit from a lease price that is less than the market value for a period that is beyond the lease period, thereby giving the lessee a portion of the residual value of the leased asset that would otherwise belong to the equity holders.

If a lease (or embedded feature in a lease) is for an asset of the VIE that represents less than 50 percent of the fair value of the VIE's total assets. If the embedded feature (residual guarantee, option, or renewal option) is based on leased assets that consist of less than 50 percent of the fair value of the VIE's total assets, the lease is not a variable interest in the VIE. Instead, the lease represents a variable interest in specified assets.

Flowchart 4.1

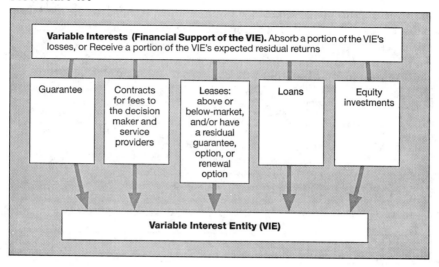

A variable interest, by definition, absorbs some of the "variability" due to changes in the VIE's net asset values. That means that if the VIE's net asset values change, the variable interest holder may be required to absorb a portion of the VIE's expected losses, or it will receive a portion of expected residual returns.

Receivables

VIE loan to another entity. If a VIE makes a loan to another entity is that loan a variable interest in the VIE? Remember that a variable interest results in an entity (a variable interest holder) absorbing some of the expected losses or receiving some of the residual returns of a VIE. A loan receivable to a VIE does not absorb expected losses or residual returns of that VIE. Instead, as an asset, it creates variability in that it is part of the change in the fair value of the VIE's net assets. In general, liabilities and equity of a VIE absorb the change in the fair value of the VIE, thus usually being considered variable interests. Assets of the VIE do not absorb any variability because they create it.

Typical Degree of Variability – Variable Interests

Some variable interests are stronger than others in that they give greater financial support to the VIE. Those stronger variable interests absorb a greater portion of expected losses or receive a greater portion of residual returns.

Some variable interest holders will never be categorized as the primary beneficiary of a VIE because they do not provide the majority of the VIE's financial support. Conversely, certain variable interest holders may provide greater support and may be considered the primary beneficiary of the VIE.

Although most variable interests will absorb some of the VIE's expected losses or receive a portion of its residual returns, some share in the VIE's expected losses and residual returns more than others, as noted in the following chart.

Comparison of Variable Interests By Typical Degree of Variability

Variable Interest	Typical Degree of Variability	Likelihood of Being the Primary Beneficiary of the VIE
Equity ownership, unrestricted	Usually highest degree of variability and most likely to be the primary beneficiary. Usually the equity owners will absorb the majority of expected losses and receive the majority of residual returns of the VIE.	Highest
Unsecured and subordinated loans	Usually next highest degree of variability and typically absorbs expected losses right after equity owners	Higher
Guarantees	Typically absorbs expected losses right after unsecured loans	Moderate
Residual value guarantee embedded as part of a lease	Typically absorbs expected losses right after unsecured loans	Moderate
Option to purchase at a fixed or predetermined price that is embedded as part of a lease	Lease option to purchase at a fixed or predetermined price could have a high degree of variability if the value of the underlying leased property fluctuates relative to the fixed option purchase price.	Moderate
Lease renewal option at a fixed or predetermined lease rate	Could have a high degree of variability if the value of the underlying lease rate fluctuates relative to the fixed or predetermined lease rate in the renewal option	Moderate
Management fees and service provider contract that are considered a variable interest	Might share in losses or residual gains if payments fluctuate based on a percentage of the VIE's assets or some other floating factor	Low
Above- or below-market lease	Lessee might share in losses if payments are above market or share in the residual returns if the lease is below market.	Low
Secured debt (including bank debt)	Least likely to absorb any VIE expected losses or receive its residual gains unless loan agreement has a variable feature (residual fee based on sale of property, etc.) Because the loan is secured, the bank is the least likely to absorb the majority of a VIE's expected losses or receive the majority of VIE residual returns.	Lowest

Implicit Variable Interests

Variable interests that directly absorb the losses or receive the returns of a VIE through contracts, are considered explicit variable interests, such as loans, guarantees, and equity interests. Most variable interests are explicit variable interests.

Explicit variable interests are those that have been discussed throughout this chapter.

There are instances in which an enterprise may have an implicit variable interest in a VIE, which is an indirect variable interest that is not identified by contract. For example, an enterprise may have an implicit guarantee of another entity's loan even though there is no contractual obligation to do so.

In identifying variable interests, an enterprise must consider all variable interests, including both explicit and implicit variable interests. That is, even though a particular enterprise holds no (explicit) variable interest, it may hold an implicit variable interest if it has either or both an obligation or incentive to protect other variable interest holders from losses even though it has no contractual obligation to do so.

An implicit variable interest is given the same weight as an explicit variable interest even though it is far more difficult to identify an implicit variable interest in comparison to an explicit variable interest.

The reader should focus on those instances in which an implicit variable interest may exist, which is occurs when there are the following elements:

- Related parties exist.
- One party is guaranteeing the loan of another party.
- Another party within the group is likely to have to step in to satisfy the guarantee of the other party.

FASB Staff Position (FSP) FIN 46(R)-5- *Implicit Variable Interests*, as amended, provides the limited guidance that exists in connection with implicit variable interests.

The FSP is focused on interpreting Paragraph B-10 of FIN 46(R) which states:

> Guarantees of the value of the assets and liabilities of a variable interest entity, written put options on the assets of the entity, or similar obligations such as some liquidity commitments or agreements (explicit or *implicit*) to replace impaired assets held by the entity are variable interests if they *protect holders of other interests from suffering losses.*

The FSP deals with an implicit variable interest, such as an implicit guarantee of debt.

The general concepts of an implicit variable interest follow:

- If a reporting enterprise has an implicit variable interest in a VIE, the reporting enterprise may be required to absorb the variability of the VIE or potential VIE.

> **EXAMPLE**
>
> Through its relationship with a common owner guarantor, an operating company may be called upon to satisfy the owner's guarantee of a VIE's debt even though the operating company has not executed a contract to guarantee that debt.

- An implicit variable interest (e.g., indirect guarantee) acts the same as an explicit variable interest (direct guarantee) except that an implicit variable interest involves absorbing and/or receiving the variability indirectly from the VIE, rather than directly from the VIE.
- If an enterprise has an implicit variable interest in a VIE, the enterprise is brought into the related party rules and could be considered the primary beneficiary of the VIE.

> **OBSERVATION**
>
> The most common example of where there is an implicit variable interest is where a common owner guarantees the debt of a lessor VIE. The related party lessee may be deemed to have an implicit guarantee of that VIE's debt even though no contractual guarantee exists between the lessee and lessor. The argument in favor of the lessee being an implicit guarantee is based on the assumption that because of the related-party relationship, the lessee operating entity would do whatever is needed to ensure that the lessee's underlying asset(s) (e.g., real estate) was protected on behalf of the common shareholder. For example, if the lessor VIE were unable to support its debt service and the owner's guarantee were called by the bank, the lessee operating company would provide the additional financial support needed to satisfy the guarantee.

FIN 46R, as amended, states:

> The identification of explicit variable interests involves determining which contractual, ownership, or other pecuniary interests in a VIE directly absorb or receive the variability of the VIE. An implicit variable interest acts the same as an explicit variable interest except it involves the absorbing and (or) receiving of variability indirectly from the VIE, rather than directly from the VIE. Therefore, the identification of an implicit variable interest involves determining

whether an enterprise may be indirectly absorbing or receiving the variability of the VIE. The determination of whether an implicit variable interest exists is a matter of judgment that depends on the relevant facts and circumstances. For example, an implicit variable interest may exist if the reporting enterprise can be required to protect a variable interest holder (such as a common owner) in a VIE from absorbing losses incurred by the VIE.

FIN 46R gives limited guidance as to how to determine whether an entity actually has an implicit variable interest in a VIE. Instead, it states that such a determination is based on the facts and circumstances.

Factors to consider in determining whether an enterprise holds an implicit variable interest in a VIE. IN46(R)-5 states that the determination of whether an implicit variable interest exists should be based on "all facts and circumstances in determining whether the reporting enterprise may absorb variability of the VIE or potential VIE."

Although it may be difficult to ascertain whether an enterprise holds an implicit variable interest, FSP FIN 46(R)-5 states that the analysis should take into consideration all relevant facts and circumstances, which should include asking the following questions. Even though there is no contractual obligation:

- Does the enterprise have the obligation to protect another entity against loss?
- Does the enterprise have an economic incentive to protect another entity against loss?
- Has the enterprise acted as a protector in similar situations in the past?
- Would the enterprise acting as a protector be a conflict of interest or be illegal?

Example

John owns Company Y and Company X John guarantees a bank loan for Company X John's primary asset to fulfill the guarantee would be the 100 percent ownership in Y.

Conclusion

Y may have an implicit guarantee of X's bank loan, which is an implicit variable interest. If John's guarantee were to be called, Y, as the primary asset of John, would be called upon to satisfy the guarantee. In determining whether Y has an implicit guarantee, Y should ask the following questions. Even though there is no contractual obligation for Y,

- Does Y have the obligation to protect X against loss?
- Does Y have an economic incentive to protect X against loss?

- Has Y acted as a protector in similar situations in the past?
- Would Y acting as a protector of X be a conflict of interest or be illegal?

If some of the above factors are affirmative, Y has an implicit guarantee of X's bank loan.

STUDY QUESTIONS

1. A variable interest is:
   a. A pecuniary interest in a VIE that does not change with changes in the fair value of the VIE's net assets
   b. A means through which one entity provides financial support to a VIE
   c. A means through which one entity absorbs a portion of the VIE's expected losses but does not receive a portion of the VIE's expected residual returns

2. Variable interests include:
   a. Sales at market value
   b. Equity investments that are at risk
   c. Most assets that create variability
   d. All fees paid to decision makers

3. In many cases, which of the following may hold the largest variable interest other than equity ownership?
   a. Derivative instruments
   b. Forward contracts related to assets owned
   c. Guarantees
   d. Unsecured and subordinated debt

4. What type of variable interest holder has the lowest likelihood of being the primary beneficiary of a VIE?
   a. A guarantor
   b. An equity holder
   c. A holder of secured debt
   d. A holder of unsecured loans

5. Which of the following determines whether an entity is a VIE?
   a. Whether it is labeled as an asset
   b. Whether it is reported in the equity section of the balance sheet
   c. Whether the role of the item is to absorb/receive the entity's variability in net assets

---

6. What type of variable interest might an entity have in a VIE if it did not have a contractual obligation to the VIE?

   a. Inferior
   b. Implicit
   c. Non-financial

REQUIREMENT 3 FOR CONSOLIDATION

The third and final requirement to consolidating a VIE is to identify the enterprise that will consolidate the VIE. The general rule is that a reporting enterprise shall consolidate a VIE when that reporting enterprise has a variable interest (or a combination of variable interests) that provides the reporting enterprise with a controlling financial interest in the VIE.

The reporting enterprise that holds the controlling financial interest in a VIE is called a primary beneficiary. Essentially, the primary beneficiary is the entity or individual that has a controlling financial interest in the VIE, and, therefore, consolidates that VIE. If the primary beneficiary is an entity, it consolidates the VIE into its financial statements. If the primary beneficiary is an individual, no consolidation of the VIE is required.

OBSERVATION

In many instances, an individual is the primary beneficiary. In such a case, the VIE will not be consolidated because an individual does not consolidate even if it issues personal financial statements. In reality, an individual is not going to perform a test to determine whether it is the primary beneficiary because the result has no impact on the individual; that is, the individual does not consolidate the VIE in any case. Instead, only a variable interest holder that is an enterprise will test the VIE to determine if the enterprise is the primary beneficiary that should consolidate the VIE.

Definition of a Primary Beneficiary

FIN 46R defines a primary beneficiary as the following:

An enterprise or individual is considered *the primary beneficiary* of the VIE if it has a variable interest (or a combination of variable interests) in a VIE and has a *controlling financial interest* in that VIE.

An entity has a controlling financial interest in a VIE if it has both of the following criteria:

- The power to direct the activities of a VIE that most significantly impact the entity's economic performance (the power criterion)
- The obligation to absorb losses of the VIE or the right to receive benefits from the VIE that could potentially be significant to the VIE (the loss/benefits criterion)

Although many variable interest holders may have to test to determine whether they are primary beneficiaries, only one enterprise or individual can ultimately be deemed the primary beneficiary.

> **NOTE**
>
> There may be many variable interest holders that may have an obligation to absorb some of the losses of the VIE or have the right to receive some of the benefits from the VIE (loss/benefits criterion mentioned above), but there is only one enterprise or individual, if any, that has the power to direct the activities of a VIE that most significantly impact the entity's economic performance (power criterion noted above).

Shared power rules. If a reporting enterprise determines that power is shared among multiple unrelated parties such that no one party has the power to direct the activities of a variable interest entity that most significantly impact the entity's economic performance, then no party is the primary beneficiary and the VIE is not consolidated. Power is shared if both of the following are true:

- Two or more unrelated parties together have the power to direct the activities of a VIE that most significantly impact the VIE's economic performance.
- Decisions about those activities require the consent of each of the parties sharing power.

If a reporting enterprise concludes that power is not shared but the activities that most significantly impact the entity's economic performance are directed by multiple unrelated parties and the nature of the activities that each party is directing is the same, then the party, if any, with the power over the majority of those activities shall be considered to have the power to direct the activities.

Power is not shared if the entities are related parties.

Rules for Determining the Primary Beneficiary

Each variable interest holder must perform its own assessment of whether that reporting enterprise has a controlling financial interest in the VIE and thus is the primary beneficiary.

The assessment should be performed first at the time when a reporting enterprise obtains a variable interest (or combination of variable interests) in a VIE, and should be continued on an ongoing basis while the entity is a variable interest holder.

The assessment of whether the holder has a controlling financial interest includes a review of several factors:

- The characteristics of the reporting enterprise's variable interest(s) in the VIE
- Involvement of the reporting enterprise's related parties and de facto agents, and other variable interest holders in the VIE
- The VIE's purpose and design, including the risks that the VIE was designed to create and pass through to its variable interest holders
- The extent to which the reporting enterprise was involved in the initial design of the VIE including preparing the governing documents
- Which activities most significantly impact the entity's economic performance and determine whether it has the power to direct those activities

A reporting enterprise is also required to perform a test to determine whether an entity in which it has a variable interest is actually a VIE.

> **NOTE**
>
> Recall that in performing an assessment, each variable interest holder, in addition to performing a test to determine whether it is the primary beneficiary of the VIE, must also perform a test to determine whether the entity is a VIE. If it is not a VIE, the test as to whether the variable interest holder is a primary beneficiary is moot. Therefore, if there are several variable interest holders, each would perform a separate test of the VIE and, presumably, each could arrive at a different conclusion as to whether the entity is a VIE and whether the holder is the primary beneficiary that should consolidate that VIE.

There can be only one primary beneficiary of a VIE. Inherent in the application of FIN 46R is the risk that two variable interests holders, with the same facts, could each reach the same conclusion that it is the primary beneficiary of the same VIE. The result is that the same VIE could be consolidated with two different variable interest holders. Note further that in some instances, there will be no primary beneficiary that consolidates a VIE. Examples include:

- An individual is considered the primary beneficiary and does not consolidate the VIE.
- One variable interest holder meets the "power" criterion, while another satisfies the second criterion, obligation to absorb losses or right to receive benefits, but no party satisfies both criteria.

- A party meets the power criterion but holds no variable interest in the VIE and does not satisfy the second criterion.
- Power is shared among various parties.

A variable interest holder is required to continually reconsider whether it is the primary beneficiary of a VIE. FAS 167 requires that a variable interest holder reconsider whether it is a primary beneficiary on a continued basis. This is a departure from the originally issued FIN 46R which requires that reconsideration be done when certain triggering events occur such as a change in the governing documents or if the primary beneficiary sells all or a part of its variable interest.

A variable interest holder in a VIE does not have to test to determine if it is the VIE's primary beneficiary if it knows that it will not absorb the majority of the VIE's expected losses, or receive the majority of its residual returns.

FAS 167 amends FIN 46R to provide that in applying FIN 46R, only substantive terms, transactions, and arrangements (whether contractual or noncontractual), shall be considered.

What this means is that if a reporting enterprise holds a variable interest in a VIE (an arrangement) and knows that such an interest will not have a substantive effect on that reporting entity's power over the VIE, obligation to absorb losses or right to receive benefits of the VIE, then that reporting enterprise is not required to test to determine whether it is a primary beneficiary of the VIE.

Criterion 1 (power criterion). Power to direct the activities of the VIE that most significantly impact the VIE's Economic performance. In order to satisfy the "power criterion," a variable interest holder must:
- Identify those activities that most significantly impact the VIE's economic performance.
- Identify who has the power to direct those activities.

FIN 46R does not give guidance on the types of activities that "most significantly impact the VIE's economic performance." However, the examples found in Appendix C to FAS 167 suggest that activities that most significantly impact a VIE's economic performance are those that impact the performance of the underlying assets, including retention of the value of those assets.

Thus, activities that protect, maintain, and maximize the value of the entity's assets would be considered significant, while those activities involving ongoing administration may not be considered significant.

One way to look at whether an activity is significant is to ask the following question: Does the activity protect, safeguard, maintain or enhance the value of the underlying assets? If it does, then that activity is likely to significantly impact the VIE's economic performance. If not, it does not.

Following are some guidelines that might assist in determining which variable interest holder satisfies the power criterion:

- Look for activities that protect, maintain, and maximize the value of the entity's assets.
- A party's power to direct those activities of the VIE that most significantly impact the VIE's economic performance is based on the facts and circumstances.
- The power can be dormant in that it is available to be used regardless of whether that party actually uses it. In some instances, the power may not be day-to-day decision making and it may be contingent on certain events occurring such as a power that is triggered in the event of a default or other event occurring.
- There can only be one variable interest holder that satisfies the power criterion.

Criterion 2 (losses/benefits criterion). The obligation to absorb losses of the VIE or the right to receive benefits from the VIE that could potentially be significant to the VIE. In order for a variable interest holder to be a primary beneficiary that consolidates a VIE, it must satisfy the two criteria (power criterion, and losses/benefits criterion).

If a variable interest holder satisfies the power criterion (Criterion 1), it must also satisfy the losses/benefits criterion (Criterion 2) in order for that enterprise to be the primary beneficiary that consolidates a VIE. In some instances, an individual will meet both criteria in which case the VIE is not consolidated.

Conversely, if a variable interest holder does not satisfy the power criterion, there is no need for that holder to test the losses/benefits criterion because that holder cannot be the primary beneficiary.

In order for a variable interest holder to satisfy the losses/benefits criterion (criterion 2), that variable interest holder must have:

> The obligation to absorb losses of the VIE or the right to receive benefits from the VIE that could potentially be significant to the VIE (losses/benefits criterion)

Prior to the issuance of FAS 167, FIN 46R allowed a variable interest holder to perform its assessment of who absorbed losses and received residual benefits by using either a quantitative method (expected losses method) or a qualitative method based on the facts and circumstances without performing a detailed quantitative analysis.

In FAS 167, the FASB eliminated use of a quantitative method. Now, a variable interest holder makes an assessment of which variable interest holder absorbs losses and receives residual benefits of the VIE by using a qualitative method based on facts and circumstances.

Following are some guidelines in assessing whether a variable interest holder satisfies the losses/benefits criterion.

- The holder has to satisfy either the obligation to absorb losses of the VIE, or the right to receive benefits of the VIE that could potentially be significant to the VIE. It is possible that one variable interest holder has the obligation to absorb losses, while another has the right to receive benefits that could potentially be significant to the VIE.
- FIN 46R, as amended, does not define the term "significant."

> **NOTE**
>
> The FASB intentionally did not define the term "significant" to avoid creating a "bright line" that would be used in practice as the sole factor to determine a significant threshold. In its Basis for Conclusions (Appendix A to FAS 167), the FASB did make the following observations:
>
> Whether the obligation to absorb losses, or right to receive benefits of the VIE, could potentially be significant to the VIE requires judgment and consideration of all facts and circumstances about the terms and characteristics of the variable interests. Further, the design and characteristics of the VIE, and the other involvements of the enterprise with the VIE might be considered.

The following examples illustrate the application of the primary beneficiary rules.

Example 1: Basic Application

Company S is established under the following structure.

Debt, five-year fixed note, personally guaranteed by Company P	$250,000
Equity- 100 percent owned by Company P	750,000
Total debt and equity	$1,000,000

Company S purchased $1 million of real estate with the debt and equity. Company P pays $750,000 for 100 percent of the voting shares of Company S. It is a given fact that S is not a VIE.

Conclusion

FIN 46R does not apply because there is no VIE. However, P would consolidate S under ARB No. 51 consolidation rules because it owns more than 50 percent of the voting shares of S.

Example 2

Assume the same facts as in Example 1 except that Company S is a VIE in that its total equity investment at risk is not sufficient to permit it to finance its activities without obtaining additional subordinated financial support in the form of a guarantee of its loan by Company P. Company P has full control over its voting rights in S's equity.

Conclusion

Because S is a VIE, FIN 46R applies. Thus, each variable interest holder must make an assessment to determine whether it has a controlling financial interest in S and thus consolidates S.

A variable interest holder has a controlling financial interest in a VIE if the holder has both of the following characteristics:
- The power to direct the activities of a VIE that most significantly impact the entity's economic performance
- The obligation to absorb losses of the VIE, or the right to receive benefits from the VIE that could potentially be significant to the VIE

In this example, the variable interest holders consist of:
- Debt holder
- Equity holder- Company P

The first step is to determine which variable interest holder has the power to direct the activities of Company S that most significantly impact S's economic performance. Clearly, Company P has the power to direct the activities of S that most significantly impact S's economic performance. In fact, P has the power to control all of S's activities.

Second, in order for P to be the primary beneficiary, it must have the obligation to absorb S's losses or the right to receive S's benefits that could potentially be significant to S. Because P owns 100 percent of the voting shares, it has the obligation to absorb the first losses of S before the debt holder absorbs losses. Further, P has the right to receive all the residual returns (the upside) from its investment in S.

P is the primary beneficiary that consolidates S, because it has a controlling financing interest in S due to having:
- The power to direct the activities of a S that most significantly impact the entity's economic performance
- The obligation to absorb losses and the right to receive benefits from S that could potentially be significant to the VIE

> **OBSERVATION**
>
> In an instance in which one reporting enterprise or individual owns 100 percent of the voting equity of a VIE and there are no restrictions on that equity, it is easy to ascertain that the primary beneficiary is the 100-percent shareholder. Typically, no test or analysis is needed in such a situation.

Example 3 (from Appendix of FAS 167, as modified by the author)

An entity (Company X) is created and financed as follows.

Financing, five-year fixed rate loan	$950
Equity	50
Total	$1,000

The $1,000 is used to purchase a property that is leased to a lessee that has a AA credit rating.

The equity is subordinate to the debt as the debt is paid off first before any cash flow is paid to the equity holders. The equity holder is an enterprise.

Company X is tested and it is considered a VIE because it cannot finance its activities without additional subordinated financial support from other parties.

The lease has a five-year lease term. The lessee provides a residual value guarantee of the leased property at the end of the five-year lease term and has an option to purchase the property at the residual value (the option price).

If the lessee does not exercise its option and the lessor sells it at less than the option price, the lessee must pay the lessor the shortfall in selling price and remarket the property for the lessor (X). If the property is sold for an amount greater than the option price, the lessee receives the excess of the selling price over the option price. The lease agreement and governing documents of X (lessor):

- Do not permit X to purchase additional assets or sell existing assets during the five-year holding period
- Do not provide the equity holders with the power to direct any activities of X

X was formed so that the lessee would have rights to use the property under an operating lease and would retain substantially all of the risks and rewards from appreciation or depreciation in value of the leased property. The lessee was involved in the design of X (lessor). The transaction was marketed to the debt and equity holders as follows:

- **Debt holders.** As an investment in a portfolio of AA-rated assets collateralized by leased property that would provide a fixed-rate return to debt holders equivalent to AA-rated assets
- **Equity holders.** As an investment with a return slightly higher than that of the debt holders because the equity is subordinate to the debt

Conclusion

In this example, following is the analysis that should be performed by the variable interest holders who consist of:

- Debt investors
- Equity investors
- Lessee

The lease is a variable interest because it has a residual value guarantee and an option to purchase at a fixed price. Each variable interest holder is required to make an assessment to determine whether it is the primary beneficiary of X that should consolidate X.

General assessment of the facts. In making that assessment, each variable interest holder performs a review of several factors:

- The characteristics of the reporting enterprise's variable interest(s) in X
- Involvement of the reporting enterprise's related parties and de facto agents, and other variable interest holders in X
- X's purpose and design, including the risks that X was designed to create and pass through to its variable interest holders
- The extent to which the reporting enterprise was involved in the initial design of X including preparing the governing documents
- Which activities most significantly impact X's economic performance and whether it has the power to direct those activities

Each variable interest holder should determine the purpose and design of X, including the risks that X designed to create a pass-through to its variable interest holders. In this case, the primary purpose for which X was created was to provide the lessee with use of the property for five years with substantially all of the rights and obligations of ownership, including tax benefits

X was marketed to potential investors as an investment in a portfolio of AA-rated assets collateralized by leased property that provides a fixed-rate return to debt holders. The return to equity investors is expected to be slightly higher than the return to debt investors.

The residual guarantee by the lessee essentially transfers most of the risk associated with the underlying property (decreases and increases in value) to the lessee.

X was designed to be exposed to the risks associated with a cumulative change in fair value of the leased property at the end of the five-year lease as well as credit risk related to the potential default by the lessee of its contractually required lease payments.

Determining who is the primary beneficiary. Each variable interest holder (debt holder, equity holder, and lessee) is required to assess whether it is a primary beneficiary of X by having a controlling financial interest in X. That controlling financial interest is achieved based on having both:

- The power to direct the activities of X that most significantly impact X's economic performance
- The obligation to absorb losses of X or the right to receive benefits from X that could potentially be significant to X

Step 1. Who has the power to direct the activities of X (the VIE) that most significantly impact X's economic performance? The most significant activities of X include:

- Managing the property, including maintenance
- Marketing the property for sale

The lessee has the power to direct both of the above activities under the lease. Moreover, the lessee was involved in the initial design of X and its governing documents might suggest that the lessee had the ability to establish power for itself within that design and documents.

Step 2. Who absorbs the losses or has the right to receive benefits from X that could potentially be significant to X? Since the lessee has the power to direct the activities of X (lessee) that are most significant, the only variable interest holder that could be the primary beneficiary is the lessee, but only if the lessee has the obligation to absorb losses and the right to receive benefits that could potentially be significant to X.

In this case, the lessee has both the obligation to absorb losses and the right to receive benefits that could potentially be significant to X through the residual value guarantee and the purchase option.

On the basis of the facts and circumstances, the lessee is considered the primary beneficiary of X because of the following:

- It is a variable interest holder with the power to direct the activities of X that most significantly impact X's economic performance, through its power to maintain and manage the property, and market it for sale.
- Through its residual value guarantee and purchase option, the lessee has the obligation to absorb losses of X and the right to receive benefits from X that could potentially be significant to the variable interest entity.

Why isn't the equity holder the primary beneficiary in Example 3? Typically, one would look to the equity holder(s) as being the variable interest holder that has both the power to direct the VIE's significant activities, and the obligation to absorb losses or right to receive residual returns of the VIE.

In Example 3, the lessee, through its contractual rights and obligations, overrides the equity holder's rights and obligations. Through the lease, the lessee has the power, obligations and rights that catapult it to being the primary beneficiary even though it does not have ownership.

What if in Example 3, the lessee had a simple market-rate lease with no residual value guarantee or option to purchase? If the lessee has a market-rate lease, it has no variable interest in X in that it will not absorb any losses of X nor receive any right to residual returns of X. Once the lessee is out of the picture as a variable interest holder, the equity holder is most likely the primary beneficiary.

What if in Example 3, the lessee has a triple net market-rate lease and is responsible for managing the property? Assume the lessee has a triple net market-rate lease under which the lessee pays all the operating expenses and maintains the leased property. However, there is neither a residual guarantee nor option to purchase the leased property.

Even though the lessee has the responsibility to pay all the bills and to manage the property, it would appear that the lessee does not have the power to direct the activities that are most significant to X. The most significant activities would be those that retain or enhance the value of X. Although the lessee does have the power to manage the property during the lease term, such management is not an activity that is significant to X as there is no responsibility to maintain or enhance the value of the property unless there is a residual value guarantee, which there is not.

Thus, the power to direct the activities that are significant to X (power criterion) lies with the equity holder. If the equity holder holds the power, then does it also have the obligation to absorb losses or right to receive residual value that is significant to X? The equity holder has the obligation to absorb losses and right to receive the residual benefits of X because no other entity has that right through contract or otherwise.

The equity holder (an enterprise) is the primary beneficiary that consolidates X.

Related-Party Rules—Primary Beneficiaries

There is trap in FIN 46R under which related parties, in particular, brother-sister entities, may be required to consolidate with each other solely due to their related-party affiliation.

FIN 46R states that in determining whether a reporting enterprise (or individual) is the primary beneficiary of a VIE, an enterprise (or individual) with a variable interest shall treat variable interests in that same VIE held by its related parties as its own interests. A related party includes:

- Related parties defined in FAS 57, *Related Party Disclosures* (ASC 850), and
- De facto agents or principals of the variable interest holder.

FAS 57 (ASC 850) defines related parties as:

> affiliates of the reporting enterprise, equity investments, trusts for the benefit of employees, the principal owners of the reporting enterprise, its management, *members of the immediate families of the principal owners* of the reporting enterprise and its management, and other parties with which the reporting enterprise may deal if one party controls or can significantly influence the management or operating policies of the other to an extent that one of the transacting parties might be prevented from fully pursuing its own separate interests, or another party that can significantly influence the management or operating policies of the transacting parties or if it has an ownership interest in one of the transacting parties and can significantly influence the other to an extent that one or more of the transacting parties might be prevented from fully pursuing its own separate interests.

The list of related parties includes:

- Parent company and its subsidiaries
- Subsidiaries of a common parent
- A reporting enterprise and trusts for the benefit of employees, such as pension and profit-sharing trusts that are managed by or under the trusteeship of the entity's management
- An entity and its principal owners, management, or members of their immediate families
  - Principal owners are owners of record or known beneficial owners of more than 10 percent of the voting interests in the entity.
  - Immediate family members are those who a principal owner or a member of management might control or influence or by whom they might be controlled or influenced because of the family relationship.
- Affiliates of the reporting enterprise, including a party that, directly or indirectly, through one or more intermediaries, controls, is controlled by, or is under common control with an entity

De facto agents and principals of a variable interest holder consist of any of the following:

- A party that cannot finance its operations without subordinated financial support from the variable interest holder, for example, another VIE of which the entity is the primary beneficiary
- A party that received its variable interests in the VIE through a contribution or loan from the variable interest holder
- An officer, employee, or member of the governing board of the variable interest holder
- A party that has an agreement that it cannot sell, transfer, or encumber its interests in the VIE without the prior approval of the variable interest holder

> **NOTE**
>
> The right of prior approval creates a de facto agency relationship only if that right could constrain the other party's ability to manage the economic risks or realize the economic rewards from its rewards in a VIE through the sale, transfer, or encumbrance of those interests. However, a de facto agency relationship does not exist if both the reporting enterprise and the party have right of prior approval and the rights are based on mutually agreed terms by willing, independent parties.

- A party that has a close business relationship with the variable interest holder such as a professional service provider (accountant or lawyer) relationship with one of its significant clients

The following series of examples illustrate the allocation of the related party rules in conjunction with the other rules found in FIN 46R.

Example 1

Company Y is the primary beneficiary of Company X through being the majority holder of various variable interests including guarantees, subordinated loans, and management fees. Y does not want to consolidate X and comes up with a plan to avoid consolidation. Y decides to transfer several of its variable interests in X to Y's attorney who provides significant legal services to Y. After the transfer, Y is no longer the primary beneficiary and believes it is not required to consolidate with X.

Conclusion

This is the wrong conclusion. Under FIN 46R, the variable interests of a variable interest holder are combined with those of all related parties and de facto agents. The definition of a de facto agent includes any party that has a "close business relationship" with the variable interest holder such as a professional service provider. In this case, Y's attorney is considered a de facto agent of Y and thus, the attorney's variable interest in X is combined with Y's to determine whether Y is the primary beneficiary of X.

Example 2

Company Y has a various variable interest in Company X but is not the primary beneficiary. Y wishes to purchase an equity investment in Company X but is concerned that, by doing so, it will be considered the primary beneficiary of X, requiring consolidation.

Y asks Company C to purchase the equity investment in Company X on its behalf and makes a loan to C for it to fund the purchase. Y believes that it has circumvented the consolidation rules by having C purchase the equity investment in X, and, thus it is not considered the primary beneficiary of X.

Conclusion

This conclusion is also incorrect. C is considered a de facto agent of Y because it received a loan from Y in order to purchase the equity investment in X. Therefore, C's equity investment in X is combined with Y's other variable interests in X in determining whether Y is the primary beneficiary of X.

Because Y now has several variable interests in X, including the equity investment held by C, Y may be the primary beneficiary of X, thus requiring consolidation of X.

Tie-Breaker Rule for Related Parties

FIN 46R provides a tie-breaker rule as a method to determine the primary beneficiary among several related parties. The tie-breaker rule applies only if there are several related parties, and no party within the group satisfies both criteria to being a primary beneficiary (the power criterion and losses/benefits criterion), but as a group, both criteria are met. Thus, collectively the related parties satisfy the two criteria for being a primary beneficiary but individually, no one party within the group meets both criteria. The tie-breaker rule works as follows.

If a reporting enterprise concludes that neither it nor any other of its related parties individually satisfies the two criteria to be a primary beneficiary, but, as a group, the enterprise and its related parties (including de facto agents) do satisfy the two criteria, the tie-breaker rule shall be used to determine which party within the related party group is the primary beneficiary that consolidates the VIE.

Under the tie-breaker rule, the related party that is designated to be the primary beneficiary is the party within the related party group, that is most closely associated with the VIE.

The determination of which party within the related party group is most closely associated with the VIE requires judgment and should be based on an analysis of all relevant facts and circumstances including:

- The existence of a principal-agency relationship between parties within the related party group
- The relationship and significance of the activities of the VIE to the various parties within the related party group
- A related party's exposure to the variability associated with the anticipated economic performance of the VIE
- The design of the VIE, such as the purpose for which the entity was created

The FASB's inclusion of the "most closely associated" provision within the tie-breaker rule is ambiguous and gives a group of related parties tremendous latitude in designating a primary beneficiary to consolidate a VIE. In the first Interpretation, the determination was based on "activities most closely associated with the VIE." In the revised Interpretation, the concept of activities was eliminated and replaced with "the related party most closely associated with the VIE." What does this mean? FIN 46R gives little guidance on how to select the finalist as the primary beneficiary among a group of related parties. Factors it does include are:

- The existence of a principal-agency relationship between parties within the related party group
- The relationship and significance of the activities of the VIE to the various parties within the related party group
- A related party's exposure to the variability associated with the anticipated economic performance of the VIE
- The design of the VIE, such as the purpose for which the entity was created

After the initial Interpretation was issued, the FASB Staff reviewed a series of case studies submitted to them in which conclusions were reached as to which entity had activities most closely associated with those of the VIE. In many instances, the FASB Staff determined that the conclusions reached were not consistent with the intent of the FASB. That is, in many instances, the wrong entity or individual was selected as having activities most closely associated with the VIE, and thus, the wrong entity or individual was deemed the primary beneficiary.

In the revised Interpretation, the FASB decided to make the "most closely associated" criteria vague. By doing so, entities have greater flexibility to determine which entity or individual is most closely associated with the VIE and would be able to evaluate all facts and circumstances in making that decision.

The following example illustrate the application of the related party and tie-breaker rules.

Example 1

Company X is a VIE. Companies Y and Z are related parties that have variable interests in X. Y has the power to direct the activities of X that are significant to X's economic performance. Z has the obligation to absorb the losses of X and/or the right to receive the residual returns of X. Neither Y nor Z individually satisfies both criteria.

Conclusion

Y and Z must use the tie-breaker rule to determine which of them is the primary beneficiary. In doing so, Y and Z determine which of them is most closely associated with X using the four factors. That entity is the primary beneficiary that consolidates X.

Change the Facts

Y satisfies both criteria to being a primary beneficiary (power criterion and losses/benefits criterion). Z satisfies the second criterion only (losses/benefits criterion).

Conclusion

The tie-breaker rule is not applicable because individually, one of the related parties (Y) satisfies both criteria. Y is the primary beneficiary and consolidates X.

Example 2

Company X, a manufacturer of packaging materials, is a VIE as it does not have sufficient equity to finance its activities without additional subordinated financial support from other parties.

X's 100 percent shareholder is John. Companies A and B are related parties of X. Company A is a manufacturer of golf clubs. Periodically, X sells packaging and boxes to Company A. Company B is a consulting company. B does no day-to-day business with X.

Both Companies A and B have variable interests in X. Company A is the guarantor of X's bank loan and has also made a significant unsecured loan to X. In return, A receives 90 percent of the residual returns of X if X is ultimately sold. John receives the other 10 percent. Company B has made a subordinated (second mortgage) loan to X. John's variable interest is through his equity ownership in X. In general, John has the power to direct X's significant activities.

There are variable interests held by other unrelated entities that, individually, are not significant.

Conclusion

Because X is a VIE, it does not have a sufficient equity investment to finance its activities without additional subordinated financial support from other parties.

Presently, X receives its support from outside entities including A (through its guarantee and loan), B (through its subordinated debt), and other variable interest holders.

Who is the primary beneficiary of X? Is it Company A, Company B, John, or none? FIN 46R states that each variable interest holder is required to assess whether it is a primary beneficiary of a VIE by having a controlling financial interest in a VIE. That controlling financial interest is achieved based on having both:

- The power to direct the activities of a VIE that most significantly impact the entity's economic performance
- The obligation to absorb losses of the VIE or the right to receive benefits from the VIE that could potentially be significant to the VIE.

In this example, John appears to have the power to direct the activities of X that most significantly impact X's economic performance. Further, Company A appears to be the entity that has the obligation to absorb the losses and right to receive most of the residual returns of X if it is ultimately sold. Thus, the two criteria for determining who is the primary beneficiary are split between John and Company A.

Under the tie-breaker rule, the related party within the related party group that is most closely associated with the VIE is the primary beneficiary.

The determination of which party within the related party group is most closely associated with the VIE requires judgment and should be based on an analysis of all relevant facts and circumstances including:

- The existence of a principal-agency relationship between parties within the related party group
- The relationship and significance of the activities of the VIE to the various parties within the related party group
- A related party's exposure to the variability associated with the anticipated economic performance of the VIE (the extent to which the party will absorb the VIE's losses or receive the VIE's residual returns)
- The design of the VIE, such as the purpose for which the entity was created

In this case, the initial conclusion is that Company A is most closely associated with Company X for several reasons.

First, there is no principal-agency relationship between Company A and X, so that the first factor is irrelevant.

Second, X and A are both manufacturers and, therefore, have activities that are more closely associated with each other than X has with either B or John.

Third, Company A has more variable interests in X (through both the guarantee and the unsecured loan) than John, and presumably, is exposed to a significant amount of losses of X.

Fourth, there is no information as to the purpose of X's design and whether such design was created for X's relationship with Company A. Thus, assume that this fourth factor provides no bias toward any of the variable interest holders.

Assuming there are no other important factors, Company A should be designated as the primary beneficiary and should consolidate Company X. This conclusion is based on the above factors that suggest that Company A is more closely associated with X than John.

Is it possible that two entities each consider themselves the primary beneficiary? One of the risks associated with FIN 46R is that two enterprises, each with imperfect information, could each independently reach the same conclusion—that each is the primary beneficiary of the same VIE. If this occurs, the same VIE could be consolidated twice. FIN 46R does not deal with the issue of having two primary beneficiaries. In fact, it states that there can be only one primary beneficiary.

Breaking the Tie Between Two Related Party Entities— Implicit Guarantees

There may be instances where it is difficult to determine which related-party enterprise or individual is the primary beneficiary when there is an implicit guarantee. Consider the following examples.

Example 1

John is the 100 percent owner of three entities the value of which represents a significant portion of John's personal net worth:

- Company X is a real estate leasing company, which is a VIE.
- Company Y is a manufacturer and a lessee of X.
- Company Z is a marketing company that has no pecuniary involvement with X or Y.

Y and X have an operating lease. John has guaranteed X's bank debt. Y and Z have not guaranteed X's bank debt. John could not satisfy the guarantee of X's debt without using his ownership in Y and Z. Company Y has limited assets and could not entirely satisfy the guarantee of John. Company Z has significant net assets and could easily satisfy the guarantee of John.

Conclusion

Both Y and Z have implicit guarantees of X's debt in that both Y and Z may be called upon to fund John's guarantee even though Y may not be able to fund the entire guarantee shortfall. Thus, Y, Z and John all could be X's primary beneficiary and must be tested under the tie-breaker rules. The next question is who is the primary beneficiary, which is the party that has both:

- The power to direct the activities of X that most significantly impact X's economic performance
- The obligation to absorb losses of X or the right to receive benefits from X that could potentially be significant to X

Who has the power to direct X's significant activities? Through its lease, relationship with John and implicit guarantee, it appears that Y has the power to direct the significant activities of X. Although John may have some power to direct X's activities, through its lease, Y would been deemed to have the power to direct X's significant activities involving the leased property. Note that shared power is not applicable to related parties.

Who has the obligation to absorb losses of X or the right to receive benefits from X that could potentially be significant to X? It appears that Z and John have the obligation to absorb losses of X that could potentially be significant; Z through its implicit guarantees and John through his (explicit) guarantee and equity ownership. Because Y does not have significant assets, it would not have the obligation to absorb significant losses of X through its implicit guarantee.

Further, John has the right to receive benefits from X that could be potentially significant to X, through his equity ownership.

A summary of which parties satisfy the two criteria for determining the primary beneficiary follows.

Criteria for Determining the Primary Beneficiary	Y	Z	John
Power to direct the activities of X that most significantly impact X's economic performance	Yes	No	No
Obligation to absorb losses of X that could potentially be significant to X	No	Yes	Yes
Right to receive benefits from X that could potentially be significant to X	No	No	Yes

In this example, one related party (Y) has the power to direct X's significant activities, and both Z and John have the obligation to absorb losses or right to receive benefits that are significant to X. Individually, no one related party satisfies both criteria for being a primary beneficiary but collectively, the related party group satisfies those criteria. The tie-breaker rule must be used to select the related party (Y, Z or John) as the primary beneficiary.

Under the tie-breaker rule, the related party that is designated to be the primary beneficiary is the party within the related party group, that is most closely associated with the VIE.

The determination of which party within the related party group is most closely associated with X requires judgment and should be based on an analysis of all relevant facts and circumstances including:

- The existence of a principal-agency relationship between parties within the related party group
- The relationship and significance of the activities of the VIE to the various parties within the related party group
- A related party's exposure to the variability associated with the anticipated economic performance of the VIE
- The design of the VIE, such as the purpose for which the entity was created

The following analysis reflects the four factors noted above.

Factor	Analysis
The existence of a principal-agency relationship between parties within the related party group	Not applicable as none of the related parties has a principal-agency relationship with X
The relationship and significance of the activities of the VIE to the various parties within the related party group	Favors Y being the primary beneficiary. Because X and Y have a lessor-lessee relationship, X's activities are more significant to Y than any other party.
A related party's exposure to the variability associated with the anticipated economic performance of the VIE	Favors Z being the primary beneficiary. Because Z has significant value, it is most likely to absorb the guarantee. John cannot fund the guarantee without Z or Y.
The design of the VIE, such as the purpose for which the entity was created	Favors Y being the primary beneficiary as X was purchased or developed for the purpose of leasing to Y

Because Factors 2 and 4 favor Y being the primary beneficiary while Factor 3 favors Z being the primary beneficiary, Y is deemed the primary beneficiary that consolidates X.

Example 2

Assume the same facts as in the previous Example except that John has significant personal assets to satisfy the guarantee without using the equity ownership in Y or Z.

Conclusion

Neither Y nor Z have implicit guarantees of X's debt as it is unlikely that either will have to fund John's guarantee. Thus, John is the primary beneficiary in that John will absorb the expected losses of X.

Getting around the implicit guarantee. In many instances, it may not be clear whether an implicit guarantee exists. For example, using the above scenario, John, the owner, has some personal assets that include the equity in Y, the operating entity. Y, along with other related party entities, could be called upon to fund the guarantee of X's debt.

There are possibly three ways around this issue to ensure that an implicit guarantee does not exist:

- Bank carve out of the guarantee
- Indemnification agreement from a related party entity outside the reporting group
- Representation from common shareholder that he/she has sufficient assets to satisfy the guarantee

One way to eliminate the risk that Y has an implicit guarantee is to have the bank specifically exclude from the guarantee the equity in Y, thereby ensuring that Y is not called upon to fund the guarantee.

A second way is to have Y sign an indemnification agreement with another entity owned by John. Under this agreement, the other related party entity agrees to indemnify Y for any losses it incurs from having to fund John's guarantee.

Example

John is the 100 percent owner of Company Y (operating company lessee), Company X (VIE lessor), and Company Z. Z is a related party of both Y and X but has no direct involvement with either entity. Z has significant net assets that are sufficient to fund the guarantee.

Y is concerned that it has an implicit guarantee of X's debt because of its pecuniary involvement with X (through the lease) and that Y may be called upon to fund John's guarantee of X's debt.

Z and Y enter into an indemnification agreement whereby Z agrees to indemnify Y for any losses Y incurs if Y is called upon to fund John's guarantee. Y has the reporting enterprise while Z does not issue financial statements.

Conclusion

By having the indemnification agreement in place, Y will not absorb any losses from the guarantee and has no implicit guarantee. In essence, the risk of absorbing the losses from the guarantee has been shifted from Y to another related party entity that is outside the reporting group (Z).

A key factor in making this conclusion is an evaluation as to whether Z has sufficient assets to cover the indemnification agreement and guarantee.

A third way is to receive a representation from the common owner that he or she has sufficient personal assets to fund the guarantee without using equity in the operating lessee or other common entities.

Example

John Smith is the 100 percent owner of Company Y (lessee) and Company X (VIE lessor). John has significant personal assets consisting of investments in securities, etc. that are sufficient to fund the guarantee. Mary is the auditor of Company Y and is concerned that Y has an implicit guarantee of X, and thus may be the primary beneficiary that consolidates X.

Flowchart 4.2

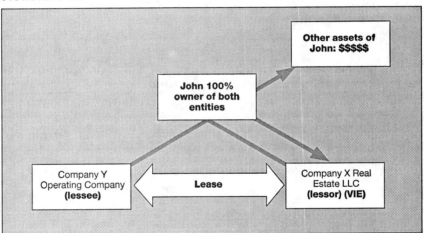

Conclusion

Mary could receive a representation from John that he has sufficient personal assets, other than his equity investment in Y, that he agrees to use to fund any guarantee shortfall prior to allowing the lender to utilize the equity in Y to fund that guarantee.

Representation of Common Owner

I, John Smith, being the 100 percent shareholder of Company Y and sole member of Company X, LLC hereby represent the following:

a. I have sufficient personal liquid assets, other than my investment in Company Y, to fund the $1 million personal guarantee that I have with No Loan Bank (the Bank) related to its note dated XXXX with Company X.

b. I agree that in the event the Bank calls my guarantee, I will immediately use my personal liquid assets to fund that guarantee making it remote that the bank would require the use of the net assets of Company Y to fund the guarantee.

c. I agree that if my financial position changes on or before March 31, 20X0, so that my personal liquid assets are less than $1 million in fair value before that date, I will immediately notify you of this change.

Signed

John Smith Date:

STUDY QUESTIONS

7. In order for an enterprise or individual to be a primary beneficiary of a VIE, that enterprise or individual must have which of the following?

  a. An equity ownership of more than 50 percent of the VIE
  b. Obligation to absorb more than 50 percent of the losses or right to receive more than 50 percent of the benefits of the VIE
  c. Controlling financial interest in the VIE

8. When an individual is the primary beneficiary:

  a. The individual may have a variable interest that will absorb very little of the VIE's expected losses.
  b. The individual must still perform a test to determine whether it is the primary beneficiary.
  c. The VIE will not be consolidated by the individual.

9. Which of the following is true?

  a. There can be only one variable interest holder.
  b. There can be only one primary beneficiary.
  c. There can be only one variable interest entity.

10. Which of the following is correct with respect to how often a variable interest holder should test to determine whether it is a primary beneficiary?

   a. A variable interest holder is required to reconsider (retest) whether it is the primary beneficiary when there is a triggering event.
   b. A variable interest holder must reconsider (retest) at least once annually.
   c. A variable interest holder is required to continually reconsider (retest).

11. Which of the following situations would require the tie-breaker rule to be used?

   a. Two unrelated parties, one of which satisfies the power criterion and the other satisfies the losses/benefits criterion
   b. Two related parties, each of whom satisfies the power and losses/benefits criteria
   c. Two related parties, one of which satisfies the power criterion and the other satisfies the losses/benefits criterion

12. Which of the following is *not* a variable interest? A lease that has:

   a. A market rate and terms with no set features
   b. A residual value guarantee
   c. An option to acquire leased assets at a fixed price

13. John is the 100 percent shareholder of X (a lessor VIE) and Y (a lessee). John guarantees X's loan. John's primary assets consist of the equity in X and Y. How should this transaction be reported?

   a. Y has an implicit guarantee of X's loan.
   b. X has an explicit guarantee of John's loan.
   c. John has an implicit guarantee of X's loan.

INITIAL TEST AND MEASUREMENT OF THE VIE BY THE PRIMARY BENEFICIARY

The rules for initial testing and measuring the VIE by the primary beneficiary vary depending on whether or not the VIE is under common control.

The first step is to determine whether an entity is a VIE, and whether a variable interest holder is the primary beneficiary. The test to determine whether an entity is a VIE and whether a variable interest holder is the primary beneficiary is performed at the time the variable interest holder becomes involved with the VIE.

The term "involved" is not defined in FIN 46R, but presumably means the time at which an entity first develops a variable interest in the VIE that requires testing to determine whether the variable interest holder is the primary beneficiary of the VIE.

The initial test is done based on the fair value of the VIE's assets and equity.

The second step involves initial measurement (consolidation) of the VIE by the primary beneficiary.

Once an entity determines that it is the primary beneficiary of a VIE, the next step is that it must consolidate the VIE into its financial statements. Note that if the primary beneficiary is an individual, no action is required because an individual does not consolidate a VIE in the individual's personal financial statements.

The initial measurement (consolidation) of the VIE's financial statements into the primary beneficiary's financial statements depends on whether or not the primary beneficiary is under common control with the VIE.

Entities Not Under Common Control

If the primary beneficiary and VIE are not under common control, the primary beneficiary of a VIE shall initially measure the assets, liabilities, and noncontrolling interests of a newly consolidated VIE at their fair values at the date the entity first becomes the primary beneficiary.

If the VIE is a business, the business combination rules found in FAS 141 (revised 2007), *Business Combinations*, should be followed:

- Assets, liabilities and noncontrolling interests are measured at fair value.
- If there is any excess of the fair values of the newly consolidated assets and the reported amount of assets transferred by the primary beneficiary to the VIE, over the sum of the fair value of the consideration paid, the reported amount of any previously held interests, and the fair value of the newly consolidated liabilities and noncontrolling interests, the resulting gain must be recognized on the income statement of the primary beneficiary, who acts as the acquirer.
- If there is any excess of the fair value of the consideration paid, the reported amount of any previously held interests, and the fair value of the newly consolidated liabilities and noncontrolling interests, over the fair value of newly consolidated identifiable assets and the reported amount of identifiable assets transferred by the primary beneficiary to the VIE, the resulting loss must be reported in the period in which the entity becomes the primary beneficiary as goodwill.

If the VIE is not a business, the following rules apply:

- The assets and liabilities of the VIE (exclusive of goodwill) are recorded at fair value using the business combination rules in FAS 141R.
- No goodwill is recognized.
- Any difference between the fair value of consideration and the fair value of the assets and liabilities shall be recognized as a gain or loss on the consolidated income statement.

Entities Under Common Control

If the primary beneficiary and the VIE are under common control (e.g., same majority shareholder or owners), the primary beneficiary must initially consolidate the VIE's assets, liabilities and noncontrolling interests at their carrying value in the financial statements of the entity that controls the VIE—assuming that entity's financial statements were prepared on a GAAP basis.

- Assuming no other entity has been consolidating the VIE prior to the time the primary beneficiary must consolidate the VIE, the primary beneficiary consolidates the VIE's carrying value (e.g., book value).
- Similarly, assets and liabilities transferred from the primary beneficiary to that VIE are transferred (at, after, or shortly before the date that the entity became the primary beneficiary) at the same value at which they were carried by the primary beneficiary. No gain or loss is recognized by the transfer even if the entity was not the primary beneficiary until shortly after the transfer occurred.

The principles of consolidation apply to the primary beneficiary's accounting for the consolidated VIE.

- After the initial measurement, the assets, liabilities, and noncontrolling interests of a consolidated VIE are accounted for in the consolidated financial statements as if the entity were consolidated based on voting interests.
- Specialized accounting requirements related to the type of business in which the VIE operates should be applied as they would be applied to a consolidated subsidiary.
- Intercompany balances, transactions, income and expenses should be eliminated, and rules for consolidations found in ARB No. 51 should be followed.
- Fees or other sources of income or expense between a primary beneficiary and a consolidated VIE shall be eliminated against the related expense or income of the VIE, and the resulting effect of that elimination on the net income or expense of the VIE shall be attributed to the primary beneficiary (and not the noncontrolling interests) in the consolidated financial statements.
- The VIE's stockholders' (or other) equity should be presented as a noncontrolling interest (or similar title) in the stockholders' equity section of the consolidated balance sheet. In accordance with FAS 160, *Noncontrolling Interests* (ASC 810) FIN 46R does not state where the VIE's stockholders' equity should be presented in the consolidated balance sheet. Because there is no elimination of the equity against an investment account, the only logical place in which to present the VIE's stockholders' equity is to present it as part of a minority interest. The author has

verified with the FASB Staff that they believe the VIE should be treated as a minority interest.

> **NOTE**
>
> FAS 160, Noncontrolling Interests (ASC 810), provides the guidance as to how a minority interest (noncontrolling interest) should be presented on the balance sheet. FAS 160 requires that the VIE's equity be presented as a noncontrolling interest within the equity section, separately from the parent's equity.

- Intercompany eliminations are assigned to the primary beneficiary and not the VIE.

> **OBSERVATION**
>
> FIN 46R deviates from ARB No. 51 with respect to the elimination of intercompany profit and loss. ARB No. 51 states that the elimination of the intercompany profit or loss may be allocated proportionately between the majority and minority interests. Yet, FIN 46R follows a different tack by requiring the effect of any elimination to be eliminated fully against the primary beneficiary. Thus, the minority interest remains untouched.

- Revenues, expenses, gains, losses, net income or loss, and other comprehensive income of the VIE are reported in the consolidated financial statements at the consolidated amounts, which include the amounts attributable to the owners of the parent and the noncontrolling interest in the VIE.
- Net income or loss and comprehensive income or loss shall be attributed to the parent and the noncontrolling interest in the VIE.
- The excess of any losses attributable to the parent and the noncontrolling interest over the equity interests shall be attributable to each interest, even if it results in a deficit noncontrolling interest balance.

If the VIE's equity is a negative amount (debit), that amount is present as a negative noncontrolling interest inside the stockholders' equity section of the balance sheet.

On the income statement of the primary beneficiary, the VIE's income statement is consolidated with the statement of the primary beneficiary. Intercompany transactions (e.g., rents, management fees, etc.) are eliminated. The net income of the VIE is backed out of the consolidated net income so that net income is the income of the primary beneficiary only. The net income of the VIE that is backed out of the consolidated net income should be net of the tax effect of the VIE's income. In instances where the VIE is a pass-through entity such as an LLC or partnership, there may be no tax effect. Where the VIE is an S corporation, the tax effect may be limited to the state income taxes on the VIE's income, inclusive of deferred state income taxes.

On the statement of cash flows, the minority interest is an adjustment to cash from operating activities.

DECONSOLIDATION

If a primary beneficiary who has consolidated a VIE is required to deconsolidate the VIE, that primary beneficiary must follow the guidance for deconsolidating subsidiaries found in FAS 160, *Noncontrolling Interests in Consolidated Financial Statements* (ASC 810).

On the date of deconsolidation, the deconsolidation shall be accounted for with the parent recognizing a gain or loss in net income, measured as follows.

Add:

+   The fair value of any consideration received (a)

+   The fair value of any retained noncontrolling investment in the former VIE at the date the VIE is deconsolidated (b)

+   The carrying amount of any noncontrolling interest in the former VIE (including any accumulated other comprehensive income attributable to the noncontrolling interest) at the date the subsidiary is deconsolidated (c)

=   Subtotal

Deduct: The carrying amount of the VIE's assets and liabilities

Equals: Gain or loss

The VIE's income shall be included in the primary beneficiary's income statement for the period up to the date of deconsolidation.

In many instances, a reporting enterprise that has been the primary beneficiary of a VIE will deconsolidate solely because it is no longer the primary beneficiary. Typically, the reason for deconsolidation is due to either or the following:

- The VIE is no longer a VIE.
- The primary beneficiary no longer has a controlling financial interest in the VIE (i.e., it is no longer the primary beneficiary) even though it continues to retain a variable interest in the VIE.

In such instances, the primary beneficiary does not receive any consideration such as if the primary beneficiary had sold its interest in the VIE, if any. Further, the primary beneficiary may not have any retention of a noncontrolling interest in the VIE. The result is that the sum of (a), (b), and (c) in the above table would be zero. Zero minus the carrying value of the VIE's net assets results in a loss equal to the carrying amount of the VIE's net assets. The result is that a reporting enterprise (primary beneficiary) that deconsolidates a VIE that it previously consolidated, will likely record a loss on its income statement equal to the carrying value of the VIE's net assets. In essence, the reporting enterprise is merely removing the net carrying amount of the VIE's net assets from its balance sheet as there is no consideration received.

UPDATING THE PRIMARY BENEFICIARY TEST

The initial test to determine whether an entity is a VIE and whether a variable interest holder is the primary beneficiary for consolidation, is done at the time the two entities are first involved with each other.

But what happens afterwards and when, if ever, must the test be updated? The reconsideration rules for a VIE; that is, the triggering events that require a reconsideration of whether an entity is still a VIE. To recap, each variable interest holder is required to reconsider whether or not an entity is still a VIE when any one of the triggering events occurs:

- The VIE's governing documents or contractual arrangements are changed in a manner that changes the characteristics or adequacy of the entity's equity investment at risk.
- The VIE's equity investment or some part thereof is returned to the equity investors, and other parties become exposed to expected losses.
- The VIE undertakes additional activities or acquires additional assets (beyond those that were anticipated at the later of the inception of the entity or the latest reconsideration event) that increase the entity's expected losses.
- The VIE receives an additional equity investment that is at risk, or the entity curtails or modifies its activities in a way that decreases expected losses.
- Changes in facts and circumstances occur such that the holders of the equity investment at risk, as a group, lose the power from voting rights or similar rights of those investments to direct the activities of the entity that most significantly impact the entity's economic performance.

NOTE

FAS 167 added the last triggering event noted above.

An entity that previously was not subject to consolidation (e.g., not previously a VIE) under FIN 46R does not become subject to consolidation because its equity deteriorates due to subsequent losses incurred that reduce the equity investment.

As for a primary beneficiary, FAS 167 made a significant change to FIN 46R regarding when a reporting enterprise who holds a variable interest in a VIE must reconsider (retest) whether it is the primary beneficiary of that VIE.

Prior to FAS 167, Interpretation 46R required a reporting enterprise that held a variable interest in a VIE to retest whether it was the primary beneficiary of a VIE only if a triggering event occurred such a change in the governing documents or if the primary beneficiary sells all or a part of its variable interest.

The new rules found in FAS 167 state:

- A variable interest holder is required to continuously reconsider whether it is the primary beneficiary of a VIE.

> **NOTE**
>
> FAS 167 does not address how often a variable interest holder must reconsider whether it is the primary beneficiary. Most companies will perform a new assessment at least once per year and at an interval that gives the reporting enterprise sufficient time to make any necessary adjustment (consolidation or deconsolidation) to issue its annual financial statements.

- The updated reconsideration of whether an entity is a primary beneficiary should be done using the fair value of the VIE at the date of the reconsideration.
- A variable interest holder that previously was not the primary beneficiary should update its test to determine if it is now the primary beneficiary.

DISCLOSURES UNDER FIN 46R

General Disclosures

Disclosures required by FAS 167 have, as principal objectives, the providing of financial statement users with the following information:

- The significant judgments and assumptions made by a reporting enterprise in determining whether it must consolidate a variable interest entity and/or disclose information about its involvement in a variable interest entity
- The nature of restrictions on a consolidated VIE's assets and on the settlement of its liabilities reported by a reporting enterprise in its balance sheet, including the carrying amounts of such assets and liabilities
- The nature of, and changes in, the risks associated with a reporting enterprise's involvement with the VIE
- How a reporting enterprise's involvement with the VIE affects the reporting enterprise's financial position, financial performance, and cash flows

In addition to disclosures required by other standards, a variable interest holder of a VIE must disclose the following information that is expected to achieve the above four objectives (The holder may have to supplement the required disclosures with additional information depending on the facts and circumstances.):

- Information about variable interest entities reported in the aggregate for similar entities if separate reporting would not provide more useful information to financial statement users. Such information shall be disclosed as to how similar entities are aggregated and shall distinguish between:
  - VIEs that are not consolidated because the reporting enterprise is not the primary beneficiary but has a variable interest
  - VIES that are consolidated

> **NOTE**
>
> In determining whether to aggregate VIEs, the variable interest holder should consider quantitative and qualitative information about the different risk and reward characteristics of each VIE and the significance of each VIE to the reporting enterprise. Further, the disclosures should be presented in a way that clearly explains the nature and extent of a reporting enterprise's involvement with VIEs.

A reporting enterprise that is a primary beneficiary of a VIE or is a variable interest holder that is not the primary beneficiary, shall disclose the following:

- Its methodology for determining whether the reporting enterprise is the primary beneficiary of a VIE, with significant judgments and assumptions made including information about the types of investments a reporting enterprise considers significant, and how the significant involvements were considered in determining whether the reporting enterprise is the primary beneficiary
- If facts and circumstances change such that the conclusion to consolidate a VIE has changed in the most recent financial statements (such as the VIE was previously consolidated and is not currently consolidated), the primary factors that caused the change and the effect on the reporting enterprise's financial statements
- Whether the reporting enterprise has provided financial or other support (explicitly or implicitly) during the periods presented to the VIE that it was not previously contractually required to provide or whether the reporting enterprise intends to provide that support, including:
  - The type and amount of support, including situations in which the reporting enterprise assisted the VIE in obtaining another type of support
  - The primary reasons for providing the support

- Qualitative and quantitative information about the reporting enterprise's involvement (giving consideration to both explicit arrangements and implicit variable interests) with the VIE, including, but not limited to, the nature, purpose, size, and activities of the VIE, and how the entity is financed
- A primary beneficiary of a VIE that is a business shall provide the disclosures required by FAS 141R.
- A primary beneficiary of a VIE that is not a business shall disclose the amount of any gain or loss recognized on the initial consolidation of the VIE.

A primary beneficiary of a VIE shall disclose the following information:
- The carrying amounts and classifications of the VIE's assets and liabilities in the balance sheet that are consolidated, including qualitative information about the relationship(s) between those assets and liabilities

> **EXAMPLE**
>
> If the VIE's assets can be used only to settle obligations of the VIE, the reporting enterprise shall disclose qualitative information about the nature of the restrictions on those assets.

- Lack of recourse if creditors (or beneficiary interest holders) of the consolidated VIE have no recourse to the general credit of the primary beneficiary
- Terms of arrangements, giving consideration to both explicit arrangements and implicit variable interests that could require the reporting enterprise to provide financial support (such as liquidity arrangements and obligations to purchase assets) to the VIE, including events and circumstances that could expose the reporting enterprise to a loss

A reporting enterprise that holds a variable interest in a VIE but is not the VIE's primary beneficiary shall disclose:
- The carrying amounts and classification of the assets and liabilities in the reporting enterprise's balance sheet that relate to the reporting enterprise's variable interest in the VIE
- The reporting enterprise's maximum exposure to loss as a result of its involvement with the VIE, including how the maximum exposure is determined and the significant sources of the reporting enterprise's exposure to the VIE. If the maximum exposure to loss cannot be quantified, that fact should be disclosed.

- A tabular comparison of the carrying amounts of the assets and liabilities that are required as noted above, and the reporting enterprise's maximum exposure to loss, as noted above. A reporting enterprise shall provide qualitative and quantitative information to allow financial statement users to understand the differences between this information. The information should include the terms of the arrangements, (addressing both explicit arrangements and implicit variable interests), that could require the reporting enterprise to provide financial support to the VIE, such as liquidity arrangements and obligations to purchase assets, as well as exposure to a loss.
- Information about any liquidity arrangements, guarantees, and/or other commitments by third parties that may affect the fair value or risk of the reporting enterprise's variable interest in the VIE is encouraged.
- If applicable, significant factors considered and judgment made in determining that the power to direct the activities of the VIE that have the most significant impact on the entity's economic performance is shared (shared power)

> **NOTE**
>
> The disclosures required by FIN 46R may be provided in more than one note to the financial statements, as long as the objectives of disclosure are satisfied. If the disclosures are provided in more than one note, the reporting enterprise shall provide a cross-reference to the other notes that provide the disclosures prescribed in FIN 46R for similar entities.

A primary beneficiary shall present separately on the face of the balance sheet the following items:

- Assets of a consolidated VIE that can be used only to settle obligations of the consolidated VIE
- Liabilities of a consolidated VIE for which creditors or beneficial interest holders do not have recourse to the general credit of the primary beneficiary

> **OBSERVATION**
>
> Generally, if a primary beneficiary consolidates a VIE into its balance sheet, the VIE's assets and liabilities lose their individual identity and in most cases are not identifiable separate and distinct from the primary beneficiary's assets and liabilities.

FAS 167 added a requirement that on the consolidated balance sheet, certain assets and liabilities of the VIE be separately presented. The assets that must be separately presented are those assets that must be used to repay the VIE's liabilities, such as real estate that is secured by the VIE's mortgage note payable.

On the liability side, the primary beneficiary must separately present on the consolidated balance sheet those liabilities of the VIE that have no claim against the primary beneficiary. Typically, unless the primary beneficiary has guaranteed or cross-collateralized a VIE liability, the creditors of the VIE have no recourse claim against the primary beneficiary. Thus, most if not all of the VIE's liabilities will be presented separately on the balance sheet.

Example

Company PB is the primary beneficiary of Company X, a VIE, which is consolidated on the balance sheet of PB. Company X's balance sheet that will be consolidated with PB is as follows.

X's Balance Sheet Prior to Consolidation	
Cash	$ 300,000
Land	$1,000,000
Building	4,000,000
Accumulated depreciation	(500,000)
	$4,800,000
Trade payables	$ 300,000
Current portion of note payable	200,000
Mortgage note payable	3,300,000
Equity	1,000,000
	$4,800,000

Conclusion

Even though X's balance sheet is consolidated with PB's balance sheet, certain assets and liabilities of X must be disclosed separately on the face of the consolidated balance sheet. Assets that must be used to settle VIE liabilities should be shown separately, and liabilities that have no recourse against the primary beneficiary are also shown separately.

In this case, the real estate of X should be presented separately as it is secured by the mortgage note and must be used to settle the VIE's obligations. Further, all of the liabilities should be shown separately because none have a claim against the primary beneficiary as PB has not guaranteed any of X's liabilities.

Company PB
Consolidated Balance Sheet
December 31, 20X2

ASSETS:	
Current assets:	
Cash and cash equivalents	$X
Trade receivables	X
Inventories	X
Other current assets	X
Total current assets	X
Property, plant and equity:	
Cost:	
Assets related to variable interest entity	**X**
Other	X
Less Accumulated depreciation:	
Assets related to variable interest entity	**X**
Other	X
Total property, plant and equipment	X
Total assets	$X
LIABILITIES AND EQUITY:	
Current liabilities:	
Accounts payable	$X
Accounts payable related to variable interest entity	**X**
Accrued expenses	X
Current portion of long-term debt	X
Total current liabilities	X
Long-term liabilities:	
Bank loans, net of current portion	X
Mortgage note payable related to variable interest entity	**X**
Deferred income taxes	X
Total long-debt liabilities	X
Stockholders' equity:	
Common stock	X
Retained earnings	X
Total XYZ Company stockholders' equity	X
Noncontrolling interest in variable interest entity	X
Total stockholders' equity	X

FAS 167 does not give any guidance as to how to present the selected assets and liabilities of the VIE on the consolidated balance sheet. Material assets and liabilities should be separated within their respective categories as shown in the above sample balance sheet.

Notice that cash is not shown separately because there is no requirement that the cash be used to settle VIE obligations. On the other side, all of the liabilities are presented separately because there is no evidence that creditors have any recourse against the primary beneficiary for those liabilities.

Finally, FAS 167 requires that the VIE assets and liabilities be presented on the face of the balance sheet thereby negating the option to present that information in the notes to financial statements.

Special Additional Disclosures—Exemption for Variable Interest Holders Who Have Difficulty Obtaining Information

The revised FIN 46R added a special exemption for certain entities that cannot obtain the necessary information to apply the rules. For those entities subject to the exemption, FIN 46R requires additional disclosures as follows:

- The number of entities to which FIN 46R is not being applied and the reason why the information required to apply FIN 46R is not available
- The nature, purpose, size (if available), and activities of the entity or entities and the nature of the variable interest holder's involvement with the entity or entities
- The reporting enterprise's maximum exposure to loss because of its involvement with the entity or entities
- The amount of income, expense, purchases, sales, or other measure of activity between the reporting entity and the entity or entities for all periods presented. However, if it is not practicable to present that information for prior periods that are presented in the first set of financial statements for which this requirements applies, the information for those prior periods is not required.

There are no required disclosures that must be included in the unconsolidated single financial statements of the VIE. The disclosures must be included in the primary beneficiary's consolidated financial statements only, or those of a variable interest holder that is not the primary beneficiary but holds a significant variable interest in a VIE. Otherwise, there are no disclosure requirements for the VIE if it issues its own financial statements.

EFFECTIVE DATE AND TRANSITION REQUIREMENTS OF FIN 46R

FAS 167 is effective as of the beginning of each reporting enterprise's first annual reporting period that begins after November 15, 2009, for interim periods within that first annual reporting period, and for interim and annual reporting periods thereafter. Earlier application is prohibited. Transition disclosures include:

- For public reporting enterprises, in periods after initial adoption, comparative disclosures for those disclosures that were not previously required by FASB SOP FAS 140-4 and FIN 46R-8 are required only for periods after the effective date. Comparative information for disclosures previously required by FSP FAS 140-4 and FIN 46R-8 that are also required by FAS 167 shall be presented.

- For nonpublic reporting enterprises, in periods after initial adoption, the reporting enterprise is required to present comparative disclosures for those disclosures that were not previously required by Interpretation 46R only for periods after the effective date.
- Further, comparative information for disclosures previously required by Interpretation 46R that are also required by FAS 167 shall be presented.

The rules for implementing FIN 46R's requirements are confusing and difficult to apply.

New Variable Interests

An entity with a variable interest in another entity that is created after the effective date of FAS 167 (created after November 15, 2009) shall apply the provisions of FIN 46R to that entity immediately. The transition rules that follow do not apply.

Example

On June 18, 2010, Company Y makes a loan guarantee for Company X.

Conclusion

Because Y creates a variable interest in X after November 15, 2009, Y must apply the provisions of FIN 46R immediately. Specifically, on June 18, 2010, Y must do the following as it relates to X:

- Test X to determine whether it is a VIE using the fair value of X's assets and equity at June 18, 2010.
- Identify all variable interest holders as of June 18, 2010.
- Determine whether Y is the primary beneficiary of X.

Assuming that Y determines it is the primary beneficiary, immediately (as of June 18, 2010), Y must consolidate X. If Y and X are not under common control, Y will consolidate X at the fair value of X's balance sheet at June 18, 2010. If they are under common control, Y will consolidate X based on the carrying value (book value) of X's balance sheet on June 18, 2010. Y will include X's income statement in its consolidated financial statements for the period June 18, 2010 to December 31, 2010, assuming Y has a calendar year end.

Transition Initial Test Existing Entities

The initial test for consolidation done by an entity with a variable interest is performed in one of two ways.

Option 1: Look-back approach. The primary beneficiary must look back to a date as if it had consolidated retroactively with the VIE (look-back date). The look-back date is the latter of:

- The date on which the primary beneficiary first became involved with the VIE
- The last date on which a reconsideration event would have occurred after the primary beneficiary first became involved with the VIE

On the look-back date, the primary beneficiary should perform its test to:

- Determine if an entity in which it has a variable interest, is a VIE
- Identify the variable interest holders
- Determine whether it is the primary beneficiary of the VIE

The test is done based on the fair value of the VIE's assets, liabilities and equity on the look-back date. If, based on the look-back date, the entity determines that it was the primary beneficiary and would have consolidated the VIE on the look-back date, the primary beneficiary should initially measure the consolidation of the VIE based on the carrying amounts of the VIE's balance sheet on the look-back date.

The carrying amounts are the amounts at which the assets, liabilities and noncontrolling interests of the VIE would have been carried in the consolidated financial statements if FIN 46R had been effective when the entity first met the conditions to be considered a primary beneficiary.

- If the entities were not under common control on the look-back date, the carrying amount of the VIE would be the fair value of its balance sheet on that date.
- If the entities were under common control on the look-back date, the carrying amount of the VIE would be the book value of the VIE's balance sheet on that date.

The carrying amounts at the look-back date must be rolled forward to the implementation date to reflect activity that has occurred on the VIE's balance sheet from the look-back date to the implementation date. The look-back balance sheet of the VIE must be adjusted for depreciation, amortization, acquisitions and sales of assets, etc.

NOTE

FIN 46R does not give any guidance as to how the retroactive look-back method should be applied. There are differing opinions as to what to do with the carrying value balance sheet of the VIE on the look-back date in terms of rolling it forward to the implementation date. The carrying value of the VIE's balance sheet on the look-back date should be adjusted to reflect all activity that has occurred from the look-back date to the implementation date. This approach is based on the logic inherent in the transition rules, which are that FIN 46R should be applied retroactively as if the entities had consolidated in previous periods.

The look-back date is the later of
- The date the primary beneficiary first became involved with the VIE
- The most recent reconsideration date (triggering event) that would have occurred had the entities consolidated retroactively.

The theory behind use of these dates is to emulate the situation that would have occurred had the entities consolidated retroactively. For example, under a retroactive consolidation, upon a triggering event occurring, the reporting enterprise would have reconsidered (retested) whether the entity was a VIE. Therefore, the latter of the initial testing date and the most recent reconsideration date should reflect the scenario that would have existed had consolidation occurred retroactively.

Option 2: Fair or carrying value of the VIE's balance sheet on the implementation date. If using the look-back method is not practicable, FIN 46R gives a second option of implementing the new rules.

Specifically, Option 2 applies the following rules, in lieu of the look-back method:
- The primary beneficiary must perform the initial test of the VIE as of the implementation date. The initial test is based on the fair value of the VIE on the implementation date to:
  - Determine whether an entity is a VIE
  - Identify variable interest holders
  - Determine whether it is the primary beneficiary that should consolidate the VIE
- The implementation date is the beginning of each reporting enterprise's first annual reporting period that begins after November 15, 2009.
- If, on the implementation date, the primary beneficiary determines it should consolidate the VIE, the primary beneficiary consolidates the VIE as of the implementation date as follows:
  - Entities that are not under common control on the implementation date consolidate the VIE based on the fair value of the VIE's balance sheet on the implementation date.
  - Entities that are under common control on the implementation date consolidate the VIE based on the carrying amounts (book value) of the VIE's balance sheet on the implementation date.
- If applicable, any difference between the net amount added to the balance sheet of the consolidating entity (primary beneficiary) and the amount of any previously recognized interest in the newly consolidated entity should be recognized as a cumulative effect adjustment to retained earnings.
- The primary beneficiary is required to describe the transition method(s) used and shall disclose the amount and classification in the balance sheet of the consolidated assets or liabilities by the transition method(s) applied.

- FIN 46R may be applied to prior years by restating previously issued financial statements for one or more years with a cumulative-effect adjustment as of the beginning of the first year restated. Restatement is encouraged but not required.

FIN 46R, however, does allow (but does not require) the rules to be applied retroactively to prior years with a cumulative effect adjustment, if any, to the beginning retained earnings in the first year restated.

Special Rules for Certain Securitization Activities

FAS 167 provides a special transition rule for those entities engaged in activities related to securitization. The rule applies to entities for which:
- It is not practicable to obtain the carrying amounts of assets and liabilities.
- The activities of the entity are primarily related to securitization or other forms of asset-backed financings.
- The assets of the entity can be used only to settle obligations of the entity.

For those entities that satisfy the criteria above, the assets and liabilities of the entity may be measured at their unpaid principal balances (as an alternative to the fair value measurement) at the date FAS 167 is first applied.

This measurement alternative does not obviate the need for the primary beneficiary to recognize any accrued interest, an allowance for credit losses, or other-than-temporary impairment, as appropriate.

Other assets, liabilities, or noncontrolling interests, if any, that do not have an unpaid principal balance, and any items that are required to be carried at fair value under other standards, shall be measured at fair value.

Transition Deconsolidation of a VIE

FAS 167 provides transition guidance for a primary beneficiary of a VIE that deconsolidates due to the new rules.

A reporting enterprise that is required to deconsolidate an entity as a result of the initial application of FAS 167 shall apply the following rules:
- The deconsolidating reporting enterprise (primary beneficiary) shall initially measure any retained interest in the deconsolidated subsidiary at its carrying amount at the transition date (beginning of the first year beginning after November 15, 2009). The carrying amount is the amount at which any retained interest would have been carried in the reporting enterprise's financial statements if FAS 167 had been effective when the reporting enterprise became involved with the entity or no longer met the conditions to be a primary beneficiary.

■ Any difference between the net amount removed from the balance sheet of the deconsolidating reporting enterprise and the amount of any retained interest in the newly deconsolidated entity shall be recognized as a cumulative effect adjustment to retained earnings. The cumulative effect adjustment due to deconsolidation shall be presented separately from any cumulative effect adjustment related to consolidation of VIEs.

Special Transition Rules Fair Value Option Under FAS 159

FAS 167 provides transitional guidance for those entities that seek to elect the fair value option allowed under FAS 159, *The Fair Value Option for Financial Assets and Financial Liabilities* (ASC 825).

Specifically, a reporting enterprise that is required to consolidate a VIE as a result of the initial application of FAS 167 may elect the fair value option under FAS 159 only if the election is made for all financial assets and liabilities of that VIE that are eligible for the option under FAS 159.

The election is made on an entity-by-entity basis.

The reporting enterprise (primary beneficiary) shall make the following disclosures:

■ Typical disclosures required by FAS 159
■ Management's reasons for electing the fair value option for a particular entity or group of entities if the election is made for some entities and not others
■ The reasons for the different elections
■ Quantitative information by line item in the balance sheet indicating the related effect on the cumulative-effect adjustment to retained earnings of electing the fair value option

Special Deferral for Certain Investment Funds

In 2010, the FASB issued an ASU, *Consolidation* (Topic 810), *Amendments to Statement 167 for Certain Investment Funds*. The ASU defers the effective date of FAS 167 indefinitely for a reporting enterprise's (investment manager's) interest in an entity that has the attributes of an investment company or for which it is industry practice to apply measurement principles for financial reporting purposes that are consistent with those followed by investment companies. The effective date of Statement 167 will be deferred for certain funds until the joint IASB/FASB consolidations project is completed (late 2010).

Specifically, FAS 167 is not effective for a reporting enterprise's interest in an entity, as long as that reporting enterprise and the entity meet all of the following conditions:

- The entity either:
  - Has all of the attributes specified in paragraph 946-10-15-2(a) through (d), *Financial Services Investment Companies*
  - Does not have all of the attributes but is an entity for which it is industry practice to apply guidance consistent with the measurement principles in Topic 946 for financial reporting purposes

> **NOTE**
>
> The attributes specified in paragraph 946-10-15-2(a) through (d) deal with whether an investment company is required to report its investment asset at fair value. Those four attributes are found in (a) through (d) are:
>
> - **Investment activity.** The investment company's primary business activity involves investing its assets, usually in the securities of other entities not under common management, for current income, appreciation, or both.
> - **Unit ownership.** Ownership in the investment company is represented by units of investments, such as shares of stock or partnership interests, to which proportionate shares of net assets can be attributed.
> - **Pooling of funds.** The funds of the investment company's owners are pooled to avail owners of professional investment management.
> - **Reporting enterprise.** The investment company is the primary reporting enterprise.

- The reporting enterprise does not have an obligation to fund losses of the entity that could potentially be significant to the entity. This condition should be evaluated considering any implicit or explicit guarantees by the reporting enterprise and its related parties, if any.
- The entity is not:
  - A securitization entity
  - An asset-backed financial entity
  - An entity that was formerly considered a qualifying special-purpose entity.

Examples of entities that may meet the conditions noted above include:
- Mutual or hedge fund
- Mortgage real estate investment fund
- Private equity fund, and
- Venture capital fund.

FAS 167 also is not effective for a reporting enterprise's interest in an entity that is required to comply with or operates in accordance with requirements that are similar to those included in Rule 2a-7 of the Investment Company Act of 1940 for registered money market funds.

STUDY QUESTIONS

14. In performing the initial measurement of the VIE by the primary beneficiary with entities not under common control, if there is any excess gain, it must be reported as which of the following?

a. As an extraordinary gain, if the VIE is not a business
b. As goodwill, if the VIE is a business
c. On the income statement of the primary beneficiary

15. A principle of consolidation that applies to the primary beneficiary's accounting for the consolidated VIE is that _____ should be eliminated.

a. Intercompany income
b. The assets of a consolidated VIE
c. The noncontrolling interests of a consolidated VIE

16. When consolidating a VIE, the VIE's stockholders' equity should be reported as which of the following?

a. Noncontrolling interest
b. As a current liability
c. In the mezzanine section of the balance sheet

17. Once a primary beneficiary is no longer required to consolidate a VIE, the proper treatment is to:

a. Deconsolidate the VIE as of the date the primary beneficiary is no longer the primary beneficiary
b. Have the new primary beneficiary wait until its new fiscal year to begin consolidation
c. Show the consolidated balance sheet through the end of the fiscal year

18. Which of the following entities is required to disclose the entity's maximum exposure to loss as a result of its involvement with a VIE?

a. Primary beneficiary of a VIE
b. An entity that holds a variable interest in a VIE but is not the primary beneficiary
c. An entity that has an investment in a VIE but holds no variable interest

19. A company is the primary beneficiary of a VIE. The VIE's balance sheet consists of real estate and a mortgage secured by that real estate. How should the VIE's real estate and mortgage be presented on the consolidated balance sheet?

   a. Combined in the assets and liabilities of the VIE
   b. Presented separately on the balance sheet
   c. Presented on the balance sheet as one "net equity or deficit" number

20. If two entities were under common control on the look-back date, the carrying amount of the VIE would be:

   a. Rolled backward to the implementation date
   b. The book value of its balance sheet on that date
   c. The fair value of its balance sheet on that date

CPE NOTE: When you have completed your study and review of chapters 3-4, which comprise Module 2, you may wish to take the Quizzer for this Module.

For your convenience, you can also take this Quizzer online at **www.cchtestingcenter.com**.

MODULE 3: RECENT ASCs AND ASUs — CHAPTER 5
Subsequent Events: FASB ASC Topic 855

LEARNING OBJECTIVES

Upon completion of this chapter, the reader will be able to:
- Describe the scope of ASC Topic 855
- List the requirements of ASC Topic 855
- Define the terms used within ASC Topic 855
- Explain the disclosure requirements of ASC Topic 855

INTRODUCTION

FAS 165 was issued in May 2009. Effective July 2009, FAS 165 was codified as FASB ASC Topic 855, *Subsequent Events*. FAS 165 was effective for interim or annual financial periods ending after June 15, 2009, and shall be applied prospectively.

Objective

The objective of this Statement is to establish GAAP principles and requirements for subsequent events. ASC Topic 855 deals with:
- The period after the balance sheet date during which management of a reporting entity shall evaluate events or transactions that may occur for potential recognition or disclosure in the financial statements
- The circumstances under which an entity shall recognize events or transactions occurring after the balance sheet date in its financial statements
- The disclosures that an entity shall make about events or transactions that occurred after the balance sheet date

BACKGROUND

In general, prior to the issuance of FAS 165, guidance for subsequent events was found in auditing literature in AU Section 560, *Subsequent Events,* which requires the auditor to evaluate subsequent events. No such guidance and requirement existed for company management even though there was some limited guidance scattered throughout other accounting literature. Examples included:
- FAS 5, *Accounting for Contingencies*
- FAS 48, *Accounting for Uncertainty in Income Taxes*
- FAS 128, *Earnings per Share.*

The FASB has undertaken several projects to incorporate accounting guidance that originated as auditing standards into the body of GAAP. In addition to FAS 165, other projects include FAS 162, *The Hierarchy of Generally Accepted Accounting Principles,* and guidance about a going concern. Including guidance in GAAP as well as in auditing standards helps to emphasize that accounting and reporting are the primary responsibility of an entity's management, and not its auditor.

Accordingly, the FASB decided to issue FAS 165 so that management now is responsible for evaluating subsequent events in connection with a company's financial statements.

In October 2008, the FASB issued an Exposure Draft, *Subsequent Events,* for a 60-day comment period. In May 2009, FAS 165, *Subsequent Events,* was issued. Effective July 2009, FAS 165 was codified as part of ASC Topic 855, *Subsequent Events.*

Because FAS 165 (now ASC Topic 855) adopted most of the same provisions found in auditing standards, as well as existing guidance spread throughout other GAAP, there should not be significant changes in the subsequent events that an entity reports either through recognition or disclosure. There are no changes made to auditing standards found in AU Section 560, so that the rules related to subsequent events now exist in both auditing and accounting standards, establishing a requirement for both the auditor and management to evaluate subsequent events.

In addition, as part of the international convergence project, FAS 165 brought U.S. GAAP more in line with international standards and in particular, IAS 10, *Events after the Reporting Period.* There still remain some small differences between FAS 165 (now ASC Topic 855) and IAS 10 in the areas of refinancing of short-term obligations and curing breaches of borrowing covenants.

REQUIREMENTS

Scope

The Statement shall be applied to the accounting for and disclosure of subsequent events not addressed in other Topics of Codification.

> **NOTE**
>
> Other Topics may address the accounting treatment of events or transactions that occur after the balance sheet date but before the financial statements are issued or are available to be issued. If an event or transaction is within the scope of another Topic, then an entity shall follow the guidance in that applicable Topic, rather than the guidance in this Topic. Examples of other Topics that also address the accounting and disclosures for specific subsequent events include:

- ■ **Income Taxes.** See FASB ASC 740-10-25-15 for guidance on changes in judgment after the balance sheet date that result in subsequent recognition, derecognition, or change in measurement of a tax position taken in a prior annual period.
- ■ **Earnings per Share.** See FASB ASC 260-10-55-12 for guidance on the effect on earnings per share of changes in the number of common shares as a result of a stock dividend or stock split that occurs after the balance sheet date but before the financial statements are issued or are available to be issued.
- ■ **Gain Contingencies.** See FASB ASC 450-30-25-1 for guidance on gain contingencies which are rarely recognized after the balance sheet date but before the financial statements are issued or are available to be issued.

STUDY QUESTIONS

1. Financial statements are considered issued when:
   a. They are issued in draft form to management in a GAAP format.
   b. They are widely distributed in an abbreviated non-GAAP format.
   c. They are widely distributed to shareholders and other users in a GAAP format.

2. If, when accounting for and determining the disclosure requirements under Topic 855 for a subsequent event, an event or transaction is also within the scope of another Topic, an entity should adhere to the requirements of Topic 855. ***True or False?***

Definitions

ASC Topic 855 defines *subsequent events* as events or transactions that occur after the balance sheet date but before financial statements are *issued or are available to be issued.*

Financial statements are considered *issued* when they are widely distributed to shareholders and other financial statement users for general use and reliance in a form and format that complies with GAAP. (SEC registrants also are required to consider the guidance in FASB ASC 855-10-S99-2)

Financial statements are considered *available to be issued* when they are:

- ■ Complete in a form and format that complies with GAAP
- ■ Have obtained all approvals necessary for issuance, such as those from management, the board of directors, and/or significant shareholders.

There are two types of subsequent events:

- **Type 1 subsequent events (recognized subsequent events).** These are events or transactions that provide additional evidence about conditions that *existed at the date of the balance sheet,* including the estimates inherent in the process of preparing financial statements.
- **Type 2 subsequent events (nonrecognized subsequent events).** These consist of events that provide evidence about conditions that *did not exist at the date of the balance sheet* but arose after that date.

Revised financial statements are revised only for either of the following conditions:
- Correction of an error
- Retrospective application of U.S. GAAP

Rules

Subsequent event period. An entity shall recognize in the financial statements the effects of all subsequent events that provide additional evidence about conditions that existed at the date of the balance sheet, including the estimates inherent in the process of preparing financial statements. An entity that meets any of the following criteria shall evaluate subsequent events through the date the financial statements are issued:

- Its debt or equity securities trade in a public market either on a stock exchange (domestic or foreign) or in an over-the-counter market, including securities quoted only locally or regionally.
- It is a conduit bond obligor for conduit debt securities that are traded in a public market (a domestic or foreign stock exchange or an over-the-counter market, including local or regional markets).
- It files with a regulatory agency in preparation for the sale of any class of debt or equity securities in a public market.
- It is required to file or furnish financial statements with the SEC.
- It is controlled by an entity covered by any of the above criteria.

If an entity does not meet any of the above criteria, it must evaluate subsequent events through the date that the financial statements are *available to be issued.*

> **NOTE**
>
> An SEC filer is required to evaluate subsequent events through the date that the financial statements are issued. An SEC filer is defined as any entity that is required to file or furnish its financial statements with either of the following:

- The Securities and Exchange Commission (SEC)
- With respect to an entity subject to Section 12(i) of the Securities Exchange Act of 1934, as amended, the appropriate agency under that Section.

The FASB generally agreed with the SEC staff's view as to when financial statements should be considered issued for SEC registrants. However, not all entities that are subject to ASC Topic 855 have their financial statements audited, and others may not widely distribute those financial statements upon completion.

As it relates to non-public entities, the concept of an "issuance date" is not meaningful because non-public companies do not have a typical issue date. For example, the audit, review or compilation work may be completed on one date, and the financial statements may be sent to users on different dates thereafter.

The Board also considered the guidance in IAS 10, under which entities must evaluate subsequent events through the date when the financial statements are authorized for issuance.

In the end, the FASB concluded that management of a reporting entity is required to evaluate subsequent events through the date that the financial statements are issued or are available to be issued. Public entities and other entities that have a current expectation of widely distributing their financial statements should evaluate subsequent events through the date that the financial statements are issued. All other entities (for example, nonpublic entities that do not widely distribute their financial statements to shareholders or other financial statement users) should evaluate subsequent events through the date that the financial statements are available to be issued. As a result, an entity that does not widely distribute its financial statements will not be required to continue to evaluate subsequent events for an extended period of time following the completion of the financial statements.

OBSERVATION

The FASB reached the conclusion that the management of a reporting entity should evaluate events or transactions occurring after the balance sheet date through the date that the financial statements are issued or are available to be issued, depending on an entity's current expectation with respect to the distribution of the financial statements. Under auditing standards (AU Section 560), subsequent events are evaluated through the issuance of financial statements. In EITF Topic No. D-86, *"Issuance of Financial Statements,"* the SEC staff stated that "financial statements are "issued" as of the date they are distributed for general use and reliance in a form and format that complies with GAAP.

Issuance of financial statements then would generally be the earlier of when the annual or quarterly financial statements are widely distributed to all shareholders and other financial statement users or filed with the Commission. Furthermore, the issuance of an earnings release does not constitute issuance of financial statements because the earnings release would not be in a form and format that complies with GAAP and GAAS.

STUDY QUESTION

3. A private entity that does not have an expectation of widely distributing its financial statements to its shareholders or any other financial statement users is required to evaluate subsequent events through the date on which the financial statements are:
   a. Issued
   b. Available to be used
   c. Printed

Recognized subsequent events. An entity shall recognize in the financial statements the effects of all subsequent events that provide additional evidence about conditions that existed at the date of the balance sheet, including the estimates inherent in the process of preparing financial statements.

EXAMPLE

The events that gave rise to litigation took place before the balance sheet date. The Company records an estimated liability for the litigation in the amount of $100,000. The litigation is settled after the balance sheet date but before the financial statements are issued or are available to be issued. The final settlement amount (after the balance sheet date) is $120,000 which is different from the $100,000 liability recorded in the balance sheet.

Conclusion. The liability at the balance sheet date should be recognized using the $120,000 settlement amount even though that amount is settled after the balance sheet date. ASC Topic 855 requires that the effects of all subsequent events that provide additional guidance about conditions that existed at the balance sheet date be recognized.

> **EXAMPLE**
>
> An entity has recorded a trade receivable in the amount of $200,000 on its balance sheet. Subsequent to the balance sheet date and before the financial statements are issued or are available to be issued, information is obtained that the trade receivable customer's financial condition has deteriorated and the customer is headed toward bankruptcy.
>
> **Conclusion.** The customer's subsequent bankruptcy filing is likely to be indicative of a condition that existed at the balance sheet date. The effects of the customer's bankruptcy filing should be considered in determining the amount of uncollectible trade receivable recognized at the balance sheet date and the portion for which an allowance should be established.

Nonrecognized subsequent events. An entity shall not recognize subsequent events that provide evidence about conditions that did not exist at the date of the balance sheet but arose after the balance sheet date but before financial statements are issued or are available to be issued. The Statement provides the following examples of non-recognized subsequent events:

Sale of a bond or capital stock issued after the balance sheet date but before financial statements are issued or are available to be issued

- A business combination that occurs after the balance sheet date but before financial statements are issued or are available to be issued
- Settlement of litigation when the event giving rise to the claim took place after the balance sheet date but before financial statements are issued or are available to be issued
- Loss of plant or inventories as a result of fire or natural disaster that occurred after the balance sheet date but before financial statements are issued or are available to be issued
- Losses on receivables resulting from conditions (such as a customer's major casualty) arising after the balance sheet date but before financial statements are issued or are available to be issued
- Changes in the fair value of assets or liabilities (financial or nonfinancial) or foreign exchange rates after the balance sheet date but before financial statements are issued or are available to be issued
- Entering into significant commitments or contingent liabilities, for example, by issuing significant guarantees after the balance sheet date but before financial statements are issued or are available to be issued

Disclosures

An entity that is not an SEC filer shall disclose the date through which subsequent events have been evaluated, as well as whether that date is the date the financial statements were issued or the date the financial statements were available to be issued

For those non-recognized subsequent events that are of such a nature that they must be disclosed to keep the financial statements from being misleading, an entity must also disclose the following:

- The nature of the event
- An estimate of its financial effect or a statement that such an estimate cannot be made.

> **NOTE**
>
> An entity also shall consider supplementing the historical financial statements with pro forma financial data. Occasionally, a non-recognized subsequent event may be so significant that disclosure can best be made by means of pro forma financial data. Such data shall give effect to the event as if it had occurred on the balance sheet date. In some situations, an entity also shall consider presenting pro forma statements, usually a balance sheet only, in columnar form on the face of the historical statements.

Reissuance of Financial Statements

An entity may need to reissue financial statements, for example, in reports filed with the SEC or other regulatory agencies. After the original issuance of the financial statements, events or transactions may have occurred that require disclosure in the reissued financial statements to keep them from being misleading.

If an entity reissues its financial statements, the entity shall not recognize events occurring between the time the financial statements were issued or available to be issued and the time the financial statements were reissued unless the adjustment is required by GAAP or regulatory requirements.

An entity shall not recognize events or transactions occurring after the financial statements were issued or were available to be issued in financial statements that are later reissued in comparative form along with financial statements of subsequent periods unless the adjustment meets the criteria stated in this paragraph.

Unless the entity is an SEC filer, an entity shall disclose the date through which subsequent events have been evaluated in both the originally issued or available to be issued financial statements and the revised (reissued) financial statements.

Effective Date and Transition

FAS 165 (ASC Topic 855) is effective for interim or annual financial periods *ending after June 15, 2009,* and shall be applied prospectively.

Certain disclosure requirements due to Accounting Standards Update No. 2010-09, *Subsequent Events (Topic 855): Amendments to Certain Recognition and Disclosure Requirements* are effective for interim or annual financial periods ending after June 15, 2010. All of the amendments in this Update are effective upon issuance of the final Update (February 2010), except for the use of the issued date for conduit debt obligors. That amendment is effective for interim or annual periods ending after June 15, 2010.

The provisions of the ASC Topic 855 do not apply to immaterial items.

STUDY QUESTIONS

4. Which of the following events would require that an entity recognize the effects of a subsequent event at the balance sheet date?

   a. Inventories loss due to a fire that occurred after the balance sheet date and after the financial statements were issued or available to be issued

   b. A litigation based on events that took place before the balance sheet date, in which a loss was realized after the balance sheet date but before the financial statements were issued.

   c. Settlement of a litigation when the event giving rise to the claim took place after the balance sheet date but before financial statements are issued or are available to be issued

5. Which of the following would be considered a non-recognized subsequent event according to ASC Topic 855?

   a. A customer that owes $300,000 before the balance sheet date files for bankruptcy after the balance sheet date but before the financial statements are issued. There is ample reason to believe that the $300,000 will not be collected.

   b. There is a material change in a foreign exchange after the balance sheet date but before financial statements are issued or are available to be issued.

   c. A lawsuit that was pending before the balance sheet date with an expected loss of $250,000 was settled for $350,000 after the balance sheet date but before the financial statements were issued.

Accounting for Transfers of Financial Assets: FASB ASC Topic 860

LEARNING OBJECTIVES

Upon completion of this chapter, the reader will be able to:

- Describe the scope of FASB 166 (ASC Topic 860)
- List what is required in order for the transfer of a financial asset to be accounted for as a sale
- Identify what constitutes an entire financial asset
- Explain the accounting required for different situations described in ASC Topic 860
- Describe the objectives for the disclosure requirements of ASC Topic 860
- Explain how to determine whether to aggregate disclosures for multiple transfers of financial assets

INTRODUCTION

FAS 166 was issued in June 2009 and is effective as of the beginning of each reporting entity's first annual reporting period that begins after November 15, 2009, for interim periods within that first annual reporting period, and for interim and annual reporting periods, thereafter. Earlier application is prohibited.

Objective

The objective of FAS 166, now codified as part of FASB ASC Topic 860, is to make changes to the accounting by a reporting entity for the transfer of financial assets and liabilities, including the effects of a transfer on its financial position, financial performance, and cash flows; and a transferor's continuing involvement in transferred financial assets.

FAS 166 amends FASB Statement No. 140, *Accounting for Transfers and Servicing of Financial Assets and Extinguishments of Liabilities* (the majority of which is now also codified as part of ASC Topic 860).

BACKGROUND

FAS 140 was issued in September 2000 and replaced FAS 125, *Accounting for Transfers and Servicing of Financial Assets and Extinguishments of Liabilities*.

FAS 140 provided accounting and reporting standards for transfers and servicing of financial assets and extinguishments of liabilities.

The purpose of FAS 140 was to prevent the transfers of financial assets from being accounted for as sales if the transferor (sponsor) had certain continuing involvement in those assets or a portion of the assets.

In particular, FAS 140 established conditions that an entity must meet to be a qualifying special-purpose entity (QSPE) and be exempt from consolidation under FIN 46(R)'s QSPE exemption. FIN 46(R) has been codified as FASB ASC Topic 810, *Consolidation.*

FAS 140 was an extension of the FASB's financial instruments project that includes off-balance-sheet financing issues. The Statement replaced FAS 125, and revised the standards for accounting for securitizations and other transfers of financial assets and collateral and required certain disclosures. Most of the provisions of FAS 125 were carried over to FAS 140 without change.

FAS 140's standards were based on application of a *financial-components approach* focusing on control.

The financial-components approach states that after a transfer of financial assets, an entity must recognize the financial and servicing assets it controls and the liabilities it has incurred, derecognize financial assets when control has been surrendered, and derecognize liabilities when extinguished. FAS 140 provided standards for distinguishing transfers of financial assets that were sales from transfers that were secured borrowings.

Since the issuance of FAS 140, the FASB has been concerned that FAS 140 did not satisfy the FASB's original objective. In particular, using FAS 140's and FIN 46's consolidation exemption for QSPEs, there were repeated examples of transferors (sponsors) who accounted for the transfer of securitized assets as sales even though the transferor had continued involvement in those transferred assets.

The FASB issued FAS 166 to deal with issues related to FAS 140, *Accounting for Transfers and Servicing of Financial Assets and Extinguishments of Liabilities.*

Since 2003, the FASB issued two FASB statements and four FASB Staff Positions that amend particular aspects of FAS 140 as follows:

- FAS 155, *Accounting for Certain Hybrid Financial Instruments*
- FAS 156, *Accounting for Servicing of Financial Assets—an amendment of FASB Statement No. 140*
- FSP FAS 140-1, *Accounting for Accrued Interest Receivable Related to Securitized and Sold Receivables under FASB Statement No. 140*
- FSP FAS 140-2, *Clarification of the Application of Paragraphs 40(b) and 40(c) of FASB Statement No. 140*
- FSP FAS 140-3, *Accounting for Transfers of Financial Assets and Repurchase Financing Transactions*
- FSP FAS 140-4, *Disclosures about Transfers of Financial Assets and Interests in Variable Interest Entities*

In December 2008, the FASB simultaneously issued an exposure draft of FAS 166 and FAS 167, *Amendments to FASB Interpretation No. 46(R)*. Within FAS 167, the FASB addressed, among many changes, elimination of the exemption from the FIN 46(R) consolidation rules for QSPEs. In June 2009, the FASB issued FAS 166 at the same time it issued FAS 167.

Prior to the issuance of FAS 166, most mortgage securitizations had been structured as sales under GAAP where the sponsor transferred the assets to a subsidiary structured as a QSPE. Usually the sponsor retained limited defined rights. The assets and related debt were removed from the sponsor's balance sheet. On the income statement, the sponsor typically recorded a gain on the sale of the securities equal to the present value of the cash flows to be received from the retained interest.

Under FAS 166 and FAS 167, the concept of QSPEs is eliminated along with the exemption from FIN 46(R). Now, a transferor (sponsor) may be required to consolidate the transferee that holds the securitized assets and liabilities.

With the elimination of the concept of a QSPE and related exemption from FIN 46(R), a sponsor is required to consolidate the securitized assets and liabilities on its balance sheet, if the sponsor is the primary beneficiary who has both:

- Power to direct the most significant activities of the QSPE entity
- The right to receive benefits or absorb losses of the QSPE entity

Transfers of financial assets by a transferor to a transferee may take one of two forms:

- The transferor has no continued involvement
- The transferor has some continued involvement with the assets transferred, or with the transferee

Examples include servicing arrangements, recourse or guarantee arrangements, agreements to purchase or redeem transferred financial assets, options written or held, derivative financial instruments, pledges of collateral, and the transferor's beneficial interests in the transferred financial assets.

Where there is continued involvement by the transferor, there are issues as to whether a sale should be recorded or whether the transaction should be accounted for as a secured borrowing.

Moreover, an entity may settle a liability by transferring assets to the creditor, obtaining an unconditional release, or entering into another arrangement designed to set aside assets dedicated to ultimately settling the liability. Such an arrangement raises the issue as to when the liability should be considered extinguished.

In accounting for transfers of financial assets, each party to the transaction (transferor and transferee) should:

- Recognize only assets it controls and liabilities it has incurred
- Derecognize assets and liabilities only when control over assets has been surrendered and when liabilities have been extinguished

The sales and other transfers of financial assets and liabilities often result in a disaggregation of the assets and liabilities into components, which become separate assets and liabilities.

For example, an entity may sell a portion of a financial asset it owns, while retaining a portion of the asset separate from the portion sold and from the assets received in the exchange.

FAS 166 amends FASB Statement No. 140, *Accounting for Transfers and Servicing of Financial Assets and Extinguishments of Liabilities,* as follows:

- Removes the concept of a QSPE from FAS 140 and removes the exception from applying FAS 46(R), *Consolidation of Variable Interest entities,* to variable interest entities that are QSPEs.
- Modifies the financial-components approach used in FAS 140 and limits the circumstances in which a transferor derecognizes a portion or component of a financial asset when the transferor has not transferred the original financial asset to an entity that is not consolidated with the transferor and/or when the transferor has continuing involvement with the financial asset.
- Introduces the concept of a participating interest.
- Establishes three conditions for reporting a transfer of a portion (or portions) of a financial asset as a sale.
- Clarifies the principle that the transferor must evaluate whether it, its consolidated affiliates included in the financial statements being presented, or its agents, effectively control the transferred financial asset directly or indirectly.
- Requires that a transferor recognize and initially measure at fair value all assets obtained (including a transferor's beneficial interest) and liabilities incurred as a result of a transfer of an entire financial asset or a group of financial assets accounted for as a sale.
- Removes the fair value practicability exception from measuring the proceeds received by a transferor in a transfer that meets the conditions for sale accounting at fair value.
- Requires enhanced disclosures to provide financial statement users with greater transparency about transfers of financial assets and a transferor's continuing involvement with transfers of financial assets accounted for as sales.

In December 2009, the FASB issued ASU 2009-16 to amend the Accounting Standards Codification (ASC) for the issuance of FAS 166.

RULES

Scope

ASC Topic 860 does not apply to the following:
- Transfers of nonfinancial assets, except for transfers of servicing assets (see Subtopic 860-50) and for the transfers noted in the following paragraph
- Transfers of unrecognized financial assets, for example, minimum lease payments to be received under operating leases
- Transfers of custody of financial assets for safekeeping
- Contributions (for guidance on accounting for contributions, see Subtopic 958-605)
- Transfers of ownership interests that are in substance sales of real estate (For guidance related to transfers of investments that are in substance a sale of real estate, see Topics 845 and 976. For guidance related to sale-leaseback transactions involving real estate, including real estate with equipment, such as manufacturing facilities, power plants, and office buildings with furniture and fixtures, see Subtopic 840-40)
- Investments by owners or distributions to owners of a business entity
- Employee benefits subject to the provisions of Topic 712
- Leveraged leases subject to Topic 840
- Money-over-money and wrap lease transactions involving nonrecourse debt subject to Topic 840.

Paragraph 815-10-40-2 states that transfers of assets that are derivative instruments and subject to the requirements of Subtopic 815-10 but that are not financial assets shall be accounted for by analogy to this Topic.

Paragraph 860-10-55-2 provides further guidance on the application of the scope of this Topic to specific transactions.

Transfers of Financial Assets and Liabilities

Transfers of financial assets can come in the form of:
- A transfer of an entire financial asset
- A transfer of a group of entire financial assets
- A transfer of a portion of a financial asset (called a participating interest)

A transfer of an entire financial asset, a group of entire financial assets, or a participating interest in an entire financial asset in which the transferor surrenders control over those assets *shall be accounted for as a sale* if and only if all of the following three conditions are met:
- The transferred assets have been isolated from the transferor. Examples include situations where assets have been put beyond the reach of the transferor and its creditors, even in bankruptcy or other receivership.

> **NOTE**
>
> Transferred financial assets are isolated in bankruptcy or other receivership only if the transferred financial assets could be beyond the reach of the powers of a bankruptcy trustee or other receiver for the transferor or any of its consolidated affiliates that are included in the financial statements being presented.

- Each transferee (or third-party holder of its beneficiary interest) has the right to pledge or exchange the assets or beneficiary interests it received, and under no condition does *both of the following*:
  - Constrains the transferee or third party holder of its beneficiary interest, from taking advantage of its right to pledge or exchange.
  - Provides more than a trivial benefit to the transferor.
- The transferor, its consolidated affiliates, or its agents *do not maintain effective control* over the transferred financial assets or third-party beneficial interests therein. Examples where a transferor has effective control over financial assets include:
  - An agreement that both entitles and obligates the transferor to repurchase or redeem them before their maturity.
  - An agreement that provides the transferor with both unilateral ability to cause the holder to return specific financial assets and a more-than-trivial benefit attributable to that ability, other than through a cleanup call.
  - An agreement that permits the transferee to require the transferor to repurchase the transferred financial assets, at a price that is so favorable to the transferee that it is probable that the transferee will require the transferor to repurchase them.

> **OBSERVATION**
>
> FAS 140 used a so-called financial-components approach for sale accounting, based on the concept that each party to a transfer recognizes the assets and liabilities that it controls after the transfer. Under the financial-components approach, both the transferor and transferee recognize the assets that it controls and liabilities that it assumes as a result of the transfer, and no longer recognizes the assets and liabilities that were surrendered or extinguished in the transfer. The key concept to the financial-components approach is that the transferor no longer recognizes the transferred financial asset if it surrendered control.

In FAS 140, the FASB provided guidance on the conditions that had to be met for a transferor to surrender control over transferred assets when the entire financial asset was transferred. However, guidance was not explicit as to how control was surrendered when a portion, but not all, of an asset was transferred. In particular, concerns were raised as to sales of undivided interests in pools of financial assets. In some such cases, such transfers were being accounted for as sales even though the transferor had some form of control, continued involvement and/or custody of the transferred asset.

To deal with the transfer of a portion of an asset, the FASB introduced the concept of a *participating interest* as a benchmark for permitting a partial transfer to use sale accounting.

In ASC Topic 860, the FASB uses the concept of a participating interest and stipulates that in a partial asset transfer, **it** is appropriate to apply the sale accounting conditions to a portion of a financial asset if the transferor and transferee proportionately share in all of the rights, risks, and benefits of the entire financial asset. The definition of a "participating interest," as well as how the rules work for partial transfers of financial assets, is discussed below.

Upon completion of a transfer of a participating interest that satisfies the three conditions for a sale, the *transferor (seller)* shall do the following:

- Allocate the previous carrying amount of the entire financial asset between the participating interests sold and those interests that continue to be held by the transferor. (The allocation should be done on a relative fair value basis at the date of the transfer.)
- Derecognize the participating interests sold.
- Recognize and initially measure at fair value servicing assets, servicing liabilities and any other assets obtained and liabilities incurred in the sale (such as cash).
- Recognize in earnings any gain or loss on the sale.
- Report any participating interest or interests that continue to be held by the transferor as the difference between the previous carrying amount of the entire financial asset and the amount derecognized.

> **NOTE**
>
> FAS 166 does not modify certain other GAAP, such as FAS 35, *Accounting and Reporting by Defined Benefit Pension Plans*, which might require accounting at the trade date for certain contracts to purchase or sell securities. In general, a transfer of securities may not be considered to be completed until the settlement date.

Upon completion of a transfer, the *transferee (buyer)* shall recognize the participating interests obtained, other assets obtained, and any liabilities incurred, and initially measure them at fair value.

Definition of a Participating Interest

A participating interest is a transfer of a portion of an asset or assets and has all of the following characteristics.

From the date of the transfer, it represents a proportionate (pro rata) ownership interest in an entire financial asset. The percentage of ownership interests held by the transferor in the entire financial asset may vary over time, while the entire financial asset remains outstanding as long as the resulting portions held by the transferor (including any participating interest retained by the transferor, its consolidated affiliates included in the financial statements being presented, or its agents) and the transferee(s) meet the other characteristics of a participating interest. For example, if the transferor's interest in an entire financial asset changes because it subsequently sells another interest in the entire financial asset, the interest held initially and subsequently by the transferor must meet the definition of a participating interest.

From the date of the transfer, all cash flows received from the entire financial asset are divided proportionately among the participating interest holders (including any interest retained by the transferor, its consolidated affiliates included in the financial statements being presented, or its agents) in an amount equal to their share of ownership. An allocation of specified cash flows is not an allowed characteristic of a participating interest unless each cash flow is proportionately allocated to the participating interest holders. In determining proportionate cash flows:

- Cash flows allocated as compensation for services perfo rmed, if any, shall not be included provided those cash flows meet both of the following conditions:
  - They are not subordinate to the proportionate cash flows of the participating interest.
  - They are not significantly above an amount that would fairly compensate a substitute service provider, should one be required, which includes the profit that would be demanded in the marketplace.
- Any cash flows received by the transferor as proceeds of the transfer of the participating interest shall be excluded provided that the transfer does not result in the transferor receiving an ownership interest in the financial asset that permits it to receive disproportionate cash flows.

The priority of cash flows has all of the following characteristics:

- The rights of each participating interest holder (including the transferor in its role as a participating interest holder) have the same priority.
- No participating interest holder's interest is subordinated to the interest of another participating interest holder.
- The priority does not change in the event of bankruptcy or other receivership of the transferor, the original debtor, or any other participating interest holder.

- Participating interest holders have no recourse to the transferor (or its consolidated affiliates included in the financial statements being presented or its agents) or to each other, other than any of the following:
  - Standard representations and warranties
  - Ongoing contractual obligations to service the entire financial asset and administer the transfer contract
  - Contractual obligations to share in any set-off benefits received by any participating interest holder
- That is, no participating interest holder is entitled to receive cash before any other participating interest holder under its contractual rights as a participating interest holder. For example, if a participating interest holder also is the servicer of the entire financial asset and receives cash in its role as servicer, that arrangement would not violate this requirement.

No party has the right to pledge or exchange the entire financial asset unless all participating interest holders agree to pledge or exchange the entire financial asset.

A set-off right is not an impediment to meeting the participating interest definition. For implementation guidance on the application of the term *participating interest,* see paragraph 860-10-55-17D

Upon completion of a transfer of an entire financial asset or a group of entire financial assets that satisfies the three conditions to be accounted for as a sale, the transferor (seller) shall do the following:

- Derecognize the transferred financial assets
- Recognize and initially measure at fair value servicing assets, servicing liabilities, and any other assets obtained (including a transferor's beneficial interest in the transferred financial assets) and liabilities incurred in the sale (FAS 166 identifies other assets obtained and liabilities incurred to include cash, put or call options, forward commitments, and swaps, among others.)
- Recognize in earnings any gain or loss on the sale

Upon completion of a transfer of an entire financial asset or a group of entire financial assets that satisfies the three conditions to be accounted for as a sale, the transferee (buyer) shall recognize all assets obtained and any liabilities incurred and initially measure them at fair value.

Transfer Not Accounted for as a Sale

If there is a transfer that *does not satisfy* the three conditions to qualify as a sale, the transaction is accounted for as a *secured borrowing with pledge of collateral.*

Under the secured borrowing with pledge of collateral rules, a debtor grants a security interest in certain assets to a lender to serve as collateral under the obligation, with or without recourse to other assets of the debtor.

- If the secured party (transferee) has the right by contract or custom to sell or repledge the collateral, the debtor (transferor) shall reclassify that asset and report that asset in its statement of financial position separately from other assets not so encumbered.
- If the secured party (transferee) sells collateral pledged to it, it shall recognize the proceeds from the sale and its obligation to return the collateral. The sale of the collateral is a transfer subject to the provisions of a sale noted above.
- If the debtor (transferor) defaults under the terms of the secured contract and is no longer entitled to redeem the pledged asset, it shall derecognize the pledged asset, and the secured party (transferee) shall recognize the collateral as its asset initially measured at fair value or, if it has already sold the collateral, derecognize its obligation to return the collateral.
- Except for the previous item above, the debtor (transferor) shall continue to carry the collateral as its asset, and the secured party (transferee) shall not recognize the pledged asset.

STUDY QUESTIONS

1. Which of the following is an example where a transferor has effective control over financial assets? An agreement that:
   a. Permits the transferee to require the transferor to repurchase the transferred financial assets at an elevated price
   b. Provides the transferor with a trivial benefit attributable to transferred asset
   c. Entitles and obligates the transferor to redeem the financial asset before its maturity

2. A transferor transfers a portion of a financial asset. The transfer does not meet the definition of a participating interest. How should the transaction be accounted for?
   a. Record the transfer as a sale for the entire asset
   b. Record the transfer as a secured borrowing
   c. Record the transfer as a nonmonetary transaction

3. When accounting for the carrying amount of a financial asset in a transfer of a participating interest, which of the following is the appropriate basis that should be used?
   a. Allocate the carrying amount based on a relative fair value basis
   b. Allocate the carrying amount based on residual value
   c. Transfer the entire carrying amount to the transferee

> **4.** According to ASC Topic 860, which of the following represents the effective date related to FAS 166, *Accounting for Transfers of Financial Assets, an amendment of FASB Statement No. 140*?
>   **a.** September 2000
>   **b.** June 2009
>   **c.** November 2009

Servicing Financial Assets and Liabilities

An entity shall recognize and initially measure at fair value a servicing asset or liability each time it undertakes an obligation to service a financial asset, by entering into a servicing contract in either of the following two situations:

- A servicer's transfer of an entire financial asset, group of entire financial assets, or a participating interest in an entire financial asset that meets the three requirements for a sale.
- An acquisition or assumption of a servicing obligation that does not relate to financial assets of the servicer or its consolidated affiliates included in the financial statements being presented.

> **NOTE**
>
> If an entity transfers its financial assets to an unconsolidated entity in a transfer that qualifies as a sale in which the transferor obtains the resulting securities and classifies them as debt securities held-to-maturity in accordance with ASC Topic 320, it may either separately recognize its servicing assets or liabilities, or report those servicing assets or liabilities together with the asset being serviced.

An entity shall subsequently measure each class of servicing assets and liabilities using one of the following methods:

- **Amortization method.** Service assets and liabilities are amortized in proportion to and over the period of estimated net servicing income (if servicing revenues exceed costs) or net servicing loss (if servicing costs exceed servicing revenues). At each reporting date, the servicing assets or liabilities are assessed for impairment or increased obligation based on fair value at each reporting date.
- **Fair value method.** Servicing assets and liabilities are measured at fair value at each reporting date and the changes in fair value are reported in earnings in the period in which the change occurs.

> **NOTE**
>
> The election to use either the amortization method or the fair value method is made separately for each class of servicing assets and servicing liabilities. An entity shall apply the same subsequent measurement method to each servicing asset and servicing liability in a class. Classes of servicing assets and servicing liabilities shall be identified based on:
>
> - The availability of market inputs used in determining the fair value of servicing assets or servicing liabilities
> - An entity's method for managing the risks of its servicing assets or servicing liabilities or
> - Both
>
> Once an entity elects the fair value measurement method for a class of servicing assets and servicing liabilities, that election shall not be reversed.

Special Rules for Financial Assets Subject to Prepayment

Those financial assets, other than instruments that are within the scope of ASC Topic 815, that can contractually be prepaid or otherwise settled in such a way that the holder would not recover substantially all of its recorded investment shall be subsequently measured like investments in debt securities classified as available-for-sale or trading under ASC Topic 320. Examples of such financial assets include interest-only strips and other beneficial interests.

Disclosures

The objectives of the disclosures required by ASC Topic 860 are to provide users with an understanding of all of the following:
- A transferor's continuing involvement with transferred financial assets.
- The nature of any restrictions on assets reported by an entity in its statement of financial position that relate to a transferred financial asset, including the carrying amounts of those assets.
- How servicing assets and liabilities are reported.
- For transfers accounted for as sales when a transferor has continuing involvement with the transferred assets, and for transfers accounted for as secured borrowings, how the transfer affects a transferor's financial position, financial performance, and cash flows.

> **NOTE**
>
> The above-noted objectives apply regardless of whether ASC Topic 860 requires specific disclosures. The specific disclosures required are minimum requirements and an entity may need to supplement the required disclosures depending on the facts and circumstances of a transfer, the nature of an

entity's continuing involvement with the transferred financial assets, and the effect of an entity's continuing involvement on the transferor's financial position, financial performance, and cash flows. Disclosures required by other U.S. generally accepted accounting principles (GAAP) for a particular form of continuing involvement shall be considered when determining whether the disclosure objectives of this Statement have been met.

The disclosures shall be presented in a manner that clearly and fully explains the transferor's risk exposure related to the transferred financial assets and any restrictions on the assets of the entity.

Finally, to apply the disclosures, an entity shall consider all involvements by the transferor, its consolidated affiliates included in the financial statements being presented, or its agents to be involvements by the transferor.

General rules associated with the format of disclosures follow:

- Disclosures may be reported in the aggregate for similar transfers if separate reporting of each transfer would not provide more useful information.
- A transferor shall disclose how similar transfers are aggregated.
- A transferor shall distinguish transfers that are accounted for as sales from transfers that are accounted for as secured borrowings.
- In determining whether to aggregate the disclosures for multiple transfers, the reporting entity shall consider quantitative and qualitative information about the characteristics of the transferred financial assets. For example, consideration should be given, but not limited, to:
  - The nature of the transferor's continuing involvement, if any
  - The types of financial assets transferred
  - Risks related to the transferred financial assets to which the transferor continues to be exposed after the transfer and the change in the transferor's risk profile as a result of the transfer
  - The guidance in paragraph 310-10-50-25 (for risks and uncertainties) and paragraphs 825-10-55-1 through 55-2 (for concentrations involving loan product terms)

Specific disclosures for collateral include:

- If the entity has entered into repurchase agreements or securities lending transactions, its policy for requiring collateral or other security.
- If the entity has pledged any of its assets as collateral that are not reclassified and separately reported in the statement of financial position, the carrying amounts and classifications of both those assets and associated liabilities as of the date of the latest statement of financial position presented, including qualitative information about the relationship(s) between those assets and associated liabilities. For example, if assets are restricted solely to satisfy a specific obligation, the carrying amounts of

those assets and associated liabilities, including a description of the nature of restrictions placed on the assets, shall be disclosed.

- If the entity has accepted collateral that it is permitted by contract or custom to sell or repledge, the fair value as of the date of each statement of financial position presented of that collateral and of the portion of that collateral that it has sold or repledged, and information about the sources and uses of that collateral.

Specific disclosures for in-substance defeasance of debt include:

- If debt was considered to be extinguished by in-substance defeasance under the provisions of FAS 76, *Extinguishment of Debt,* prior to the effective date of previously issued and superseded FAS 125, a general description of the transaction and the amount of debt that is considered extinguished at the end of each the period as long as that debt remains outstanding.

Specific disclosures for all servicing assets and servicing liabilities include:

- Management's basis for determining its classes of servicing assets and servicing liabilities.
- A description of the risks inherent in servicing assets and servicing liabilities and, if applicable, the instruments used to mitigate the income statement effect of changes in fair value of the servicing assets and servicing liabilities. (Disclosure of quantitative information about the instruments used to manage the risks inherent in servicing assets and servicing liabilities, including the fair value of those instruments at the beginning and end of the period, is encouraged but not required.)
- The amount of contractually specified servicing fees (defined as all amounts that, per contract, are due to the servicer in exchange for servicing the financial asset and would no longer be received by a servicer if the beneficial owners of the serviced assets or their trustees or agents were to exercise their actual or potential authority under the contract to shift the servicing to another servicer), late fees, and ancillary fees earned for each period for which results of operations are presented, including a description of where each amount is reported in the statement of income.
- Quantitative and qualitative information about the assumptions used to estimate the fair value (for example, discount rates, anticipated credit losses, and prepayment speeds). (An entity that provides quantitative information about the instruments used to manage the risks inherent in the servicing assets and servicing liabilities is encouraged, but not required, to disclose quantitative and qualitative information about the assumptions used to estimate the fair value of those instruments.)

Specific disclosures for servicing assets and servicing liabilities subsequently measured at fair value include:
- For each class of servicing assets and servicing liabilities, the activity in the balance of servicing assets and the activity in the balance of servicing liabilities (including a description of where changes in fair value are reported in the statement of income for each period for which results of operations are presented), including, but not limited to, the following:
  - The beginning and ending balances
  - Additions (through purchases of servicing assets, assumptions of servicing obligations, and recognition of servicing obligations that result from transfers of financial assets)
  - Disposals
  - Changes in fair value during the period resulting from changes in valuation inputs or assumptions used in the valuation model or other changes in fair value and a description of those changes
  - Other changes that affect the balance and a description of those changes

Specific disclosures for servicing assets and servicing liabilities subsequently amortized in proportion to and over the period of estimated net servicing income or loss and assessed for impairment or increased obligation include:
- For each class of servicing assets and servicing liabilities, the activity in the balance of servicing assets and the activity in the balance of servicing liabilities (including a description of where changes in the carrying amount are reported in the statement of income for each period for which results of operations are presented), including, but not limited to, the following:
  - The beginning and ending balances
  - Additions (through purchases of servicing assets, assumptions of servicing obligations, and recognition of servicing obligations that result from transfers of financial assets)
  - Disposals
  - Amortization
  - Application of valuation allowance to adjust carrying value of servicing assets
  - Other-than-temporary impairments
  - Other changes that affect the balance and a description of those changes
- For each class of servicing assets and servicing liabilities, the fair value of recognized servicing assets and servicing liabilities at the beginning and end of the period if it is practicable to estimate the value.
- The risk characteristics of the underlying financial assets used to stratify recognized servicing assets for purposes of measuring impairment.

- The activity by class in any valuation allowance for impairment of recognized servicing assets, including beginning and ending balances, aggregate additions charged and recoveries credited to operations, and aggregate write-downs charged against the allowance, for each period for which results of operations are presented.

Specific disclosures for securitizations, asset-backed financing arrangements, and similar transfers accounted for as sales when the transferor has continuing involvement with the transferred financial assets (defined as any involvement with the transferred financial assets that permits the transferor to receive cash flows or other benefits that arise from the transferred financial assets or that obligates the transferor to provide additional cash flows or other assets to any party related to the transfer) include:

- For each income statement presented:
  - The characteristics of the transfer (including a description of the transferor's continuing involvement with the transferred financial assets, the nature and initial fair value of the assets obtained as proceeds and the liabilities incurred in the transfer, and the gain or loss from sale of transferred financial assets. For initial fair value measurements of assets obtained and liabilities incurred in the transfer, the following information:
    - The level within the fair value hierarchy (as described in ASC Topic 820) in which the fair value measurements in their entirety fall, segregating fair value measurements using quoted prices in active markets for identical assets or liabilities (Level 1), significant other observable inputs (Level 2), and significant unobservable inputs (Level 3).
    - The key inputs and assumptions used in measuring the fair value of assets obtained and liabilities incurred as a result of the sale that relate to the transferor's continuing involvement (including, at a minimum, but not limited to, and if applicable, quantitative information about discount rates, expected prepayments including the expected weighted-average life of prepayable financial assets, and anticipated credit losses, and, if applicable, including expected static pool losses).
    - The valuation technique(s) used to measure fair value.
  - Cash flows between a transferor and transferee, (including proceeds from new transfers, proceeds from collections reinvested in revolving-period transfers, purchases of previously transferred financial assets, servicing fees, and cash flows received from a transferor's beneficial interests).

- For each statement of financial position presented, regardless of when the transfer occurred:
  - Qualitative and quantitative information about the transferor's continuing involvement with transferred financial assets that provides financial statement users with sufficient information to assess the reasons for the continuing involvement and the risks related to the transferred financial assets to which the transferor continues to be exposed after the transfer and the extent that the transferor's risk profile has changed as a result of the transfer (including, but not limited to, credit risk, interest rate risk, and other risks), such as:
    - The total principal amount outstanding, the amount that has been derecognized, and the amount that continues to be recognized in the statement of financial position.
    - The terms of any arrangements that could require the transferor to provide financial support (for example, liquidity arrangements and obligations to purchase assets) to the transferee or its beneficial interest holders, including a description of any events or circumstances that could expose the transferor to loss and the amount of the maximum exposure to loss.
    - Whether the transferor has provided financial or other support during the periods presented that it was not previously contractually required to provide to the transferee or its beneficial interest holders, including when the transferor assisted the transferee or its beneficial interest holders in obtaining support, including the type and amount of support and the primary reasons for providing the support.
    - Information is encouraged about any liquidity arrangements, guarantees, and/or other commitments provided by third parties related to the transferred financial assets that may affect the transferor's exposure to loss or risk of the related transferor's interest.
  - The entity's accounting policies for subsequently measuring assets or liabilities that relate to the continuing involvement with the transferred financial assets.
  - The key inputs and assumptions used in measuring the fair value of assets or liabilities that relate to the transferor's continuing involvement (including, at a minimum, but not limited to, and if applicable, quantitative information about discount rates, expected prepayments including the expected weighted-average life of prepayable financial assets, and anticipated credit losses, including expected static pool losses).

- For the transferor's interests in the transferred financial assets, a sensitivity analysis or stress test showing the hypothetical effect on the fair value of those interests (including any servicing assets or servicing liabilities) of two or more unfavorable variations from the expected levels for each key assumption that is reported independently from any change in another key assumption, and a description of the objectives, methodology, and limitations of the sensitivity analysis or stress test.
- Information about the asset quality of transferred financial assets and any other assets that it manages together with them. This information shall be separated between assets that have been derecognized and assets that continue to be recognized in the statement of financial position. This information is intended to provide financial statement users with an understanding of the risks inherent in the transferred financial assets as well as in other assets and liabilities that it manages together with transferred financial assets. For example, information for receivables shall include, but is not limited to delinquencies at the end of the period and credit losses, net of recoveries, during the period.

> **NOTE**
>
> The disclosures discussed in the section above on servicing assets and liabilities subsequently amortized in proportion to and over the period of estimated net servicing income or loss and assessed for impairment or increased obligation, apply to transfers accounted for as sales when the transferor has continuing involvement with transferred financial assets as a result of a securitization, asset-backed financing arrangement, or a similar transfer. If specific disclosures are required for a particular form of the transferor's continuing involvement by other U.S. GAAP, the transferor shall provide the information required as noted above with a cross-reference to the separate notes to financial statements so a financial statement user can understand the risks retained in the transfer. The entity need not provide each specific disclosure required if the disclosure is not required by other U.S. GAAP.

Specific disclosures for transfers of financial assets accounted for as secured borrowings include:

- The carrying amounts and classifications of both assets and associated liabilities recognized in the transferor's statement of financial position at the end of each period presented, including qualitative information about the relationship(s) between those assets and associated liabilities; for example, if assets are restricted solely to satisfy a specific obligation, the carrying amounts of those assets and associated liabilities, including a description of the nature of restrictions placed on the assets.

Unit of Account in Applying ASC Topic 860

The conditions that determine whether a transfer is a sale state that sale accounting conditions are applied to transfers of an entire financial asset, transfers of a group of entire financial assets, and transfers of a participating interest in an entire financial asset.

In order to be eligible for sale accounting an entire financial asset cannot be divided into components before a transfer unless all of the components meet the definition of a participating interest.

In determining what constitutes an entire financial asset, the legal form of the asset and what the asset conveys to its holders is considered. Examples that illustrate the application of what constitutes an entire financial asset include the following.

Situation	Conclusion
A loan to one borrower in accordance with a single contract that is transferred to a securitization entity before securitization	The contract is considered an entire financial asset.
A beneficial interest in securitized financial assets after the securitization process has been completed	The beneficiary interest is considered an entire financial asset.
A transferred interest in an individual loan	The transferred interest is not to be considered an entire financial asset; however, if the transferred interest meets the definition of a participating interest, the participating interest would be eligible for sale accounting.
The transferor creates an interest-only strip from a loan and transfers the interest-only strip	The interest-only strip does not meet the definition of an entire financial asset (and an interest-only strip does not meet the definition of a participating interest; therefore, sale accounting would be precluded). In contrast, if an entire financial asset is transferred to a securitization entity that it does not consolidate and the transfer meets the conditions for sale accounting, the transferor may obtain an interest-only strip as proceeds from the sale. An interest-only strip received as proceeds of a sale is an entire financial asset for purposes of evaluating any future transfers that could then be eligible for sale accounting.

Situation	Conclusion
Multiple advances are made to one borrower in accordance with a single contract (such as a line of credit, credit card loan, or a construction loan).	An advance on that contract would be a separate unit of account if the advance retains its identity, does not become part of a larger loan balance, and is transferred in its entirety. However, if the transferor transfers an advance in its entirety and the advance loses its identity and becomes part of a larger loan balance, the transfer would be eligible for sale accounting only if the transfer of the advance does not result in the transferor retaining any interest in the larger balance or if the transfer results in the transferor's interest in the larger balance meeting the definition of a participating interest. Similarly, if the transferor transfers an interest in an advance that has lost its identity, the interest must be a participating interest in the larger balance to be eligible for sale accounting.

Removal of Qualifying Special-Purpose Entity (QSPE) Concept

Perhaps one of the most significant changes made by FAS 166 is the elimination of the concept of a QSPE. Previously, FAS 140 held the concept of a QSPE and FIN 46(R) exempted QSPEs from its consolidation rules. Thus, entities that were structured to meet the definition of a QSPE were able to avoid consolidation of that entity with its transferor (seller).

FAS 140 defined a QSPE as a trust or other legal vehicle that was demonstrably distinct from the transferor; had certain permitted activities, significantly limited and specified in the legal documents; and held certain passive financial assets.

In issuing FAS 166, the FASB removed the concept of a QSPE altogether. Further, in amending FIN 46(R), FAS 167 eliminated the exemption from the consolidation rules for QSPEs.

The result may be significant for certain entities that previously met the definition of a QSPE and did not consolidate the QSPE with the transferor (seller). Now, the consolidation exemption is eliminated. Consequently, such entities are now required to be consolidated with the transferor if the FIN 46(R) (ASC Topic 810) rules for consolidation are met.

In removing the QSPE concept, the FASB noted that the application of the conditions for a qualifying special-purpose entity had been extended in some cases beyond the intent of FAS 140, thus effectively rendering the conditions no longer operational in practice.

Examples of Applications of ASC Topic 860

The following two examples have been extracted from ASC Topic 860.

Example 1

Company X transfers entire loans with a carrying amount of $1,000 to an unconsolidated securitization entity and receives proceeds with a fair value of $1,030.

The transfer meets the three conditions and is accounted for as a sale.

The Company retains no servicing responsibilities and assumes a limited recourse obligation to repurchase delinquent loans.

Company X agrees to provide the transferee a return at a floating rate of interest even though the contractual terms of the loan are fixed rate in nature (that provision is effectively an interest rate swap).

Details follow.

Fair values:	
Cash proceeds	$1,050
Interest rate swap	40
Recourse obligation	60
Net proceeds:	
Cash received	$1,050
Plus:	
Interest rate swap	40
Less: Recourse obligation	(60)
Net proceeds	$1,030
Gain on sale:	
Net proceeds	$1,030
Carrying amount of loans sold	1,000
Gain on sale	$ 30

Conclusion

The transfer represents a transfer of an entire financial asset. A given fact is that the transfer satisfies the three conditions that allow the transaction to be accounted for as a sale. Under this example, the transferor does the following:

- Derecognizes the transferred financial assets (loans) with a carrying value of $1,000
- Recognizes and initially measures at fair value any assets obtained (interest rate swap of $40) and liabilities incurred (recourse obligation of $60)
- Recognizes in earnings a gain of $30

Although not presented above, upon completion of a transfer of the loans to the transferee, the transferee (buyer) shall recognize all assets obtained and any liabilities incurred and initially measure them at fair value.

Entry:		
Cash	1,050	
Interest rate swap	40	
Loans		1,000
Recourse obligation		60
Gain on sale		30
To record transfer of loans		

Example 2: Sale of Receivables with Servicing Retained

Company X originates $1,000 of loans that yield 10 percent interest income for their estimated lives of nine years. The Company transfers the entire loans to an unconsolidated entity and the transfer is accounted for as a sale.

The company receives as proceeds $1,000 cash, a beneficiary interest to receive one percent of the contractual interest on the loans (an interest-only strip receivable), and an additional one percent of the contractual interest as compensation for servicing the loans.

The fair value of the servicing asset and the interest-only strip receivable are $40 and $60, respectively.

Conclusion

Similar to Example 1, this example represents a transfer of an entire financial asset, which is the $1,000 of loans. A given fact is that the transfer satisfies the three conditions that allow the transaction to be accounted for as a sale. Under this example, the transferor does the following:

- Derecognizes the transferred financial assets (loans) with a carrying value of $1,000
- Recognizes and initially measures at fair value any assets obtained ($60 interest-only strip receivable and $40 servicing asset) and liabilities incurred (none in this example)
- Recognizes in earnings a gain of $100

Although not presented above upon completion of a transfer of the loans to the transferee, the transferee (buyer) shall recognize all assets obtained and any liabilities incurred and initially measure them at fair value.

Details of the computations and related entries follow.

```
        Fair values:
            Cash proceeds                              $1,000
            Servicing asset                                40
            Interest-only strip receivable                 60

        Net proceeds:
            Cash proceeds                              $1,000
            Servicing asset                                40
            Interest-only strip receivable                 60
            Net proceeds                               $1,100
```

Gain on sale:

Net proceeds	$1,100	
Carrying amount of loans sold	1,000	
Gain on sale	$ 100	

Entries:

Cash	1,000	
Servicing asset	40	
Interest-only strip receivable	60	
Loans		1,000
Gain on sale		100
To record transfer		

To record transfer and recognize interest-only
strip receivable and servicing asset

Example 3: Recording Transfers of Participating Partial Interests

Company B transfers nine-tenths participating interest in a loan with a fair value of $1,100 and a carrying amount of $1,000.

It is assumed that the transfer satisfies the three conditions and is accounted for as a sale.

The servicing contract has a fair value of zero, because Company B estimates that the benefits of servicing are just adequate to compensate it for its servicing responsibilities.

Conclusion

In this example there is a transfer of a participating (partial) interest in the loans. Because the transfer satisfies the three conditions for sale accounting, the transfer is recorded as a sale. In recording the sale, the following is done:

- Allocate the $1,000 carrying amount of the entire loans between the participating interests sold (90 percent) and those interests that continue to be held by the transferor 10 percent). The allocation should be done on a relative fair value basis at the date of the transfer.

- Derecognize (remove) the participating interests sold by recording the portion of the carrying value sold, which is $900.
- Recognize and initially measure at fair value any servicing assets, servicing liabilities, and any other assets obtained and liabilities incurred in the sale. In this example, the servicing assets have a zero value.
- Recognize in earnings any gain or loss on the sale, which is a $90 gain.
- Report the participating interest that continues to be held by the transferor as the difference between the previous carrying amount of the entire financial asset ($1,000) and the amount derecognized of $900. The portion held is $100.

Fair values		Allocated Fair Value	Percent Fair Value
Portion sold: 9/10 of participating interest sold	$1,100 x 9/10	$990	90%
Portion held by transferor: 1/10 of interest	1,100 x 1/10	110	10%
		$1,100	100%

Allocation of carrying value	Percent Fair Value	Allocated Carrying Value
Portion sold: 9/10 of participating interest sold	90%	$900
Portion held by transferor: 1/10 of interest	10%	100
	100%	$1,000

Computation of gain on portion transferred	
Net proceeds	$990
Carrying value of portion sold	900
Gain on sale	$90

Entry to record transfer of loans		
Cash	990	
Loans (portion sold)		900
Gain on sale		90

Effective Date

The Statement is effective as of the beginning of each reporting entity's first annual reporting period that begins after November 15, 2009, for interim periods within that first annual reporting period, and for interim and annual reporting periods thereafter. Earlier application is prohibited.

The recognition and measurement provisions of the Statement shall be applied to transfers that occur on or after the effective date.

Additionally, on and after the effective date, existing qualifying special-purpose entities (as defined under previous accounting standards) must be evaluated for consolidation by reporting entities in accordance with the applicable consolidation guidance. If the evaluation on the effective date results in consolidation, the reporting entity shall apply the transition guidance provided in the pronouncement that requires consolidation.

The disclosure provisions of this Statement shall be applied to transfers that occurred both before and after the effective date of this Statement. An entity is encouraged, but not required, to disclose comparative information for periods earlier than the effective date for disclosures that were not previously required by FAS 140 for nonpublic entities or by FASB Staff Position FAS 140-4 and FIN 46(R)-8, *Disclosures by Public Entities (Enterprises) about Transfers of Financial Assets and Interests in Variable Interest Entities,* for public entities. Comparative disclosures for those disclosures that were not previously required by FAS 140 for nonpublic entities or by FSP FAS 140-4 and FIN 46(R)-8 for public entities are required only for periods after the effective date.

STUDY QUESTIONS

5. Using the amortization method, a service asset is amortized in proportion to and over:

a. The period of estimated net servicing income or loss

b. The estimated useful life of the transferred asset

c. An estimated straight-line period consistent with the industry practices

6. A transferor has a servicing asset in connection with a transferred asset. The servicing asset is not subsequently measured at fair value. Which of the following is *not* a disclosure required for the transferor?

a. Basis for determining the classes of servicing assets

b. A description of the risks inherent in servicing assets

c. The amount of contractually specified servicing fees

d. The activity in the balance of servicing assets

7. Which of the following is a byproduct of FAS 166's removal of the QSPE concept?

a. Financial assets will be transferred at higher values than previously used.

b. More transferors of financial assets may have to consolidate transferees.

c. More entities will meet the QSPE definition even if it is not codified.

8. Company X transfers 75 percent participating interest in a loan. The fair value of the loan is $2,000 and the carrying value is $1,200. The transfer satisfies the three conditions for a sale transaction. How much is the gain to be recognized by the transferor?

   a. Zero
   b. $800
   c. $600
   d. $2,000

9. A company (transferor) transfers 100 percent of the loans it holds, with a carrying value of $4,000, to a transferee. The transfer qualifies as a sale transaction. The company receives $5,000 cash for the transferred assets. The transferor receives two percent of the contracted interest as compensation for servicing the loans. The fair value of the servicing asset is $500. What is the gain or loss recognized on the transfer?

   a. $1,500
   b. $ 500
   c. $1,000
   d. Zero

10. If an entity chooses the fair value method to account for its servicing assets, changes in fair value are reported in which of the following?

    a. Equity
    b. The mezzanine section
    c. Current earnings

FASB Accounting Standards Updates (ASUs)

LEARNING OBJECTIVES

Upon completion of this chapter, the reader will be able to:

- Explain the purpose of an ASU
- Describe the changes made to GAAP due to recently issued ASUs
- List the specific requirements of several of the selected ASUs discussed in this chapter

INTRODUCTION

Over the past few years, the Financial Accounting Standards Board (FASB), together with its staff and other specialists, have been working on a project to codify (by topic) U.S. generally accepted accounting principles (U.S. GAAP). The FASB's purpose is to simplify U.S. GAAP, without change, by consolidating the numerous accounting rules into logically organized topics. The result of this project is the *FASB Accounting Standards Codification* (FASB Codification).

On June 3, 2009, the FASB approved the Accounting Standards Codification (ASC) and decided to make it effective for interim or annual reporting periods ending after September 15, 2009.

Effective July 1, 2009, changes to the source of authoritative U.S. GAAP, the FASB Codification, are communicated through an Accounting Standards Update (ASU). ASUs will be published for all authoritative U.S. GAAP promulgated by the FASB, regardless of the form in which such guidance may have been issued prior to release of the FASB Codification (e.g., FASB Statements, EITF Abstracts, FASB Staff Positions, etc.). ASUs also will be issued for amendments to the SEC content in the FASB Codification as well as for editorial changes. An ASU is a transient document that:

- Summarizes the key provisions of the project that led to the ASU
- Details the specific amendments to the FASB Codification
- Explains the basis for the Board's decisions

Although ASUs will update the FASB Codification, the FASB does not consider ASUs as authoritative in their own right.

Prior to the release of the FASB Codification as the single source of authoritative U.S. GAAP, the FASB amended pre-Codification standards and issued them in an "as amended" form. The FASB will not amend ASUs. It will only amend the FASB Codification.

STUDY QUESTIONS

1. Which of the following is the FASB's purpose for codifying (by topic) U.S. GAAP?

   a. To modify U.S. GAAP
   b. To simplify U.S. GAAP without changing it
   c. To make U.S. GAAP more complex
   d. To converge with IFRS

2. On which of the following effective dates are changes to the FASB ASC communicated through an ASU?

   a. June 3, 2009
   b. July 1, 2009
   c. September 15, 2009
   d. December 31, 2009

3. Which of the following is *not* included as part of an ASU?

   a. Amendments to Statements on Financial Accounting Standards
   b. A summary of the key provisions of the project that led to the ASU
   c. An explanation of the basis for the Board's decisions
   d. Details of the specific amendments to the FASB Codification

4. Which of the following statements *incorrect?*

   a. Pre-Codification, the FASB made amendments to the Statements on Financial Accounting Standards.
   b. Pre-Codification, the FASB made amendments to FASB Interpretations.
   c. The Codification is the single source of authoritative U.S. GAAP.
   d. The FASB will not amend the Codification, but will only amend the ASUs.

SUMMARY OF RECENTLY ISSUED ASUS

Following is a summary of the ASUs issued through March of 2010:

ASU	Description
No. 2009-01	This ASU amends the Codification for the issuance of FAS 168, *The FASB Accounting Standards Codification™ and the Hierarchy of Generally Accepted Accounting Principles*. This ASU includes FAS 168 in its entirety, including the ASU instructions contained in Appendix B of the Statement.

ASU	Description
No. 2009-02	This ASU represents technical corrections to various Topics, addressing feedback received.
No. 2009-03	This ASU represents technical corrections to various Topics containing SEC Staff Accounting Bulletins to update cross-references to Codification text.
No. 2009-04	This ASU represents an update to Section 480-10-S99, Distinguishing Liabilities from Equity, per EITF Topic D-98, *Classification and Measurement of Redeemable Securities.*
No. 2009-05	This ASU amends Subtopic 820-10, *Fair Value Measurements and Disclosures,* to provide guidance on the fair value measurement of liabilities.
No. 2009-06	The Board issued this ASU to provide additional implementation guidance on accounting for uncertainty in income taxes and to eliminate the disclosures required by paragraph 740-10-50-15(a) through (b) for nonpublic entities.
No. 2009-07	This ASU represents technical corrections to various Topics containing SEC guidance based on external comments received.
No. 2009-08	This ASU represents technical corrections to Topic 260-10-S99, *Earnings per Share,* based on EITF Topic D-53, *Computation of Earnings Per Share for a Period that Includes a Redemption or an Induced Conversion of a Portion of a Class of Preferred Stock* and EITF Topic D-42, *The Effect of the Calculation of Earnings per Share for the Redemption or Induced Conversion of Preferred Stock.*
No. 2009-09	This ASU represents a correction to Section 323-10-S99-4, *Accounting by an Investor for Stock-Based Compensation Granted to Employees of an Equity Method Investee.* Section 323-10-S99-4 was originally entered into the Codification incorrectly.
No. 2009-10	This ASU codifies the Observer comment in paragraph 17 of EITF 02-3, *Issues Involved in Accounting for Derivative Contracts Held for Trading Purposes and Contracts Involved in Energy Trading and Risk Management.*
No. 2009-11	This ASU represents a technical correction to the SEC Observer comment in EITF 90-22, *Accounting for Gas-Balancing Arrangements.*
No. 2009-12	This ASU amends Subtopic 820-10, *Fair Value Measurements and Disclosures,* to provide guidance on the fair value measurement of investments in certain entities that calculate net asset value per share (or its equivalent).
No. 2009-13	The objective of this ASU is to address the accounting for multiple-deliverable arrangements to enable vendors to account for products or services (deliverables) separately rather than as a combined unit.
No. 2009-14	The objective of this ASU is to address concerns raised by constituents relating to the accounting for revenue arrangements that contain tangible products and software.
No. 2009-15	The purpose of this ASU is to address the accounting for own-share lending arrangements entered into in contemplation of a convertible debt issuance or other financing.

ASU	Description
No. 2009-16	This ASU amends the FASB Accounting Standards Codification for the issuance of FAS 166, *Accounting for Transfers of Financial Assets—an amendment of FASB Statement No. 140*. The amendments in this ASU improve financial reporting by eliminating the exceptions for qualifying special-purpose entities from the consolidation guidance and the exception that permitted sale accounting for certain mortgage securitizations when a transferor has not surrendered control over the transferred financial assets. In addition, the amendments require enhanced disclosures about the risks that a transferor continues to be exposed to because of its continuing involvement in transferred financial assets. Comparability and consistency in accounting for transferred financial assets will also be improved through clarifications of the requirements for isolation and limitations on portions of financial assets that are eligible for sale accounting.
No. 2009-17	This ASU amends the Codification for the issuance of FAS 167, *Amendments to FASB Interpretation No. 46(R)*. The amendments in this ASU replace the quantitative-based risks and rewards calculation for determining which reporting entity, if any, has a controlling financial interest in a variable interest entity with an approach focused on identifying which reporting entity has the power to direct the activities of a variable interest entity that most significantly impact the entity's economic performance and (1) the obligation to absorb losses of the entity or (2) the right to receive benefits from the entity. An approach that is expected to be primarily qualitative will be more effective for identifying which reporting entity has a controlling financial interest in a variable interest entity. The amendments in this ASU also require additional disclosures about a reporting entity's involvement in variable interest entities, which will enhance the information provided to users of financial statements.
No. 2010-01	The amendments in this ASU clarify that the stock portion of a distribution to shareholders that allows them to elect to receive cash or stock with a potential limitation on the total amount of cash that all shareholders can elect to receive in the aggregate is considered a share issuance that is reflected in EPS prospectively and is not a stock dividend for purposes of applying Topics 505 and 260 (*Equity* and *Earnings Per Share*).
No. 2010-02	This ASU provides amendments to Subtopic 810-10 and related guidance within U.S. GAAP to clarify the scope of the decrease in ownership provisions of the Subtopic and related guidance. The amendments in this ASU also clarify that the decrease in ownership guidance does not apply to certain transactions, even if they involve businesses.
No. 2010-03	The objective of the amendments included in this ASU is to align the oil and gas reserve estimation and disclosure requirements of *Extractive Activities—Oil and Gas* (Topic 932) with the requirements in the Securities and Exchange Commission's final rule, Modernization of the Oil and Gas Reporting Requirements (the Final Rule). The Final Rule was issued on December 31, 2008.
No. 2010-04	This ASU represents technical corrections to SEC guidance in various Topics.

ASU	Description
No. 2010-05	This ASU codifies EITF Topic D-110, *Escrowed Share Arrangements and the Presumption of Compensation,* from the June 18, 2009 EITF meeting.
No. 2010-06	This update provides amendments to Topic 820 that will provide more robust disclosures about (1) the different classes of assets and liabilities measured at fair value, (2) the valuation techniques and inputs used, (3) the activity in Level 3 fair value measurements, and (4) the transfers between Levels 1, 2, and 3.
No. 2010-07	This ASU amends the Codification for the issuance of FAS 164, *Not-for-Profit Entities: Mergers and Acquisitions.* The amendments in this ASU provide guidance on accounting for combinations of not-for-profit entities. Those transactions or other events include mergers of two or more not-for-profit entities and acquisitions by a not-for-profit entity that result in its initially recognizing another not-for-profit entity, a business, or a nonprofit activity in its financial statements.
No. 2010-08	From time to time, the Board reviews its standards to determine if any provisions in U.S. GAAP are outdated, contain inconsistencies, or need clarifications to reflect the Board's original intent. The amendments in this ASU eliminate those inconsistencies and outdated provisions and provide the needed clarifications. The related changes to U.S. GAAP are generally nonsubstantive in nature.

STUDY QUESTIONS

5. Which of the following statements is correct?

   a. ASUs are issued using alphabetical prefixes to identify their order.

   b. Readers can identify the month an ASU was issued by the last two digits of it issuance number.

   c. An ASU pertaining to the fair value option which was issued on June 13, 2009, would be given the issuance number of "FV2009."

   d. The next ASU to be issued after "2009-06" would be numbered" 2009-07."

6. Which of the following was the key provision of the first ASU to be issued in 2009?

   a. Corrections to various Topics addressing feedback received.

   b. Amendments to Topics addressing equity and earnings per share

   c. Amendments to fair value measurement (Topic 820) requiring more robust disclosures regarding the valuation techniques used.

   d. The issuance of FAS 168, *The FASB Accounting Standards Codification™ and the Hierarchy of Generally Accepted Accounting Principles.*

ANALYSIS OF SELECTED ASUS

Accounting Standards Update No. 2009-06, Income Taxes (ASC 740): *Implementation Guidance on Accounting for Uncertainty in Income Taxes and Disclosure Amendments for Nonpublic Entities*

Objective

The FASB issued ASU 2009-06 in September 2009 to provide additional implementation guidance on the accounting for uncertainties in income taxes (previously FIN 48). The ASU addresses the following questions:

- Is the income tax paid by the entity attributable to the entity or its owners?
- What constitutes a tax position for a pass-through entity or a tax-exempt not-for-profit entity?
- How should accounting for uncertainty in income taxes be applied when a group of related entities comprise both taxable and nontaxable entities?

Further, the FASB decided to eliminate certain required disclosures found in FIN 48 for nonpublic entities.

Background

FASB Interpretation No. 48, *Accounting for Uncertainty in Income Taxes* (FIN 48, now included in ASC 740), was issued in June 2006 and was effective for fiscal years beginning after December 15, 2006.

FIN 48 clarified the accounting for uncertainty in income taxes recognized in an enterprise's financial statements in accordance with FASv109, *Accounting for Income Taxes* (ASC 740). Further FIN 48 applied to not-for-profit organizations, pass-through entities and entities whose tax liability is subject to 100 percent credit for dividends paid (for example, real estate investment trusts and registered investment companies) that are potentially subject to income taxes.

FIN 48 did not provide examples of how it applies to not-for-profit entities or pass-through entities, such as S Corporations or partnerships

Questions remain about how to apply FIN 48 to pass-through entities and not-for-profit entities. In response to those concerns, the Board issued FSP FIN 48-3, *Effective Date of FASB Interpretation No. 48 for Certain Nonpublic Enterprises* (also now included in Subtopic 740-10), in December 2008. That FSP extended the deferral of the effective date of FIN 48 to annual financial statements for fiscal years beginning after December 15, 2008. The FASB concluded that the effective date deferral provided by FSP FIN 48-3 would give the Board the time necessary to develop guidance on the implementation of FIN 48 to pass-through entities and tax-exempt not-for-profit entities.

Scope

The ASU applies to financial statements of nongovernmental entities that are presented in conformity with U.S. GAAP. The disclosure amendments will apply only to nonpublic entities as defined in ASC 740-10-20.

Amendments Made to Topic 740

Topic 740 is amended to include the following within the definition of a tax position and within the scope of Topic 740:

- Pass-through entities
- Tax-exempt not-for-profit entities
- Entities taxed in a manner similar to pass-through entities such as REITs and registered investment companies.

> **NOTE**
>
> If income taxes paid by the entity are attributable to the entity, the transaction should be accounted for consistent with the guidance for uncertainty in income taxes in ASC 740. If income taxes paid by the entity are attributable to the owners, the transaction should be recorded as a transaction with owners. The determination of attribution should be made for each jurisdiction where the entity is subject to income taxes.
>
> A reporting entity must consider the tax positions of all entities within a related party group of entities regardless of the tax status of the reporting entity.

Nonpublic entities are exempt from certain disclosures required under Topic 740.

Topic 740-10-50-15A requires that <u>public entities only</u> (not non public entities) shall disclose both of the following at the end of each annual reporting period presented:

- A tabular reconciliation of the total amounts of unrecognized tax benefits at the beginning and end of the period, which shall include at a minimum:
  - The gross amounts of the increases and decreases in unrecognized tax benefits as a result of tax positions taken during a prior period
  - The gross amounts of increases and decreases in unrecognized tax benefits as a result of tax positions taken during the current period
  - The amounts of decreases in the unrecognized tax benefits relating to settlements with taxing authorities
  - Reductions to unrecognized tax benefits as a result of a lapse of the applicable statute of limitations.
- The total amount of unrecognized tax benefits that, if recognized, would affect the effective tax rate.

Transition: ASU 2009-06

The following represents the transition and effective date information related to ASU 2009-06.

- For entities that are currently applying the standards for accounting for uncertainty in income taxes, the ASU content shall be effective for interim and annual periods ending after September 15, 2009.
- For those entities that have deferred the application of accounting for uncertainty in income taxes, the ASU changes shall be effective upon adoption of those standards.
- The effective date guidance does not affect the effective date guidance for certain nonpublic entities in ASC 740- 10-65-1.

New Examples Provided by the ASU

ASC 2009-06 amends Topic 740 to include new Examples 33-38 as presented below, as modified by the author.

Example 33: Definition of a Tax Position

Facts: Entity S converted to an S Corporation from a C Corporation effective January 1, 20X0. In 20X7, Entity S disposed of assets subject to built-in gains and reported a tax liability on its 20X7 tax returns.

Conclusion: Tax positions to consider related to the built-in gains tax include, but are not limited to:
- Whether other assets were sold subject to the built-in gains tax
- Whether the income associated with the calculation of the taxable amount of the built-in gains is correct
- Whether the basis associated with the built-in gains calculation is correct
- Whether or not Entity S is subject to the built-in gains tax.

Example 34: Definition of a Tax Position

Facts: Entity N, a tax-exempt not-for-profit entity, enters into transactions that may be subject to income tax on unrelated business income.

Conclusion: Tax positions to consider include but are not limited to:
- Entity N's characterization of its activities as related or unrelated to its exempt purpose
- Entity N's allocation of revenue between activities that relate to its exempt purpose and those that are allocated to unrelated business income
- The allocation of Entity N's expenses between activities that relate to its exempt purpose and those that are allocated to unrelated business activities
- Whether N qualifies as a tax-exempt not-for-profit entity.

Example 35: Attribution of Income Taxes to the Entity or Its Owners

Facts: Entity A, a partnership with two partners—Partner 1 and Partner 2—has nexus in Jurisdiction J. Jurisdiction J assesses an income tax on Entity A and allows Partners 1 and 2 to file a tax return and use their pro rata share of Entity A's income tax payment as a credit (that is, payment against the tax liability of the owners).

Conclusion: Because the owners may file a tax return and utilize Entity A's payment as a payment against their personal income tax, the income tax would be attributed to the owners by Jurisdiction J's laws whether or not the owners file an income tax return.

Because the income tax has been attributed to the owners, payments to Jurisdiction J for income taxes should be treated as a transaction with the owners. The result would not change even if there were an agreement between Entity A and its two partners requiring Entity A to reimburse Partners 1 and 2 for any taxes the partners may owe to Jurisdiction J. This is because attribution is based on the laws and regulations of the taxing authority rather than on obligations imposed by agreements between an entity and its owners.

Example 36: Attribution of Income Taxes to the Entity or Its Owners

Facts: Assume the fact pattern in Example 35 above is changed such that Jurisdiction J has no provision for the owners to file tax returns and the laws and regulations of Jurisdiction J do not indicate that the payments are made on behalf of Partners 1 and 2.

Conclusion: Income taxes are attributed to Entity A on the basis of Jurisdiction J's laws and are accounted for based on the guidance in Topic 740.

Example 37: Attribution of Income Taxes to the Entity or Its Owners

Facts: Entity S, an S Corporation, files a tax return in Jurisdiction J. An analysis of the laws and regulations of Jurisdiction J indicates that Jurisdiction J can hold Entity S and its owners jointly and severally liable for payment of income taxes. The laws and regulations also indicate that if payment is made by Entity S, the payments are made on behalf of the owners.

Conclusion: Because the laws and regulations attribute the income tax to the owners regardless of who pays the tax, any payments to Jurisdiction J for income taxes should be treated as a transaction with its owners and not subject to ASC Topic 740.

Example 38: Financial Statements of a Group of Related Entities

Facts: Entity A, a partnership with two partners, owns a 100 percent interest in Entity B and is required to issue consolidated financial statements.

Entity B is a taxable entity that has unrecognized tax positions and a related liability for unrecognized tax benefits.

Conclusion: Because entities within a consolidated or combined group should consider the tax positions of all entities within the group regardless of the tax status of the reporting entity, Entity A should include in its financial statements the assets, liabilities, income, and expenses of both Entity A and Entity B, including those relating to the implementation of Topic 740 to Entity B. This is required even though Entity A is a pass-through entity.

STUDY QUESTIONS

7. An entity is an S corporation that pays state income taxes on behalf of the entity. Which of the following is correct as it relates to ASU 2009-06 and ASC Topic 740?
   a. The state income taxes are not covered by ASC Topic 740.
   b. The state income taxes are covered by ASC Topic 740 only if they relate to the owners of the S corporation.
   c. The state income taxes are included within the scope of ASC Topic 740.
   d. The state income taxes are not covered by ASC Topic 740 because the entity is a non-public entity

8. What is the effective date for ASU 2009-06 for entities that are currently applying the standards for accounting for uncertainty in income taxes?
   a. June 1, 2006
   b. December 15, 2006
   c. September 15, 2009
   d. December 15, 2009

Accounting Standards Update No. 2009-12, Fair Value Measurements and Disclosures (ASC 820): *Investments in Certain Entities That Calculate Net Asset Value per Share (or Its Equivalent)*

Objective

This ASU, issued in September 2009, provides amendments to ASC Subtopic 820-10, *Fair Value Measurements and Disclosures—Overall,* for the fair value measurement of investments in certain entities that calculate net asset value per share (or its equivalent).

The amendments in this Update permit a reporting entity to measure the fair value of an investment that is within the scope of the amendments in this ASU on the basis of the net asset value per share of the investment (or its equivalent) if the net asset value of the investment (or its equivalent) is calculated in a manner consistent with the measurement principles of ASC Topic 946, *Financial Services—Investment Companies*.

The ASU also requires disclosures by major category of investment about the attributes of investments within the scope of the ASU.

Background

An investor may invest in entities that permit the investor to redeem its investments directly with the investee or receive distributions from the investee at times specified under the terms of the investee's governing documents. Many of these investments do not have readily determinable fair values because, for example, those investments are not listed on national exchanges or over-the-counter markets such as the National Association of Securities Dealers Automated Quotation System).

Examples of these investees (also referred to as *alternative investments*) include hedge funds, private equity funds, real estate funds, venture capital funds, and offshore fund vehicles.

Some of these investees provide their investors with a net asset value per share (or its equivalent, for example, member units or an ownership interest in partners' capital if the investee is a partnership to which a proportionate share of net assets is attributed) that has been calculated in a manner consistent with ASC 946.

Among other requirements, ASC 946 requires that the investee measure its underlying investments at fair value in accordance with ASC 820, *Fair Value Measurements and Disclosures*.

If fair value of the investment is not readily determinable, and the net asset value per share of the investment (or its equivalent) is calculated as of the measurement date, it is common for investors to estimate the fair value of their investment using the net asset value per share (or its equivalent) provided by the investee without further adjustment. In some cases, this is because the investee regularly stands ready (without significant restriction) to redeem the investment for net asset value per share (or its equivalent) and, thus, the net asset value per share (or its equivalent) provided by the investee is a reasonable indication of the price the investor would receive to sell its investment in an orderly transaction (fair value).

If there are restrictions to redemption, or the investment is designed for redemption to occur through distributions from the investee, many investors indicated that, in their view, the key consideration when relying on net asset value per share (or its equivalent) provided by the investee without further adjustment is that the investee's underlying investments are measured at fair value at the investor's measurement date. However, the net asset value per share (or its equivalent) provided by the investee may not represent the fair value of the investor's investment in all circumstances. Certain attributes of the investment and the presence of principal-to-principal or brokered transactions for the investment may indicate that it is necessary to make adjustments to the net asset value per share (or its equivalent) provided by the investee to estimate the fair value of the investment.

In January 2009, the AICPA's Accounting Standards Executive Committee and Alternative Investments Task Force issued a draft Issues Paper, *FASB Statement No. 157 Valuation Considerations for Interests in Alternative Investments* (ASC 820). The draft paper includes proposed nonauthoritative guidance on estimating the fair value of investments in certain alternative investments.

The draft paper indicates that when estimating fair value using the net asset value per share, an investor should consider other attributes of the investment in addition to the investee's net asset value per share. Those considerations include attributes of the investment such as:

- Redemption restrictions and unfunded commitments
- The intangible benefits of the investment (such as access to certain types of investments or investment strategies)
- The presence of principal-to-principal or brokered transactions for the investment.

There have been concerns voiced to the FASB about the requirement that investors adjust the net asset value per share (or its equivalent) for certain attributes of the investment. In particular, those parties have questioned which attributes of the investment would require an adjustment to net asset value per share and whether an adjustment would be an increase or decrease to net asset value per share.

Moreover, some adjustments may be increases to net asset value per share (for example, for access to certain types of investments or investment strategies and for access to a particular investment manager), while other adjustments, such as the imposition of a gate, may be decreases to net asset value per share (for example, for preventing an otherwise redeemable investment from being redeemed for a period of time).

Other parties have asserted that principal-to-principal or brokered transactions are uncommon for the types of investments within the scope of the ASU and often involve a distressed seller. Consequently, in their view, in many circumstances principal-to-principal or brokered transactions are not relevant observable inputs to a fair value measurement of an alternative investment within the scope of the amendments in this ASU because the investment is designed to be (a) redeemed with the investee at net asset value per share (or its equivalent) or (b) exited through distributions from the investee at times specified under the terms of the investee's governing documents, generally when the underlying investments of the investee are sold.

Because of these complexities and practical difficulties in estimating the fair value of alternative investments, the FASB decided to provide guidance on using the net asset value per share provided by the investee to estimate the fair value of an alternative investment.

Scope

The amendments in this ASU should apply to an investment that meets both of the following criteria as of the reporting entity's measurement date:

- Does not have a readily determinable fair value and
- Is an investment in an entity that has all four of the attributes specified as an investment company (in ASC 946-10-15-2), or if one or more of the investment company attributes are not present, is an investment in an entity for which it is industry practice to issue financial statements consistent with the measurement principles in ASC 946.

An example would be certain investments in real estate funds that measure investment assets at fair value on a recurring basis.

The four attributes of an investment company found in ASC 946-10-15-2 follow:

- **Investment activity.** The entity's primary business activity involves investing its assets, usually in the securities of other entities not under common management, for current income, appreciation, or both.
- **Unit ownership.** Ownership in the entity is represented by units of investments, such as shares of stock or partnership interests, to which proportionate shares of net assets can be attributed.
- **Pooling of funds.** The funds of the entity's owners are pooled to avail owners of professional investment management.
- **Reporting entity.** The entity is the primary reporting entity.

Investments in Certain Entities That Calculate Net Asset Value per Share

Classification within the fair value hierarchy of a fair value measurement of an investment within the scope of this ASU that is measured at net asset value per share (or its equivalent, for example member units or an ownership interest in partners' capital to which a proportionate share of net assets is attributed) requires judgment, with consideration of the following:

- If a reporting entity has the ability to redeem its investment with the investee at net asset value per share (or its equivalent) at the measurement date, the fair value measurement of the investment shall be categorized as a Level 2 fair value measurement.
- If a reporting entity will never have the ability to redeem its investment with the investee at net asset value per share (or its equivalent), the fair

value measurement of the investment shall be categorized as a Level 3 fair value measurement.

- If a reporting entity cannot redeem its investment with the investee at net asset value per share (or its equivalent) at the measurement date but the investment may be redeemable with the investee at a future date (for example, investments subject to a lockup or gate or investments whose redemption period does not coincide with the measurement date), the reporting entity shall consider the length of time until the investment will become redeemable in determining whether the fair value measurement of the investment shall be categorized as a Level 2 or a Level 3 fair value measurement. For example, if the reporting entity does not know when it will have the ability to redeem the investment or it does not have the ability to redeem the investment in the near term at net asset value per share (or its equivalent); the fair value measurement of the investment shall be categorized as a Level 3 fair value measurement.

Fair Value Measurements of Investments in Certain Entities That Calculate Net Asset Value per Share (or Its Equivalent)

A reporting entity is permitted to estimate the fair value of an investment within the scope of the ASU using the net asset value per share (or its equivalent, such as member units or an ownership interest in partners' capital to which a proportionate share of net assets is attributed) of the investment, if the net asset value per share of the investment (or its equivalent) is calculated in a manner consistent with the measurement principles of Topic 946 as of the reporting entity's measurement date.

The decision about whether to apply the above guidance shall be made on an investment-by-investment basis and shall be applied consistently to the fair value measurement of a reporting entity's entire position in a particular investment, unless it is probable at the measurement date that a reporting entity will sell a portion of an investment at an amount different from net asset value per share (or its equivalent). In those situations, the reporting entity shall account for the portion of the investment that is being sold in accordance with other provisions.

If the net asset value per share of the investment is not as of the reporting entity's measurement date or is not calculated in a manner consistent with the measurement principles of ASU 946, the reporting entity shall consider whether an adjustment to the most recent net asset value per share is necessary.

The objective of any adjustment is to estimate a net asset value per share for the investment that is calculated in a manner consistent with the measurement principles of Topic 946 as of the reporting entity's measurement date.

A reporting entity is not permitted to estimate the fair value of an investment (or a portion of the investment) using the net asset value per share of the investment (or its equivalent) if, as of the reporting entity's measurement date, it is probable that the reporting entity will sell the investment for an amount different from the net asset value per share (or its equivalent). A sale is considered probable only if all of the following criteria have been met as of the reporting entity's measurement date:

- Management, having the authority to approve the action, commits to a plan to sell the investment.
- An active program to locate a buyer and other actions required to complete the plan to sell the investment are initiated.
- The investment is available for immediate sale subject only to terms that are usual and customary for sales of such investments (for example, a requirement to obtain approval of the sale from the investee or a buyer's due diligence procedures).
- Actions required to complete the plan indicate that it is unlikely that significant changes to the plan will be made or that the plan will be withdrawn.

Disclosures

For investments that are within the scope of the ASU and measured at fair value on a recurring or nonrecurring basis during the period, the reporting entity shall disclose information that enables users of its financial statements to understand the nature and risks of the investments and whether the investments are probable of being sold at amounts different from net asset value per share (or its equivalent, such as member units or an ownership interest in partners' capital to which a proportionate share of net assets is attributed).

To meet that objective, to the extent applicable, the reporting entity shall disclose all of the following information for each interim and annual period separately for each major category of investment (major category of investment shall be determined on the basis of the nature and risks of the investments in a manner consistent with the guidance for major security types):

- The fair value of the investments in the major category, and a description of the significant investment strategies of the investee(s) in the major category.
- For each major category of investment that includes investments that can never be redeemed with the investees, but the reporting entity receives distributions through the liquidation of the underlying assets of the investees, the reporting entity's estimate of the period of time over which the underlying assets are expected to be liquidated by the investees.

- The amount of the reporting entity's unfunded commitments related to investments in the major category.
- A general description of the terms and conditions upon which the investor may redeem investments in the major category (for example, quarterly redemption with 60 days' notice).
- The circumstances in which an otherwise redeemable investment in the major category (or a portion thereof) might not be redeemable (for example, investments subject to a lockup or gate). Also, for those otherwise redeemable investments that are restricted from redemption as of the reporting entity's measurement date, the reporting entity shall disclose its estimate of when the restriction from redemption might lapse. If an estimate cannot be made, the reporting entity shall disclose that fact and how long the restriction has been in effect.
- Any other significant restriction on the ability to sell investments in the major category at the measurement date.
- If a reporting entity determines that it is probable that it will sell an investment(s) for an amount different from net asset value per share (or its equivalent), the reporting entity shall disclose the total fair value of all investments that meet that criteria and any remaining actions required to complete the sale.
- If it is probable that a group of investments would otherwise be sold for an amount different from net asset value per share, but the individual investments to be sold have not been identified (for example, if a reporting entity decides to sell 20 percent of its investments in private equity funds but the individual investments to be sold have not been identified), the reporting entity shall disclose its plans to sell and any remaining actions required to complete the sale(s).

Case D: Disclosure—Fair Value Measurements of Investments in Certain Entities That Calculate Net Asset Value per Share (or Its Equivalent)

For investments that are within the scope of this ASU measured at fair value on a recurring or nonrecurring basis during the period, in addition to the disclosures required elsewhere, this ASU requires disclosure of information that enables users to understand the nature and risk of the investments by major category and whether the investments are probable of being sold at amounts different from net asset value per share (or its equivalent, such as member units or an ownership interest in partners' capital to which a proportionate share of net assets is attributed). That information may be presented as follows.

Category	Fair Value in Millions	Unfunded Commitments	Redemption Frequency, if Currently Eligible	Redemption Notice Period
Equity long/short hedge	$55		Quarterly	30-60 days
Event driven hedge funds	45		Quarterly and annually	30-60 days
Global opportunities hedge funds (c) 35 quarterly 30–45 days	35		Quarterly	30-45 days
Multi-strategy hedge	40		Quarterly	30-60 days
Real estate funds	47	$20		
Private equity funds—international	43	15		
	265	35		

Effective Date

The amendments in this ASU are effective for interim and annual periods ending after December 15, 2009. Early application is permitted in financial statements for earlier interim and annual periods that have not been issued. If an entity elects to early adopt the measurement amendments in this ASU, the entity is permitted to defer the adoption of the disclosure provisions until periods ending after December 15, 2009.

STUDY QUESTIONS

9. Under the fair value rules, if the fair value is not readily determinable, a reporting entity is permitted to estimate the fair value of an investment using the _____ if it is calculated in a manner consistent with the measurement principles of Topic 946 as of the reporting entity's measurement date.

    a. Net asset value per share
    b. Book value per share
    c. Present value method
    d. Quoted market price

10. Which of the following would *not* be considered an "alternative investment" as defined and covered under ASU 2009-12?

    a. Hedge funds
    b. Private equity funds
    c. Offshore fund vehicles
    d. Funds listed on a national exchange

Accounting Standards Update No. 2009-13, Revenue Recognition (ASC 605): *Multiple-Deliverable Revenue Arrangements a consensus of the FASB Emerging Issues Task Force*

Objective

The objective of this ASU, issued in October 2009, is to address the accounting for multiple-deliverable arrangements to enable vendors to account for products or services (deliverables) separately, rather than as a combined unit. Vendors often provide multiple products or services to their customers. Those deliverables often are provided at different points in time or over different time periods.

Background

Subtopic 605-25, *Revenue Recognition—Multiple-Element Arrangements*, establishes the accounting and reporting guidance for arrangements under which the vendor will perform multiple revenue-generating activities. Specifically, this Subtopic addresses how to separate deliverables and how to measure and allocate arrangement consideration to one or more units of accounting.

Existing U.S. GAAP requires a vendor to use vendor-specific objective evidence or third-party evidence of selling price to separate deliverables in a multiple-deliverable arrangement. Vendor-specific objective evidence of selling price is the price charged for a deliverable when it is sold separately or, for a deliverable not yet being sold separately, the price established by management with the relevant authority. Third-party evidence of selling price is the price of the vendor's or any competitor's largely interchangeable products or services in standalone sales to similarly situated customers. If a vendor does not have vendor-specific objective evidence or third party evidence of selling price for the undelivered elements in an arrangement, the revenue associated with both delivered and undelivered elements are combined into one unit of accounting. Any revenue attributable to the delivered products is then deferred and recognized as the undelivered elements are delivered by the vendor. An exception to this guidance exists if the vendor has vendor-specific objective evidence or third-party evidence of selling price for the undelivered elements in the arrangement but not for the delivered elements. In those situations, the vendor uses the residual method to allocate revenue to the delivered element, which results in the allocation of the entire discount in the arrangement, if any, to the delivered element.

Constituents have raised concerns that this guidance results in financial reporting that does not reflect the underlying economics of transactions.

Scope

The amendments in this ASU affect accounting and reporting for all vendors that enter into multiple-deliverable arrangements with their customers when those arrangements are within the scope of ASC Subtopic 605-25.

- The amendments affect vendors that are affected by the guidance in Accounting Standards Update No. 2009-14, Software (ASC 985): *Certain Revenue Arrangements That Include Software Elements,* which affect vendors that sell tangible products that include software.
- The amendments do not affect arrangements for which industry-specific allocation and measurement guidance exists, such as ASC Subtopic 605-35 for long-term construction contracts and ASC 985 for software transactions.

Amendments of the ASU

The ASU amends the criteria in ASC Subtopic 605-25 for separating consideration in multiple-deliverable arrangements. Multiple-deliverable arrangements will be separated in more circumstances than under existing U.S. GAAP.

The amendments establish a selling price hierarchy for determining the selling price of a deliverable. The selling price used for each deliverable is based on the following hierarchy:

- First, use vendor-specific objective evidence if available, then
- Second, third-party evidence if vendor-specific objective evidence is not available, then
- Third, estimated selling price if neither vendor-specific objective evidence nor third-party evidence is available.

The amendment replaces the term *fair value* in the revenue allocation guidance with *selling price* to clarify that the allocation of revenue is based on entity-specific assumptions rather than assumptions of a marketplace participant.

The amendment eliminates use of the residual method of allocation and requires that arrangement consideration be allocated at the inception of the arrangement to all deliverables using the relative selling price method.

- Relative selling price method allocates any discount in the arrangement proportionally to each deliverable on the basis of each deliverable's selling price.
- A vendor determines its best estimate of selling price in a manner that is consistent with that used to determine the price to sell the deliverable on a standalone basis.

> **NOTE**
>
> The ASU does not prescribe any specific methods that vendors must use to accomplish this objective; however, examples have been provided to illustrate the concept of estimated selling price and the relative selling price method.

Disclosures

The ASU expands the disclosures related to a vendor's multiple-deliverable revenue arrangements. A vendor is required to disclose the following information by similar type of arrangement:

- A description of the entity's multiple-deliverable arrangements, which includes the nature and terms of the arrangement
- The significant deliverables within its arrangements
- The general timing of their delivery or performance of deliverables
- The significant factors and estimates used to determine vendor-specific objective evidence, third-party evidence, or estimated selling price, and significant changes in the selling price or the methodology or the assumptions used to estimate selling price
- The general timing of revenue recognition for separate units of accounting.

In the year of adoption, vendors are required to disclose information that enables users of its financial statements to understand the effect of adopting the amendments in this ASU. To satisfy that objective, vendors are required to disclose at a minimum the following qualitative information by similar types of arrangements:

- A description of any change in the units of accounting
- A description of the change in how a vendor allocates the arrangement consideration to various units of accounting
- A description of the changes in the pattern and timing of revenue recognition
- Whether the adoption of this Update is expected to have a material effect on financial statements in periods after the initial adoption.

If the adoption of the amendments in this Update does have a material effect on financial statements, vendors will be required to supplement the qualitative information with quantitative information to satisfy the objective of describing the effect of the change in accounting principle. Depending on a vendor's facts and circumstances, the following are examples of methods (but not the only potential methods) that may individually or in combination provide quantitative information to satisfy that objective:

- Disclosure of the amount of revenue that would have been recognized in the year of adoption if the related arrangements entered into or materially modified after the effective date were subject to the measurement requirements of Subtopic 605-25 (before the amendments in this Update)

- Disclosure of the amount of revenue that would have been recognized in the year preceding the year of adoption if the arrangements accounted for under Subtopic 605-25 (before the amendments in this Update) were subject to the measurement requirements of the amendments in this Update

- Disclosure of the amount of revenue recognized in the reporting period and the amount of deferred revenue as of the end of the reporting period from applying (a) the guidance in Subtopic 605-25 (before the amendments in this Update) and (b) the amendments in this Update.

STUDY QUESTIONS

11. Under ASU 2009-13, which of the following correctly identifies the selling price hierarchy for a deliverable in a multiple-element arrangement?

   a. Estimated selling price, then third-party evidence, then, vendor-specific objective evidence

   b. Third-party evidence, then vendor-specific objective evidence, then, estimated selling price

   c. Vendor-specific objective evidence, then third-party evidence, then estimated selling price

   d. Vendor-specific objective evidence, then estimated selling price, then third-party evidence

12. ASU 2009-13 replaces the term *fair value* in the revenue allocation guidance with *selling price* to clarify that the allocation of revenue is based on which of the following?

   a. Vendor-specific assumptions

   b. Entity-specific assumptions

   c. Assumptions of a marketplace participant

   d. Assumptions of an active exchange market

Accounting Standards Update No. 2009-14, Software (ASC 985): *Certain Revenue Arrangements That Include Software Elements a consensus of the FASB Emerging Issues Task Force*

Objective

This Update was issued in October 2009. Its objective is to address concerns raised by constituents relating to the accounting for revenue arrangements that contain tangible products and software.

Currently, products that contain software that is "more than incidental" to the product as a whole are within the scope of the software revenue guidance in ASC Subtopic 985-605, *Software—Revenue Recognition*.

Background

ASC Subtopic 985-605 requires a vendor to use vendor-specific objective evidence of selling price to separate deliverables in a multiple-element arrangement.

A vendor must sell, or intend to sell, a particular element separately to assert vendor-specific objective evidence for that element. If a vendor does not have vendor-specific objective evidence for the undelivered elements in an arrangement, the revenue associated with both the delivered and undelivered elements is combined into one unit of accounting. Any revenue attributable to the delivered products is then deferred and recognized at a later date, which in many cases is as the undelivered elements are delivered by the vendor.

There have been concerns that:

- The current accounting model does not appropriately reflect the economics of the underlying transactions because no revenue is recognized for products for which the vendor has already completed the related performance.
- The guidance in ASC Subtopic 985-605 was originally developed primarily for traditional software arrangements when more software-enabled products now fall or will fall within the scope of that guidance than originally intended because of ongoing technological advances.

Amendments of the ASU

The amendments affect vendors that sell or lease tangible products in an arrangement that contains software that is more than incidental to the tangible product as a whole. The amendments clarify what guidance should be used in allocating and measuring revenue.

The amendments do not provide guidance on when revenue should be recognized even though it is likely that vendors affected by the amendments recognize revenue earlier than they had previously because of the different allocation, measurement, and recognition guidance that exists in different revenue guidance including the amendments resulting from Accounting Standards Update No. 2009-13, Revenue Recognition (ASC 605): *Multiple-Deliverable Revenue Arrangements (A Consensus of the FASB Emerging Issues Task Force)*, as further described below.

The amendments do not affect:

- Software revenue arrangements that do not include tangible products.
- Software revenue arrangements that include services if the software is essential to the functionality of those services.

The ASU amendments change the accounting model for revenue arrangements that include both tangible products and software elements:

- Tangible products containing software components and non-software components that function together to deliver the tangible product's

essential functionality are no longer within the scope of the software revenue guidance in ASC Subtopic 985-605.
- Hardware components of a tangible product containing software components are always excluded from the software revenue guidance.

The ASU amendments provide additional guidance on how to determine which software, if any, relating to the tangible product also would be excluded from the scope of the software revenue guidance.

If the software contained in the tangible product is essential to the tangible product's functionality, the software is excluded from the scope of the software revenue guidance.

> **NOTE**
>
> This exclusion includes essential software that is sold with or embedded within the product and undelivered software elements that relate to that tangible product's essential software.

> **EXAMPLE**
>
> If a vendor sells a computer that includes an operating system that is deemed essential to that computer's functionality and also sells post-contract customer support services for that operating system, both the operating system and the support services in the arrangement are excluded from the scope of the software revenue guidance.

Following are factors to consider in determining whether the tangible product contains software that works together with the non-software components of the tangible product to deliver the tangible product's essential functionality:
- If sales of the tangible product without the software elements are infrequent, a rebuttable presumption exists that software elements are essential to the functionality of the tangible product.
- A vendor may sell products that provide similar functionality, such as different models of similar products. If the only significant difference between similar products is that one product includes software that the other product does not, they will be considered the same product for the purpose of evaluating the factors noted above.
- A vendor may sell software on a standalone basis. The vendor also may sell a tangible product containing that same software. The separate sale of the software does not lead to a presumption that the software is not essential to the functionality of the tangible product.

- Software elements do not need to be embedded within the tangible product to be considered essential to the tangible product's functionality.
- The non-software elements of the tangible product must substantively contribute to the tangible product's essential functionality. For example, the tangible product should not simply provide a mechanism to deliver the software to the customer.

The amendments provide guidance on how a vendor should allocate arrangement consideration to deliverables in an arrangement that includes both tangible products and software.

If a tangible product contains software that is not essential to the product's functionality, that nonessential software and any other deliverables within the arrangement (other than the non-software components of the tangible product) that relate to that nonessential software are within the scope of the software revenue guidance in Subtopic 985-605.

If an undelivered element relates to a deliverable within the scope of Subtopic 985-605 and a deliverable excluded from the scope of Subtopic 985-605, the undelivered element shall be bifurcated into a software deliverable and a non-software deliverable.

The software deliverable is within the scope of Subtopic 985-605 and the non-software deliverable is not within the scope of Subtopic 985- 605. The amendments also provide further guidance on how to allocate arrangement consideration when an arrangement includes deliverables both included and excluded from the scope of the software revenue guidance.

Disclosures

Vendors that are affected by the amendments in this Update are required to provide disclosures that are included within the amendments in ASU 2009-13, which was issued concurrently with this Update. The amendments in ASU 2009-13 significantly expand the disclosure requirements for multiple-deliverable revenue arrangements.

Effective Date

The amendments in the ASU are effective prospectively for revenue arrangements entered into or materially modified in fiscal years beginning on or after June 15, 2010. Early adoption is permitted.

If a vendor elects early adoption and the period of adoption is not the beginning of the vendor's fiscal year, the vendor is required to apply the amendments in this ASU retrospectively from the beginning of the vendor's fiscal year.

A vendor may elect, but is not required, to adopt the amendments in this ASU retrospectively to prior periods. In order to apply this ASU retrospectively to a period, it must not be impracticable for a vendor to report the change through retrospective application to that prior period.

A vendor is required to adopt the amendments in this Update in the same period using the same transition method that it uses to adopt the amendments in ASU 2009- 13.

STUDY QUESTION

---

13. Which of the following is **not** a factor to consider in determining whether a tangible product contains software that works together with its non-software components to deliver the tangible product's essential functionality?

   a. If sales of the tangible product without the software are rare, it is assumed that the software elements are essential to the functionality of the tangible product.

   b. If the only major difference between similar products is that one includes software that the other does not, the products will be considered the same product for the purpose of evaluation.

   c. The separate sale of the software does not mean that the software is inessential to the functionality of the tangible product.

   d. In order for software elements to be considered essential to the functionality of the tangible product, they must be embedded within the tangible product.

ASU 2010-02: Accounting Standards Update (ASU) 2010-02: *Consolidation (ASC 810): Accounting and Reporting for Decreases in Ownership of a Subsidiary—a Scope Clarification*

Objective

The objective of ASU 2010-02, issued in January 2010, is to address implementation issues related to the changes in ownership provisions in the *Consolidation—Overall* Subtopic (Subtopic 810-10) of the FASB Codification, originally issued as FAS 160, *Noncontrolling Interests in Consolidated Financial Statements*.

Background

Subtopic 810-10 establishes the accounting and reporting guidance for noncontrolling interests and changes in ownership interests of a subsidiary. The general rule is as follows:

- An entity is required to deconsolidate a subsidiary when the entity ceases to have a controlling financial interest in the subsidiary.
- Upon deconsolidation of a subsidiary, an entity recognizes a gain or loss on the transaction in the income statement and measures any retained investment in the subsidiary at fair value. The gain or loss includes any gain or loss associated with the difference between the fair value of the retained investment in the subsidiary and its carrying amount at the date the subsidiary is deconsolidated.

- If, instead, there is a decrease in the ownership interest of a subsidiary that does not result in a change of control of the subsidiary, the offset to the decrease is an equity transaction and does not impact the income statement.

Although Subtopic 810-10 provides general guidance on accounting for the decreases in ownership of a subsidiary, including a deconsolidation, some constituents raised concerns that the guidance appears to conflict with the gain or loss treatment or derecognition criteria of other U.S. GAAP, such as the guidance for sales of real estate, transfers of financial assets, conveyances of oil and gas mineral rights, and transactions with equity method investees.

Some constituents also questioned whether the Board intended for the decrease in ownership provisions of Subtopic 810-10 to apply to all entities because a subsidiary is defined as an entity, including an unincorporated entity such as a partnership or trust, in which another entity, known as its parent, holds a controlling financial interest. Those constituents were concerned that such an interpretation could result in the accounting for a transaction being driven by its form rather than its substance. For example, different accounting might be applied to a transaction involving the same underlying assets depending on whether those assets were transferred in asset or entity form.

Scope

The ASU provides amendments to Subtopic 810-10 and related guidance within U.S. GAAP to clarify that the scope of the decrease in ownership provisions of the Subtopic and related guidance applies to the following:

- A subsidiary or group of assets that is a business or nonprofit activity
- A subsidiary that is a business or nonprofit activity that is transferred to an equity method investee or joint venture
- An exchange of a group of assets that constitutes a business or nonprofit activity for a noncontrolling interest in an entity (including an equity method investee or joint venture).

The ASU does not apply to the following transactions (even if they involve businesses) with:

- Sales of in substance real estate. Entities should apply the sale of real estate guidance in Subtopics 360-20, *Property, Plant, and Equipment*, and 976-605, *Retail—Land*, to such transactions.
- Conveyances of oil and gas mineral rights. Entities should apply the mineral property conveyance and related transactions guidance in Subtopic 932-360, *Oil and Gas—Property, Plant, and Equipment* to such transactions.

> **NOTE**
>
> The amendments clarify, but do not necessarily change, the scope of current U.S. GAAP. The FASB thought that by clarifying the decrease in ownership provisions of Subtopic 810-10, it would remove the potential conflict between guidance in that Subtopic and asset derecognition and gain or loss recognition guidance that may exist in other U.S. GAAP.

Rules

Decrease in ownership in a subsidiary that is not a business or nonprofit activity:

- If a decrease in ownership occurs in a subsidiary that is not a business or nonprofit activity, an entity first needs to consider whether the substance of the transaction causing the decrease in ownership is addressed in other U.S. GAAP, such as transfers of financial assets, revenue recognition, exchanges of nonmonetary assets, sales of in substance real estate, or conveyances of oil and gas mineral rights, and apply that guidance as applicable.
- If no other guidance exists, an entity should apply the guidance in Subtopic 810-10, below.

Decrease in ownership in a subsidiary that is a business or nonprofit activity (Guidance of Subtopic 810-10):

- If a parent deconsolidates a subsidiary or derecognizes a group of assets through a nonreciprocal transfer to owners, such as a spinoff, the accounting guidance in Subtopic 845-10, *Nonmonetary Transactions*, and not 810-10 applies.
- Otherwise, a parent shall account for the deconsolidation of a subsidiary or derecognition of a group of assets by recognizing a gain or loss in net income attributable to the parent, measured as the difference between (A) and (B), below:
  - (A) The aggregate of all of the following:
    - The fair value of any consideration received
    - The fair value of any retained noncontrolling investment in the former subsidiary or group of assets at the date the subsidiary is deconsolidated or the group of assets is derecognized
    - The carrying amount of any noncontrolling interest in the former subsidiary (including any accumulated other comprehensive income attributable to the noncontrolling interest) at the date the subsidiary is deconsolidated.
  - (B) The carrying amount of the former subsidiary's assets and liabilities or the carrying amount of the group of assets.
  - (A) − (B) = GAIN OR LOSS (PART OF NET INCOME)

Disclosures

The amendments in the ASU expand the disclosures about the deconsolidation of a subsidiary or derecognition of a group of assets within the scope of Subtopic 810-10.

In addition to existing disclosures, an entity should disclose the following for such a deconsolidation or derecognition:

- The valuation techniques used to measure the fair value of any retained investment in the former subsidiary or group of assets and information that enables users of its financial statements to assess the inputs used to develop the measurement
- The nature of continuing involvement with the subsidiary or entity acquiring the group of assets after it has been deconsolidated or derecognized
- Whether the transaction that resulted in the deconsolidation of the subsidiary or the derecognition of the group of assets was with a related party, or whether the former subsidiary or entity acquiring the group of assets will be a related party after deconsolidation.

An entity also should disclose the valuation techniques used to measure an equity interest in an acquiree held by the entity immediately before the acquisition date in a business combination achieved in stages.

Effective Date

The amendments in this Update are effective beginning in the period that an entity adopts FAS 160 (now included in Subtopic 810-10).

If an entity has previously adopted FAS 160 as of the date the amendments in this ASU, the amendments in this ASU are effective beginning in the first interim or annual reporting period ending on or after December 15, 2009. The amendments in this Update should be applied retrospectively to the first period that an entity adopted FAS 160.

Interrelation with International Standards

The amendments in this ASU may result in differences in accounting and between U.S. GAAP and IFRS.

> **NOTE**
>
> IFRS guidance on accounting for decreases in ownership of subsidiaries is similar to guidance in U.S. GAAP. IFRS guidance, however, applies to all subsidiaries, even those that are not businesses or nonprofit activities or those that involve sales of in substance real estate or conveyances of oil and gas mineral rights. The decrease in ownership guidance in IFRS also

does not address whether that guidance should be applied to transactions involving nonsubsidiaries that are businesses or nonprofit activities. Despite those potential differences, the FASB concluded that the guidance should be clarified so that it is applied consistently and does not conflict with other guidance in U.S. GAAP.

STUDY QUESTION

14. Which of the following is covered under the guidance in ASU 2010-02 with respect to decrease in ownership of a subsidiary?

a. Sales of in substance real estate
b. Conveyances of oil mineral rights
c. An exchange of a group of assets that does not constitute a business for a noncontrolling interest in an entity
d. A subsidiary that is a business

Accounting Standards Update No. 2010-06:
Fair Value Measurements and Disclosures (ASC 820):
Improving Disclosures about Fair Value Measurements

Objective

This ASU was issued in January 2010 and its objective is to improve disclosure requirements related to *Fair Value Measurements and Disclosures—Overall* (Subtopic 820-10) of the FASB Codification, originally issued as FAS 157, *Fair Value Measurements.*

Background

U.S. GAAP requires that a reporting entity provide disclosures about fair value measurements used in financial statements. Most of those requirements are set out in Subtopic 820-10.

Various third parties have asked the FASB to enhance the disclosures for fair value measurements.

During 2008, the Securities and Exchange Commission's (SEC) Division of Corporation Finance issued letters to some public companies that encouraged additional disclosures in the management's discussion and analysis (MD&A) section of their SEC filings about the application of the fair value measurement standards in U.S. GAAP.

In October 2008, in responding to FSP FAS 157-3, *Determining the Fair Value of a Financial Asset When the Market for That Asset Is Not Active,* some financial statement users urged the Board to enhance the disclosure requirements in U.S. GAAP on fair value measurements.

In October 2008, the International Accounting Standard Board's (IASB) Expert Advisory Panel issued a report titled *Measuring and Disclosing the Fair Value of Financial Instruments in Markets That Are No Longer Active.* On the basis of that report, the IASB issued proposals to improve the fair value disclosures in IFRS 7.

In December 2008, the SEC released its *Report and Recommendations Pursuant to Section 133 of the Emergency Economic Stabilization Act of 2008: Study on Mark-To-Market Accounting.* This report recommended that the FASB consider enhancing the disclosure requirements in U.S. GAAP on fair value measurements.

In February 2009, the FASB's Valuation Resource Group met to discuss various issues on the implementation of fair value disclosure requirements in U.S. GAAP and suggested additional disclosures.

In March 2009, the International Monetary Fund issued the Working Paper, *Procyclicality and Fair Value Accounting.* The authors of that Paper recommend that fair value measurements be supplemented with adequate disclosures.

In March 2009, the IASB issued *Improving Disclosures about Financial Instruments (Amendments to IFRS 7).* The amendments require new disclosures and improve convergence with the fair value hierarchy and the related disclosures in Subtopic 820-10.

In response, the FASB concluded that changes were needed to provide a greater level of disaggregated information and more robust disclosures about valuation techniques and inputs to fair value measurements.

Amendments of the ASU

The ASU applies to all entities that are required to make disclosures about recurring or nonrecurring fair value measurements. The ASU amends Subtopic 820-10 by requiring new disclosures as follows:

- **Transfers in and out of Levels 1 and 2.** A reporting entity should disclose separately the amounts of significant transfers in and out of Level 1 and Level 2 fair value measurements and describe the reasons for the transfers.
- **Activity in Level 3 fair value measurements.** In the reconciliation for fair value measurements using significant unobservable inputs (Level 3), a reporting entity should present separately information about purchases, sales, issuances, and settlements (that is, on a gross basis rather than as one net number).

The ASU amends Subtopic 820-10 to clarify existing disclosures as follows:

- **Level of disaggregation.** A reporting entity should provide fair value measurement disclosures for each class of assets and liabilities. A class is often a subset of assets or liabilities within a line item in the statement of financial position. A reporting entity needs to use judgment in determining the appropriate classes of assets and liabilities.
- **Disclosures about inputs and valuation techniques.** A reporting entity should provide disclosures about the valuation techniques and inputs used to measure fair value for both recurring and nonrecurring fair value measurements. Those disclosures are required for fair value measurements that fall in either Level 2 or Level 3.

The ASU includes conforming amendments to the guidance on employers' disclosures about postretirement benefit plan assets (Subtopic 715-20). The amendments to Subtopic 715-20 change the terminology from *major categories* of assets to *classes* of assets and provide a cross reference to the guidance in Subtopic 820-10 on how to determine appropriate classes to present fair value disclosures.

Effective Date

The new disclosures and clarifications of existing disclosures are effective for interim and annual reporting periods beginning after December 15, 2009, except for the disclosures about purchases, sales, issuances, and settlements in the roll forward of activity in Level 3 fair value measurements. Those disclosures are effective for fiscal years beginning after December 15, 2010, and for interim periods within those fiscal years.

STUDY QUESTION

> **15.** ASU 2010-06 amends disclosures for fair value measurements to include transfers:
> **a.** In and out of Level 4 fair value measurements
> **b.** In and out of Levels 1 and 2 fair value measurements
> **c.** In and out of Level 3 fair value measurements.

> **CPE NOTE:** When you have completed your study and review of chapters 5–7, which comprise Module 3, you may wish to take the Quizzer for this Module.
>
> For your convenience, you can also take this Quizzer online at **www.cchtestingcenter.com**.

TOP ACCOUNTING ISSUES FOR 2011 CPE COURSE
Answers to Study Questions

MODULE 1 — CHAPTER 1

1. a. Incorrect. Although the FASB and the IASB are working on converging U.S. GAAP and IFRS, the IASB is not replacing the FASB.
b. Incorrect. The Financial Reporting Interpretations Committee replaced the SIC.
c. Correct. The International Accounting Standards Board (IASB) was created in 2001 and replaced the International Accounting Standards Committee (IASC), which was created in 1973.

2. a. Incorrect. One of the IASB objectives is to develop global accounting standards, in the public interest.
b. Correct. The IASB wants to be actively involved in the convergence of the accounting standards of other nations with IFRS. The Board is currently heavily involved in the convergence project with the United States.
c. Incorrect. The IASB is very clear that its objective is to improve the transparency and comparability of financial statements, so that better economic decisions can be made globally.

3. True. Incorrect. The Trustees are selected on the basis of geographical representation.
False. Correct. The members of the Board are selected based on their expertise and background rather than where they are located (unlike the Trustees).

4. a. Incorrect. Currently, only listed companies in Hong Kong and Singapore are reporting in compliance with IASB GAAP.
b. Correct. The majority of the users are located in Europe which, since 2005, has required all corporations listed on stock exchanges in the EU to comply with IASB GAAP.
c. Incorrect. While the United States and Canada are beginning to converge to IASB GAAP, and the SEC is requiring certain corporations to be in compliance by 2011, they are not the majority of the users.

5. True. Incorrect. The IASB and the FASB are currently working together to increase the use of fair value measurement.

False. *Correct.* The IASB is interested in increasing the use of fair value measurement. Although they do have the backing of the United States in this endeavor, many preparers and regulators in a number of other countries are much more cautious.

6. a. *Incorrect.* While the IASB tends to be more principles-based, the IASB's policy is not to use the word "can" when developing its standards.
b. *Correct.* **The standards are generally written using the word "should." The Board feels that this is more of a descriptive rather than prescriptive style.**
c. *Incorrect.* The IASB policy is more principles-based rather than rules-based.

7. a. *Incorrect.* While employees may have an interest in the financial statements for bonus or profit-sharing purposes, their needs are not what the Framework is based upon.
b. *Correct.* **Financial statements should meet the objectives of investors. In addition, they should also generally be prepared on an accrual and "going concern" basis.**
c. *Incorrect.* Not all of the public will have an interest in specific financial statements, and those that do may have varying objectives.

8. a. *Incorrect.* Materiality is a feature of relevance.
b. *Incorrect.* Substance over form is a feature of reliability.
c. *Correct.* **Completeness and faithful representation are both features of reliability.**

9. a. *Correct.* **Because the Framework states that preparers of financial statements should assume that users of those statements have a reasonable knowledge of business, when reporting complex matters relevance should be considered before understandability.**
b. *Incorrect.* "Substance over form" means the financial statements reflect the financial reality of the entity rather than the legal form of the underlying transactions of the entity. It is not noted as being more important than understanding.
c. *Incorrect.* Faithful representation is a feature of reliability. It is not noted as being more important than understanding.

10. a. *Incorrect.* Although directors', managements', and chairman's reports may be included in financial statements, the Framework does not consider them to be financial statements.
b. *Incorrect.* Although supplementary schedules may be included when reporting financial statements, they are not required as part of a full set of financial statements.

c. *Correct.* Financial statements include an income statement, balance sheet and a statement of changes in financial position. Supplementary schedules may also be included.

11. a. *Incorrect.* Both depreciation and amortization decrease future economic benefit.
b. *Incorrect.* In the Framework, equity is defined as a residual interest after liabilities are subtracted from assets.
c. *Correct.* Paragraphs 47–80 define the elements of financial statements. In those paragraphs, income and expenses are defined as "increases and decreases in economic benefits that are equated with changes in assets and liabilities."

12. a. *Incorrect.* Assets, which appear on the balance sheet, are considered elements of financial position.
b. *Incorrect.* Liabilities (amounts owed) are considered elements of financial position.
c. *Correct.* Expenses (including losses) and income are both considered elements of performance.

13. a. *Incorrect.* The financial concept (the amount invested or invested purchasing power) is one of the two main concepts.
b. *Incorrect.* The physical concept (the notion of the productivity or operating capabilities of an entity) is one of the two main concepts.
c. *Correct.* Maintenance is not one of the concepts of capital according to the Framework, although the choice of a concept of capital is related to the most meaningful concept of capital maintenance.

14. a. *Incorrect.* Probability relates to the likeliness of a specific outcome.
b. *Incorrect.* While assessments are generally made when reporting financial statements, assessments are not related to the elements of the financial statements.
c. *Correct.* The elements of financial statements relate to both performance and the measurement of financial position, according to the Framework.

15. a. *Incorrect.* The income statement includes the elements of revenue and expenses, as well as gains and losses.
b. *Incorrect.* The balance sheet includes elements of financial position.
c. *Correct.* Because the statement of changes in financial position includes both income statement elements and changes in balance sheet elements, the Framework does not identify any elements.

MODULE 1 — CHAPTER 2

1. a. *Incorrect.* Although earlier application is permitted, the standard did not become effective this early.

b. *Incorrect.* While many standards do take effect at the end of the calendar year, this is not the case with the new version of IFRS 1.

c. *Incorrect.* The new version was issued in November but this is not its effective date.

d. *Correct.* Due to the inefficiency of the originally issued standard, the IASB issued a new version of IFRS 1 in November 2008 with an effective date of July 1, 2009.

2. a. *Incorrect.* IFFRS financials should be transparent for users and comparable over all periods presented.

b. *Incorrect.* Providing a suitable starting point for accounting under IFRSs, is important according to the IFRS 1 objectives.

c. *Incorrect.* An entity's first IFRS statements should be generated at a cost that does not exceed the benefits to users.

d. *Correct.* IFRS is generally believed to be less complex than the rules-based U.S. GAAP.

3. a. *Incorrect.* While first-time financial statements should be in compliance with IFRS, statements which are not in compliance may also be considered first-time IFRS financial statements.

b. *Incorrect.* While first-time financial statements should be in compliance with International Accounting Standards (IASs), statements which are not in compliance may also be considered first-time IFRS financial statements.

c. *Correct.* "First IFRS financial statements" is defined in IFRS 1 as "The first annual financial statements in which an entity adopts International Financial Reporting Standards, by an explicit and unreserved statement of compliance with IFRSs."

d. *Incorrect.* Not all first-time IFRS statements were originally reported in U.S. GAAP.

4. a. *Incorrect.* Purchase price would be used if using historical cost to value an asset. However, this is not what is defined in IFRS as the amount for which an asset could be exchanged or a liability settled, between knowledgeable, willing parties in an arm's-length transaction.

b. *Correct.* Fair value in IFRS is the amount an asset could be exchanged for or a liability could be settled for, between knowledgeable, willing parties in an arm's-length transaction. This is very similar to the U.S. GAAP definition.

c. Incorrect. Deemed cost is an amount used as a substitute for cost or depreciated cost at a given date. Any depreciation or amortization taken later assumes that the entity had originally recognized the asset or liability at the given date and that its cost was equal to the deemed cost.

5. a. Incorrect. While some first-time adopters may be required to present more than one year comparative data, this is not the correct date.
b. Incorrect. While a minimum of one year comparative data must be presented, this is not the correct date.
c. Correct. An entity shall not apply different versions of IFRSs that were effective at earlier dates. Since the reporting date in this example is December 31, 2009 the statements should be prepared under Standards effective at December 31, 2009.

6. a. Incorrect. Although retrospective application is sometimes allowed for business combinations, this is not the correct date range.
b. Incorrect. The application would not be limited to the fiscal or calendar year in which the restated combination took place.
c. Correct. A first-time adopter is not required to apply IFRS 3, "Business Combinations," retrospectively to business combinations that occurred before the date of transition to IFRSs. However, if a first-time adopter restates any business combination to comply with IFRS 3, it must restate all subsequent business combinations.

7. a. Incorrect. Remember that the objective of IFRS 1 is to ensure that an entity's first IFRS financial statements, and its interim financial reports for part of the period covered by those financial statements, contain high quality information.
b. Correct. To avoid retrospective analysis, a first-time IFRS adopter may recognize all cumulative actuarial gains and losses at the date of transition to IFRS in the income statement, even if it uses the corridor approach for later actuarial gains and losses. If this election is made, it will apply it to all plans.
c. Incorrect. This would be a strict application of the "corridor" approach allowed by IAS 19, "Employee Benefits." However, this is not required by a first-time adopter.

8. a. Incorrect. Per IFRS 1, paragraphs B4-B6, retrospective application of hedge accounting is prohibited.
b. Incorrect. Per IFRS 1, paragraphs 14-17, retrospective application of estimates is prohibited.
c. Correct. A first-time adopter may apply the transitional provisions of IFRS 4, "Insurance Contracts."

9. a. Incorrect. At least two statements of comprehensive income must be presented.

b. Correct. A minimum of three statements of financial position must be presented. In addition, two statements of comprehensive income, two separate income statements (if presented), two statements of cash flows, and two statements of changes in equity and related notes, including comparative information, are required.

c. Incorrect. Only two statements of cash flow are required.

10. a. Correct. Reconciliations are required of its equity reported under previous GAAP to its equity under IFRSs for the date of transition to IFRSs and the end of the most recent period presented in the entity's latest annual financial statements under previous GAAP.

b. Incorrect. A reconciliation to its total comprehensive income under IFRSs for the latest period in the entity's most recent annual financial statements is required. The starting point for that reconciliation is the total comprehensive income under previous GAAP for the same period or profit or loss under previous GAAP.

c. Incorrect. If the entity recognized or reversed any impairment losses for the first time in its opening IFRS statement of financial position, disclosures that would have been required by IAS 36 if the entity had recognized those impairment losses or reversals in the period beginning with the date of transition to IFRSs must be made.

MODULE 2 — CHAPTER 3

1. a. Incorrect. While there is a rule regarding percentage of ownership and consolidation requirements, the requirements of ARB No. 51 do not require a minimum of 75 percent ownership.

b. Correct. The general rule for consolidation of entities found in ARB No. 51, _Consolidated Financial Statements_, is that consolidation occurs when one entity directly or indirectly has a controlling financial interest in another entity.

c. Incorrect. Consolidation does not occur at less than 50 percent ownership. Instead, either the equity or cost method is used.

d. Incorrect. Typically, an entity that has controlled another, but not owned the majority of its voting equity, has not consolidated that entity provided certain criteria were met.

2. a. Incorrect. Previously, an entity was not required to consolidate another even though ownership exceeded the 50 percent threshold if there was foreign ownership. That exception has been eliminated.

b. Incorrect. Previously, an entity was not required to consolidate another even though ownership exceeded the 50 percent threshold if there were non-homogeneous operations. That exception has been eliminated.

c. Incorrect. Previously, an entity was not required to consolidate another even though ownership exceeded the 50 percent threshold where control was temporary or did not rest with the majority owner. That exception has been eliminated.

d. Correct. Presently, there are no exceptions to the consolidation rules. Therefore, an entity that owns more than 50 percent of the voting shares of another entity must consolidate that entity's financial statements with its own.

3. a. Correct. A non-variable interest entity is consolidated based only on the traditional consolidation rules (more than 50 percent ownership in voting equity). The reason is because a non-VIE is self supportive and does not have to be consolidated under the FIN 46R rules.

b. Incorrect. A non-variable interest entity can finance its activities without additional subordinated financial support from others.

c. Incorrect. A non-variable interest entity *is* self-supportive, while a VIE is not-self-supportive.

d. Incorrect. A non-VIE is not required to be consolidated under FIN 46R. Outside of the traditional consolidation rules, a VIE, and not a non-VIE, must be consolidated under FIN 46R.

4. a. Incorrect. Prior to the issuance of FAS 167, QSPEs were excluded from FIN 46R's scope. Under FAS 167, QSPEs are now included under FIN 46R.

b. Correct. Under FAS 167, QSPEs are included within FIN 46R's scope.

c. Incorrect. FIN 46R, as amended by FAS 167, does address QSPEs.

5. a. Correct. FAS 167 revised FIN 46R and replaced the term SPE with VIE. As a result, FIN 46R had greater breadth, but is still based on the concept that companies that control another entity through interests other than voting interests should consolidate the controlled entity.

b. Incorrect. The term "non issuer" is being used to replace the term for a private entity.

c. Incorrect. Although subsidiaries are usually consolidated, subsidiary is a term for a company in which the majority of the voting rights are held by a parent company.

6. a. Correct. Because consolidated financial statements give a bigger picture of the company's total net worth, they are generally more meaningful to a financial statement user than unconsolidated statements would be.

b. Incorrect. Although more aspects of a company's financial interests are included in consolidated financial statements, this actually eliminates confusion as to what other interests the company may have.

c. Incorrect. While the fair value option may be used in reporting consolidated financial statements, it may also just as easily be used in reporting unconsolidated financial statements. There is no additional incentive when providing consolidated financial statements.

7. a. Incorrect. A variable interest (VI) is a form of financial support given by one entity or individual to a VIE in the form of a guarantee, loan, lease payments, management fees, etc.

b. Correct. A primary beneficiary is an entity or individual that has a controlling financial interest in a VIE. That controlling financial interest is based on the primary beneficiary having power to direct the VIE's significant activities, the obligation to absorb the VIE's losses, and the right to receive the VIE's residual benefits that are significant to the VIE.

c. Incorrect. A variable interest entity (VIE) is an entity that is not self-supportive in that it cannot finance its activities without receiving additional subordinated financial support.

8. a. Incorrect. A VIE is an entity that is not self-supportive in that it has an insufficient amount of equity for it to finance its activities with additional support from others.

b. Incorrect. A VIE must be an entity, not an individual.

c. Correct. A VIE is an entity that is not self-supportive if its owners do not hold the typical power, risks and rights of equity owners.

9. a. Incorrect. An entity is considered a VIE by design if, as a group, the holders of equity investments at risk have *no* obligation to absorb the expected losses of the entity.

b. Correct. An entity is considered a VIE by design if, as a group, the holders of equity investments at risk lack one of three characteristics. The lack of the right to receive the expected residual returns of the entity is one of those characteristics.

c. Incorrect. A VIE's equity holders may lack the direct ability to make decisions about the entity's activities that have a significant effect on the success of the entity. However, this criterion is not a factor in determining whether an entity is a VIE.

10. a. Incorrect. A guarantee is considered additional subordinated financial support.

b. Incorrect. A subordinated loan is considered additional subordinated financial support.

c. Incorrect. Above-market lease payments are considered a form of additional subordinated financial support.

d. Correct. The FASB has indicated that one way an entity is able to "finance its activities" is if it can obtain non-recourse financing from an unrelated party, such as in the case of obtaining bank or other independent financing.

11. a. Incorrect. Only in instances in which a conclusion cannot be reached using either qualitative or quantitative methods, should a combination of both types be used.

b. Incorrect. The expected losses method is one method that can be used to demonstrate sufficiency of equity but it is not the first method that should be used to determine if an entity is a VIE.

c. Correct. FIN 46R suggests that the qualitative methods be used first. There are three examples of qualitative methods.

d. Incorrect. There is one quantitative method that can be used to determine if an entity is a VIE, but it is not the first method that should be used according to FIN 46R.

12. a. Incorrect. The similar entity method is a qualitative method under which one determines whether the entity has at least as much equity as a similar entity that finances its operations with no additional subordinated financial support.

b. Correct. The expected losses method is the only quantitative method discussed in Interpretation 46R.

c. Incorrect. The 10- percent equity threshold rule is a threshold and not a method to determine whether an entity is a VIE.

d. Incorrect. The non-recourse financing exception is a qualitative method under which an entity demonstrates that it can obtain non-recourse, investment-grade financing from an unrelated party, without additional subordinated financial support.

13. a. Incorrect. A variable interest holder *retests* when a triggering event occurs, but this is not the date on which the variable interest holder first performs the test.

b. Correct. Each variable interest holder should perform their respective test of the VIE on the date the holder first becomes involved with the VIE, which, in this case, is June 30, 20X1. A variable interest holder does not know if it is the primary beneficiary of a VIE until it performs the test.

c. Incorrect. Company X should not wait a full year to perform the VIE test. The annual date of the loan has no significance where the test is concerned.

14. a. Incorrect. Carrying value of equity is not used. Rather fair value would be used.

b. Incorrect. An entity would not wait until the beginning of the year or refer back to the beginning of the year.

c. Correct. In a reconsideration, the fair value of equity and total assets at the date on which the reconsideration is performed is the value used. Any adjustments would be made as of that date.

15. a. Correct. The entity would be considered self-supportive and therefore not considered to be a VIE.

b. Incorrect. An entity that met any of the qualitative or qualitative methods would not be considered a VIE because it satisfied those methods. A VIE would not satisfy any of those methods.

c. Incorrect. Even though an entity may meet the requirements of one of the methods, it still may not own the majority of its voting rights. These methods do not test for an entity's level of control.

MODULE 2 — CHAPTER 4

1. a. Incorrect. A variable interest is a contractual, ownership, or other pecuniary interest in a VIE that changes with changes in the fair value of the VIE's net assets, exclusive of variable interests.

b. Correct. A variable interest is a means through which one entity (or individual) provides financial support to a VIE that could result in the providing entity (or individual) absorbing a portion of the VIE's expected losses or receiving a portion of the VIE's expected residual returns.

c. Incorrect. A variable interest holder generally absorbs a portion of the VIE's expected losses and also the VIE's expected residual returns.

2. a. Incorrect. A variable interest excludes certain contracts such as casual purchases and sales at market value.

b. Correct. Variable interests are equity investments that are at risk. If the investment is not at risk, then it is not a variable interest.

c. Incorrect. A variable interest excludes most assets that create variability (e.g., create the change in fair value of assets).

d. Incorrect. Most contracts related to fees paid to decision makers and service providers are not variable interests provided they satisfy six criteria, including that the contract must be arms length and at market value, among other requirements.

3. a. Incorrect. Derivative instruments held or written by a VIE should be analyzed in terms of their option-like, forward-like, or other variable characteristics. Generally such instruments do not hold the largest variable interest.

b. Incorrect. Forward contracts to sell assets that are owned by the VIE at a fixed price will usually absorb the variability in the fair value of the asset that is the subject of the contract. However, rarely are forward contracts the largest variable interests as they do not have the greatest degree of variability.

c. Incorrect. A guarantee is a variable interest but typically does not result in it being the largest variable interest other than equity ownership.

d. Correct. Unsecured and subordinated debt are variable interests that in many cases may hold the largest variable interest other than equity ownership. The reason is because unsecured and subordinated debt is at the "bottom of the food chain" in being paid in the event of a decline in the net asset values of the VIE.

4. a. Incorrect. A guarantor has a moderate likelihood of being the primary beneficiary of a VIE. It typically absorbs expected losses right after unsecured loans.

b. Incorrect. An equity holder who is at risk has a high likelihood of being the primary beneficiary as that holder has the greatest risk of absorbing losses and receiving residual returns of the VIE.

c. Correct. A secured debt holder has the lowest likelihood of being the primary beneficiary of a VIE. The reason is because the holder is the last one to absorb any VIE expected losses, and generally does not receive its residual gains unless loan agreement has a variable feature.

d. Incorrect. A holder of unsecured loans has a higher likelihood of being the primary beneficiary of a VIE. Right after equity holders, it usually has the next highest degree of variability and typically absorbs expected losses.

5. a. Incorrect. Although an investment may be labeled as an asset, this does not mean that it would then be considered a VIE.

b. Incorrect. Remember that some VIE investments do not include equity-type investments.

c. Correct. It is the role of the item and not the labeling of it that determines whether it is a VIE. If the role of the item is to absorb or receive the entity's variability due to the change in its net assets, it is then most likely a VIE.

6. a. Incorrect. A contractual obligation is not necessarily superior to a non-contractual obligation. The degree of obligation would be the determining factor.

b. Correct. For example, an implicit variable interest may still exist without a contractual obligation if the entity is still obligated to protect the VIE against loss.

c. Incorrect. Even without a contract, an entity may be still be obligated financially to a VIE to perform certain duties.

7. a. Incorrect. A primary beneficiary has to have a variable interest, which does not require ownership in a VIE.

b. Incorrect. A primary beneficiary must meet the loss/benefits criterion which requires the enterprise to have the obligation to absorb losses of the VIE or right to receive benefits from the VIE that could potentially be significant to the VIE. There is no "more than 50 percent" threshold.

c. Correct. A primary beneficiary is that individual or enterprise that has a controlling financial interest in the VIE, which is achieved by satisfying both the power criterion and losses/benefits criterion.

8. a. Incorrect. A primary beneficiary must have either the obligation to absorb losses or right to receive benefits that are potentially significant to a VIE. The term "significant' is greater than "very little."

b. Incorrect. An individual is not required to perform a test to determine whether it is the primary beneficiary. Remember that the results of a test would not have an impact on an individual's personal financial statements.

c. Correct. When an individual is the primary beneficiary, the VIE will not be consolidated. Only if an enterprise is the primary beneficiary will the VIE be consolidated. The consolidation rules do not apply to personal financial statements.

9. a. Incorrect. There can be many variable interest holders. For example, one entity may have an equity interest, while another may be a guarantor.

b. Correct. Although at times there may be competing interests, there can be only one primary beneficiary.

c. Incorrect. An entity or individual may have interest in several entities and each entity is tested to determine whether it is a VIE.

10. a. Incorrect. The test to determine whether an entity is a VIE, and not whether a variable interest holder is a primary beneficiary, is based on whether there is a triggering event.

b. Incorrect. There is no annual retest required even though some companies may choose to perform an annual retest.

c. Correct. FIN 46R requires that a variable interest holder continually reconsider (retest) whether it is the primary beneficiary of a VIE. The VIE status would be reconsidered whenever there is a triggering event.

11. a. Incorrect. The tie-breaker rule applies only to related parties.

b. Incorrect. The tie-breaker rule applies only if there are two or more related parties, and individually none of the parties satisfy both criteria.

c. Correct. If there are two related parties, and one satisfies the power criterion while the other satisfies the losses/benefits criterion, but neither satisfies both criteria, the tie-breaker rule applies.

12. a. *Correct.* A lease at a market rate and terms with no embedded features is not a variable interest.

b. *Incorrect.* A lease with a residual value guarantee is a variable interest. The lessee is absorbing some of the loss of the leased asset that would otherwise be absorbed by the equity holders.

c. *Incorrect.* An option to acquire leased assets at a fixed or predetermined price is a variable interest. However, if the option was to acquire at fair market value at the end of the lease it would not be a variable interest.

13. a. *Correct.* Y has an implicit guarantee of X's loan because John may have to call upon Y's assets to satisfy John's guarantee.

b. *Incorrect.* Remember that X has not signed a contract guaranteeing any of John's loans.

c. *Incorrect.* John has an explicit guarantee, not an implicit guarantee of X's loan

14. a. *Incorrect.* This transaction would not be considered extraordinary since it would occur in the normal course of business and is not unusual in nature.

b. *Incorrect.* If there is any excess *loss*, it must be reported as goodwill if the VIE is a business.

c. *Correct.* If there is any excess of the fair values of the newly consolidated assets and the reported amount of assets transferred by the primary beneficiary to the VIE, over the total of the fair value of the consideration paid, the reported amount of any previously held interests, and the fair value of the newly consolidated liabilities and noncontrolling interests, the resulting gain must be reported on the income statement of the primary beneficiary, who acts as the acquirer.

15. a. *Correct.* Intercompany income and expenses, as well as other intercompany balances, should be eliminated under the rules of consolidation.

b. *Incorrect.* Neither the assets nor the liabilities of the consolidated entity should be eliminated.

c. *Incorrect.* A principle of consolidation that applies to the primary beneficiary's accounting for the consolidated VIE is that the noncontrolling interests of a consolidated VIE are accounted for in the consolidated financial statements as if the entity were consolidated based on voting interests. Thus, there is no elimination of the noncontrolling interests.

16. a. *Correct.* The VIE's equity should be presented as a noncontrolling interest in the stockholders' equity section of the consolidated balance sheet.

b. *Incorrect.* The VIE's equity is not reported as a current liability, although it may be at risk.

c. *Incorrect.* Although the FASB once considered a mezzanine section for reporting purposes, it decided against this idea.

17. a. *Correct.* Once a primary beneficiary is no longer required to consolidate a VIE, the proper treatment is to deconsolidate the VIE as of the date that the primary beneficiary is no longer the primary beneficiary.

b. *Incorrect.* There is no rule in effect that suggests the new primary beneficiary should wait until its new fiscal year to begin consolidation.

c. *Incorrect.* While an interest in the VIE may still exist, consolidation of the balance sheet would not be an acceptable treatment.

18 a. *Incorrect.* The maximum exposure to loss disclosure is not required for a primary beneficiary of a VIE.

b. *Correct.* The disclosure of the maximum exposure to loss is required for a reporting enterprise that holds a variable interest in a VIE but is not the primary beneficiary.

c. *Incorrect.* An entity that has an investment in a VIE but holds no variable interest would not be exposed to the obligation of the VIE's losses.

19. a. *Incorrect.* Remember that the mortgage will be used to settle the real estate transaction.

b. *Correct.* Any assets that must be used to settle the liabilities of the VIE must be presented separately on the balance sheet along with the related liability. In this example, the real estate will be used to settle the mortgage obligation.

c. *Incorrect.* Remember that transparency of the transactions is the goal of the reporting process.

20. a. *Incorrect.* The carrying amounts at the look-back date must be rolled *forward* to the implementation date to reflect activity that has occurred on the VIE's balance sheet from the look-back date to the implementation date.

b. *Correct.* If the entities were under common control on the look-back date, the carrying amount of the VIE would be the book value of its balance sheet on the look-back date.

c. *Incorrect.* If the entities were *not* under common control on the look-back date, the carrying amount of the VIE would be the fair value of its balance sheet on that date.

MODULE 3 — CHAPTER 5

1. a. *Incorrect.* Financial statements issued in draft form to management in a GAAP format are not considered issued, because they were only distributed internally.

b. *Incorrect.* To be considered issued, financial statements must be issued in accordance with GAAP.

c. *Correct.* Financial statements are considered issued if they are both widely distributed to shareholders and other users and are in a GAAP format. There are also additional requirements for SEC filers which can be found in FASB ASC 855-10-S99-2.

2. True. *Incorrect.* There are a few circumstances in which the requirements of Topic 855 would not be applied to the treatment of a subsequent event. One example would be the accounting for income tax related subsequent events. That guidance would be found in Topic 740.

False. *Correct.* For example, when accounting for a subsequent event regarding the effect on earnings per share, Topic 260 requirements covering earnings per share would apply.

3. a. *Incorrect.* Only an entity that has a current expectation of widely distributing its financial statements should use the "issued" date.

b. *Correct.* If there is no wide distribution of the financial statements, the "available to be used" date should be used. This would generally be the date that no more entries were expected to be made to the books for that period.

c. *Incorrect.* Financial statements may be printed several times before they are considered complete.

4. a. *Incorrect.* Because the loss occurred after the balance sheet date, the effect would not be recognized at the balance sheet date. Moreover, its effect was not discovered until the financial statements were issued.

b. *Correct.* Because the loss was based on events that took place before the balance sheet date, its effect would be recorded at the balance sheet date.

c. *Incorrect.* The settlement was based on an event that took place after the balance sheet date. The result is that its effect should not be recorded at the balance sheet date.

5. a. *Incorrect.* Because the $300,000 was owed before the balance sheet date, and it is estimated that the receivable will not be collected, the entity should recognize the loss prior to the issuance of the financial statements.

b. Correct. Because the change occurred after the balance sheet date but before financial statements were issued, the change in the foreign exchange rate would not be recognized as a subsequent event. This would be the case even if the financial statements were available to be issued, but still not issued.

c. Incorrect. Because the settlement was based on an event that took place before the balance sheet date, and the amount of the settlement was known before the financial statements were issued, the actual settlement amount should be recognized.

MODULE 3 — CHAPTER 6

1. a. Incorrect. An example would be an agreement that permits the transferee to require the transferor to repurchase the transferred financial assets, but at a very favorable price.

b. Incorrect. An agreement that provides the transferor with *more-than-trivial* benefit, and not just a trivial benefit, is an example where a transferor has effective control.

c. Correct. One example is an agreement that entitles and obligates the transferor to redeem the financial asset before its maturity.

2. a. Incorrect. The transfer must be a participating interest to be treated as a sale. Further, if it were recorded as a sale, it would not be recorded for the entire asset.

b. Correct. Because it does not meet the definition of a participating interest, it is recorded as a secured borrowing instead of as a sale.

c. Incorrect. ASC Topic 860 does not provide for the transfer to be recorded as a nonmonetary transaction, because a transfer of an asset actually exists.

3. a. Correct. ASC Topic 860 requires that the carrying amount be allocated between participating interests sold and those interests that continue to be held by the transferor, based on a relative fair value basis.

b. Incorrect. There is no authorization to make an allocation based on residual value. Residual value is the amount an entity would expect to be paid for an asset at the end of its useful life.

c. Incorrect. A participating interest is a partial transfer and requires an allocation of the carrying amount, and not a transfer of the entire carrying amount.

4. a. Incorrect. Although September 2000 was when FAS 140 was issued, ASC 860 does not allow for retroactive application.

b. Incorrect. Although major changes were issued in June 2009, this is not the effective date of FAS 166 requirements.

c. Correct. FAS 166 requirements are effective November 15, 2009 for interim periods within that first annual reporting period, and for interim and annual reporting periods, thereafter.

5. a. Correct. Service assets and liabilities are amortized over the period of estimated net servicing income or loss. If servicing income exceeds costs, it is based on net servicing income. If servicing costs exceed income, it is based on net servicing loss.

b. Incorrect. The asset transferred is a financial asset and does not have a useful life.

c. Incorrect. While industry practices may have certain circumstantial tendencies, there is no requirement to use a straight-line period based on industry practices.

6. a. Incorrect. Management's basis for determining the classes of servicing assets (and liabilities) is a requirement for all servicing assets and liabilities.

b. Incorrect. A description of the risks inherent in servicing assets as well as the instruments used to mitigate the income statement effect of the changes in fair value is a required disclosure for all service assets.

c. Incorrect. The amount of contractually specified servicing fees, as well as late and ancillary fees earned for which results of operations are presented, is required for all servicing assets.

d. Correct. A disclosure of the activity in the balance of servicing assets is required only if the servicing assets (and liabilities) are subsequently measured at fair value. If not, the disclosure is not required. That activity includes the beginning and ending balances, additions, disposals, changes in fair value during the period, and other changes.

7. a. Incorrect. While FAS 166 did affect the accounting for asset transfers, there will be no effect on the values at which financial assets will be transferred.

b. Correct. Because the QSPE exemption is eliminated, more transferors of financial assets may have to consolidate transferees if certain conditions are met. Companies had structured their asset transfers to get under the QSPE exemption. Now that exemption is gone and the impact could be significant.

c. Incorrect. There is no change to the definition of a QSPE. Instead, the entire concept is eliminated under FAS 166 (now codified as part of ASC Topic 860).

8. a. Incorrect. Because the transaction qualifies as a sale transaction, a gain or loss is recognized. Thus, zero is an incorrect answer.

b. Incorrect. $800 is the gain on the total transaction. X transferred only 75 percent of the asset so that recognition of the total gain is not appropriate under the participating interest rules.

c. Correct. Because the transaction is a participating interest, the participating interest transferred (75 percent) is derecognized. In doing so, 75 percent of the fair value ($2,000 x 75% = $1,500), and 75 percent of the carrying value ($1,200 x 75% = $900) are derecognized resulting in a gain of $600.

d. Incorrect. $2,000 represents the total fair value and ignores the derecognized portion of the carrying value of the interest transferred.

9. a. Correct. The gain is equal to $5,000 cash proceeds plus the $500 fair value of the servicing asset, minus the $4,000 carrying value.

b. Incorrect. The $500 assumes that the $500 fair value of the servicing asset is deducted in determining the gain, when in fact it is added as part of net proceeds.

c. Incorrect. The $1,000 gain would be the correct answer if the $500 servicing asset fair value were not considered.

d. Incorrect. Zero is not an option. When a transfer of an entire asset is made, a gain or loss is recognized.

10. a. Incorrect. The changes would not be treated as a correction of an error, which would require a change in equity.

b. Incorrect. While the FASB has previously considered the application of a mezzanine section on the balance sheet, they have decided against such application.

c. Correct. The change in fair value would be recorded in earnings for the current period (income statement) and not as an adjustment to retained earnings (balance sheet).

MODULE 3 — CHAPTER 7

1. a. Incorrect. Although the FASB is making many changes to GAAP, this is not the purpose of the Codification.

b. Correct. In the FASB's view, "the issuance of this Statement and the Codification will not change GAAP, except for those nonpublic nongovernmental entities that must now apply the American Institute of Certified Public Accountants Technical Inquiry Service Section 5100," "Revenue Recognition," paragraphs 38–76." (FAS 168, Summary)

c. Incorrect. Although the SEC does believe that U.S. GAAP is very rules-based and complex, this is not the purpose of the Codification

d. Incorrect. Although the FASB is working on several projects to converge with IFRS, this is not the purpose of the Codification.

2. a. *Incorrect.* June 3 is when the FASB approved the ASC.

b. *Correct.* Effective July 1, 2009, all changes made to the ASC are communicated through ASUs. However, FASB has stated that the ASUs in themselves are not authoritative.

c. *Incorrect.* The ASC is effective for interim or annual reporting periods ending after September 15, 2009.

d. *Incorrect.* Although many of the FASB standards are made effective for interim or annual reporting periods ending after December 31st of a particular year, this is not the case with the ASC.

3. a. *Correct.* The ASUs do not amend pre-Codification FASs. The FASs have already been codified as part of the ASC and are now superseded by the ASC.

b. *Incorrect.* Each ASU describes the key provisions that led to the issuance of the ASU. For example, the FASB issued ASU 2009-06 to provide additional implementation guidance on the accounting for uncertainties in income taxes.

c. *Incorrect.* As was the case with previously issued FASs, ASUs also explain the basis of the FASB Board's decisions.

d. *Incorrect.* Each amendment made to the Codification is communicated through the issuance of an ASU. Each ASU which is issued will detail the specifics of the amendments which will be made as a result to the ASC.

4. a. *Incorrect.* Prior to the ASC, the FASB would amend existing FASs. An example would be the issuance of FAS 166, *Accounting for Transfers of Financial Assets—an amendment of FASB Statement No. 140.*

b. *Incorrect.* Prior to the ASC, the FASB would amend existing Interpretations. An example would be the issuance of FAS 167, *Amendments to FASB Interpretation No. 46(R).*

c. *Incorrect.* The Codification is the single source of authoritative U.S. accounting and reporting standards, except for rules and interpretive releases of the Securities and Exchange Commission (SEC) under authority of federal securities laws, which are sources of authoritative GAAP for SEC registrants.

d. *Correct.* Prior to the release of the FASB Codification as the single source of authoritative U.S. GAAP, the FASB amended pre-Codification standards and issued them in an "as amended" form. The FASB will not amend ASUs. It will only amend the FASB Codification.

5. a. *Incorrect.* The FASB is making several changes to GAAP; however it continues to use a numerical system to number its releases.

b. *Incorrect.* The FASB does not identify the month of issuance in an ASU's identification number, although the year of issuance is included.

c. Incorrect. The issuance number would begin with the year of issuance.
d. Correct. The ASU identification includes the year of issuance first and then the sequence of its issuance within that year.

6. a. Incorrect. The second ASU provided for amendments based on feedback received.
b. Incorrect. The first ASU issued in 2010 amended the Topics *Equity* and *Earnings Per Share.*
c. Incorrect. These amendments to Topic 820 were not made until 2010 and provide more robust disclosures about (1) the different classes of assets and liabilities measured at fair value, (2) the valuation techniques and inputs used, (3) the activity in Level 3 fair value measurements, and (4) the transfers between Levels 1, 2, and 3.
d. Correct. This ASU amends the FASB Accounting Standards Codification for the issuance of FAS 168, *The* FASB Accounting Standards Codification™ *and the Hierarchy of Generally Accepted Accounting Principles.* This ASU includes Statement 168 in its entirety, including the ASU instructions contained in Appendix B of the Statement.

7. a. Incorrect. ASU 2009-06 amends ASC Topic 740 to include pass-through entities within the scope.
b. Incorrect. Taxes paid on behalf of the owners are not covered under ASC 740.
c. Correct. Pass-through entities and the taxes they pay (e.g., state income taxes) are included within the scope of ASC Topic 740.
d. Incorrect. ASC Topic 740 applies to non-public entities even though there are certain disclosures that apply to public entities only.

8. a. Incorrect. FIN 48 was issued in June of 2006, but this is not the effective date for ASU 2009-06.
b. Incorrect. FIN 48, not ASU 2009-06, was effective for interim and annual periods ending after December 15, 2006.
c. Correct. The ASU content is effective for interim and annual periods ending after September 15, 2009.
d. Incorrect. The FASB did not allow this much time from the issuance of ASU 2009-06 to the effective date.

9. a. Correct. The net asset value per share may be used to determine fair value when the fair value is not readily available by other means.
b. Incorrect. Because fair value is the goal, using book value or historical cost per share is not an option.

c. Incorrect. Use of the present value may be applicable in some fair value models but not in connection with transactions covered by Topic 946.

d. Incorrect. Quoted market prices are not readily available thereby requiring another method to arrive at fair value.

10. a. Incorrect. A hedge fund would be considered an alternative investment under ASU 2009-12. Venture capital funds are another example of an alternative investment.

b. Incorrect. Private equity funds, or funds invested in the equity of a private entity, would be considered alternative investments.

c. Incorrect. Offshore fund vehicles would be considered alternative investments. Real estate funds are another example of an alternative investment.

d. Correct. Funds listed on a national exchange, such as public stocks, would not be considered alternative investments.

11. a. Incorrect. Estimated selling price is not first in the hierarchy.

b. Incorrect. Third-party evidence is not first in the hierarchy.

c. Correct. Vendor-specific objective evidence is first, third-party evidence is second, and estimated selling price is third, which is correctly stated. The amendment also replaces the term *fair value* **in the revenue allocation guidance with** *selling price.*

d. Incorrect. Estimated selling price is not second in the hierarchy.

12. a. Incorrect. While vendor information may be considered, it would not be the total basis of the revenue allocation assumptions.

b. Correct. Entity-specific assumptions rather than assumptions of a marketplace participant are what the allocation is based on.

c. Incorrect. Allocation of revenue is not based on assumptions of a marketplace participant.

d. Incorrect. Revenue recognition for multiple deliverables would not be based on prices or assumptions of an exchange market, although fair value may be.

13. a. Incorrect. The amendments affect vendors that sell or lease tangible products in an arrangement that contains software that is a necessary part of the tangible product. If sales of the tangible product without the software are rare, the software elements are considered essential to the functionality of the tangible product.

b. Incorrect. This is a factor to consider. If the only major difference between similar products is that one includes software that the other does not, the products are assumed to be the same product for evaluation purposes. Another factor to consider is whether the non-software elements of the tangible property contribute significantly to its essential functionality.

c. Incorrect. This is a factor to consider. Just because a vendor sells software on a standalone basis, this is not necessarily an indication that the software is not essential to the functionality of the tangible product.

d. Correct. The amendments clarify what guidance should be used in allocating and measuring revenue. It is not necessary for software to be embedded within the tangible product for it to be considered essential to the tangible product's functionality.

14. a. Incorrect. Sales of in substance real estate are covered by the guidance in Subtopics 360-20, *Property, Plant, and Equipment,* and 976-605, *Retail—Land.*

b. Incorrect. Conveyances of oil and gas mineral rights are covered by the guidance in Subtopic 932-360, *Oil and Gas—Property, Plant, and Equipment.*

c. Incorrect. An exchange of a group of assets that does not constitute a business for a noncontrolling interest in an entity is not covered by ASU 2010-02. If a there is a decrease in ownership in a subsidiary that is not a business or nonprofit activity, an entity should first consider whether the substance of the transaction causing the decrease is addressed in other U.S. GAAP.

d. Correct. A subsidiary or a group of assets that is a business or nonprofit activity is included within the scope of ASU 2010-02.

15. a. Incorrect. There are only 3 levels in the hierarchy. Level 3 fair value measurements use significant unobservable inputs.

b. Correct. New disclosures are required for transfers in and out of Levels 1 and 2 fair value measurements. The amounts of significant transfers and the reasons for those transfers must be disclosed.

c. Incorrect. The disclosures require that activity in Level 3 fair value measurements be presented on a gross basis.

TOP ACCOUNTING ISSUES FOR 2011 CPE COURSE

Index

A

Accounting Standards Codification (FASB Codification) ... 187–217
changes to, communicating ... 187
future amendments of ... 188

Accounting standards updates (ASUs) ... 187–217
recently issued, table summarizing ... 188–191
to update FASB Codification ... 187

Accrual basis for preparing financial statements ... 18

Additional subordinated financial support ... 78–79

Amortization of service assets and liabilities ... 171–172

Analyzed combined statement ... 8–9

ARB No. 51, *Consolidated Financial Statements* ... 59, 60
rule for consolidation in ... 67

ASC Topic 810, *Consolidated Financial Statements* (ARB No. 51) ... 59–150
determining whether entity is VIE under ... 59–94
identifying variable interests in ... 95–150
update to ... 62

ASC Topic 855, *Subsequent Events* ... 151–159
background of ... 151–152
effective date of ... 159
issuance of ... 152
objective of ... 151
requirements of ... 152–159
responsibility for evaluating subsequent events under ... 152
scope of ... 152–153
transition to ... 159

ASC Topic 860 ... 161–186
changes initiated by ... 164
disclosures required by ... 172–179
effective date of ... 184–185
examples of applying ... 181–184
issuance of ... 162, 163
objective of ... 161
rules of, for financial assets subject to prepayment ... 172
scope of ... 165
unit of account in applying ... 179–180

ASC Topic 946, measurement principles in ... 197, 199, 200

Assets
ASB Framework definition of ... 23, 25
capabilities of ... 24
derecognition of group of ... 213
disaggregation of ... 217
entire financial ... 179–180, 181–182
financial ... 50, 51, 163–164, 171–172, 177–79
intangible ... 50
leased, option to purchase ... 100
recognition of ... 31, 46–47
representation of personal ... 128–129
servicing, disclosures for ... 174–176
transfers of ... 165–169
of VIE ... 98, 101

ASU No. 2009-06, *Income Taxes* ... 192–196
ASC Topic 740 amended by ... 192–196
background of ... 192
examples of applying ... 194–196
objective of ... 192
scope of ... 193
transition to ... 194

ASU No. 2009-12, *Fair Value Measurements and Disclosures* ... 196–203
ASC Subtopic 820-10 amended by ... 196
background of ... 197–199
disclosures required by ... 201–202
effective date of ... 203
for investments in certain entities that calculate net asset value per share ... 196, 199–201, 202–203
objective of ... 196–197
scope of ... 199

ASU No. 2009-13, *Revenue Recognition* ... 208
ASC Subtopic 605-25 amended by ... 205
background of ... 204
disclosures required by ... 206–207
objective of ... 204
scope of ... 205
transition to ... 211

ASU No. 2009-14, *Software* ... 207–211
amendments for revenue arrangements including tangible products and software by ... 208210
background of ... 208
disclosures required by ... 210
effective date of ... 210–211
objective of ... 207

TOP ACCOUNTING ISSUES FOR 2011 CPE COURSE

CPE Quizzer Instructions

The CPE Quizzer is divided into three Modules. There is a processing fee for each Quizzer Module submitted for grading. Successful completion of Module 1 is recommended for **4 CPE Credits.*** Successful completion of Module 2 is recommended for **7 CPE Credits.*** Successful completion of Module 3 is recommended for **5 CPE Credits.***You can complete and submit one Module at a time or all Modules at once for a total of **16 CPE Credits.***

To obtain CPE credit, return your completed Answer Sheet for each Quizzer Module to **CCH Continuing Education Department, 4025 W. Peterson Ave., Chicago, IL 60646**, or fax it to (773) 866-3084. Each Quizzer Answer Sheet will be graded and a CPE Certificate of Completion awarded for achieving a grade of 70 percent or greater. The Quizzer Answer Sheets are located after the Quizzer questions for this Course.

Express Grading: Processing time for your Answer Sheet is generally 8-12 business days. If you are trying to meet a reporting deadline, our Express Grading Service is available for an additional $19 per Module. To use this service, please check the "Express Grading" box on your Answer Sheet and provide your CCH account or credit card number **and your fax number.** CCH will fax your results and a Certificate of Completion (upon achieving a passing grade) to you by 5:00 p.m. the business day following our receipt of your Answer Sheet. **If you mail your Answer Sheet for Express Grading, please write "ATTN: CPE OVERNIGHT" on the envelope.** NOTE: CCH will not Federal Express Quizzer results under any circumstances.

NEW ONLINE GRADING gives you immediate 24/7 grading with instant results and no Express Grading Fee.

The **CCH Testing Center** website gives you and others in your firm easy, free access to CCH print Courses and allows you to complete your CPE Quizzers online for immediate results. Plus, the **My Courses** feature provides convenient storage for your CPE Course Certificates and completed Quizzers.

Go to **www.cchtestingcenter.com** to complete your Quizzer online.

---

* Recommended CPE credit is based on a 50-minute hour. Participants earning credits for states that require self-study to be based on a 100-minute hour will receive ½ the CPE credits for successful completion of this course. Because CPE requirements vary from state to state and among different licensing agencies, please contact your CPE governing body for information on your CPE requirements and the applicability of a particular course for your requirements.

Date of Completion: The date of completion on your Certificate will be the date that you put on your Answer Sheet. However, you must submit your Answer Sheet to CCH for grading within two weeks of completing it.

Expiration Date: December 31, 2011

Evaluation: To help us provide you with the best possible products, please take a moment to fill out the Course Evaluation located at the back of this Course and return it with your Quizzer Answer Sheets.

CCH is registered with the National Association of State Boards of Accountancy (NASBA) as a sponsor of continuing professional education on the National Registry of CPE Sponsors. State boards of accountancy have final authority on the acceptance of individual courses for CPE credit. Complaints regarding registered sponsors may be addressed to the National Registry of CPE Sponsors, 150 Fourth Avenue North, Suite 700, Nashville, TN 37219-2417. Web site: www.nasba.org.

CCH is registered with the National Association of State Boards of Accountancy (NASBA) as a Quality Assurance Service (QAS) sponsor of continuing professional education. State boards of accountancy have final authority on the acceptance of individual courses for CPE credit. Complaints regarding registered sponsors may be addressed to NASBA, 150 Fourth Avenue North, Suite 700, Nashville, TN 37219-2417. Web site: www.nasba.org.

CCH has been approved by the California Tax Education Council to offer courses that provide federal and state credit towards the annual "continuing education" requirement imposed by the State of California. A listing of additional requirements to register as a tax preparer may be obtained by contacting CTEC at P.O. Box 2890, Sacramento, CA, 95812-2890, toll-free by phone at (877) 850-2832, or on the Internet at www.ctec.org.

Processing Fee:	**Recommended CPE:**
$48.00 for Module 1	4 hours for Module 1
$84.00 for Module 2	7 hours for Module 2
$60.00 for Module 3	5 hours for Module 3
$192.00 for all Modules	16 hours for all Modules

One **complimentary copy** of this book is provided with certain CCH publications. Additional copies may be ordered for $37.00 each by calling 1-800-248-3248 (ask for product 0-0970-300). Grading fees are additional.

Quizzer Questions: Module 1

1. Which of the following is a stated objective of the IASB?

   a. To harmonize accounting standards
   b. To develop accounting standards which are similar to U.S. GAAP
   c. To require all countries to be in compliance with IASB GAAP by 2011
   d. To develop a single set of enforceable global accounting standards

2. The IASB is proposing a new type of analyzed combined income statement which would allow for the transparency of which of the following?

   a. Transparency of accruals to accounts receivable
   b. Transparency of accruals to accounts payable
   c. Transparency of transactions
   d. Transparency of the effects of revaluation changes

3. The IASB Framework is written in which of the following styles?

   a. Descriptive
   b. Prescriptive
   c. Quantitative
   d. Qualitative

4. The IASB Framework states that materiality is an aspect of which of the following qualitative characteristics of financial statements?

   a. Relevance
   b. Reliability
   c. Comparability
   d. Understandability

5. Which of the following does the IASB's Framework not cover?

   a. The objective of financial statements
   b. The elements of financial statements
   c. Quantitative characteristics of financial statement information
   d. Qualitative characteristics of financial statement information

6. Which of the following statements is correct?

   a. The Framework takes the position that financial statements that are prepared to meet the needs of management will meet the needs of all users.
   b. The Framework states that financial statements should be prepared on a cash basis.
   c. The Framework states that financial statements should normally be prepared on a "going concern" basis.
   d. The Framework takes the position that financial statements that are prepared to meet the needs of customers will meet the needs of all users.

7. The Framework cites which of the following as one of the four main qualitative characteristics in its Framework?

   a. Cost
   b. Reliability
   c. Neutrality
   d. Completeness

8. According to the Framework, which of the following is a procedure for dealing with a situation in which a decrease in the future economic benefits embodied in an asset takes place over several accounting periods?

   a. Income
   b. Expenses
   c. Liabilities
   d. Depreciation

9. Which of the following is considered to be an element of financial position?

   a. Equity
   b. Income
   c. Expenses
   d. Losses

10. Which of the following does the Framework identify as a form of the financial concept of capital?

   a. Invested money
   b. Borrowed money
   c. The productive capacity of an entity
   d. The operating capability of an entity

11. The IASB is interested in increasing the usage of which of the following in financial reporting?

    a. Historical cost
    b. Fair value
    c. Net present value
    d. Acquisition cost

12. The Framework states that which of the following is less important than relevance when reporting complex financial information?

    a. Materiality
    b. Understandability
    c. Completeness
    d. Neutrality

13. Which of the following is necessary to ensure reliability, according to the Framework?

    a. Comparability
    b. Understandability
    c. Completeness
    d. Fair value measurement

14. Which of the following is directly related to the measurement of financial performance?

    a. Assets
    b. Income
    c. Liabilities
    d. Fair value

15. Which of the following is directly related to the measurement of financial position?

    a. Liabilities
    b. Expenses
    c. Gains
    d. Losses

16. IFRS requires an entity to do all of the following in the opening balance sheet that it prepares as a starting point for its accounting under IFRSs, **except:**

    a. Recognize all assets and liabilities as required by IFRSs
    b. Not recognize items as assets or liabilities if IFRSs do not permit such recognition.
    c. Apply IFRSs in measuring a minimum of 75 percent of all recognized assets and liabilities
    d. Reclassify items that it recognized under previous GAAP as one type of asset that are a different type of asset under IFRSs

17. The cost to generate an entity's first IFRS financial statements should:

    a. Not be a consideration
    b. Not exceed the cost to generate U.S. GAAP statements
    c. Not exceed the benefits to users
    d. Not be reported or explained

18. Which of the following is **not** included in the definition of IFRS?

    a. International Financial Reporting Standards
    b. International Accounting Standards
    c. Statements of Financial Accounting Standards
    d. Interpretations originated by the International Financial Reporting Interpretations Committee

19. The basis of accounting that a first-time adopter used immediately before adopting IFRSs:

    a. Must be U.S. GAAP
    b. Cannot be OCBOA
    c. Is referred to as previous GAAP under IFRS 1
    d. Is converted to fair value under IFRS 1

20. If an entity chooses or is otherwise required to produce comparative figures on a comparable basis for more than one year, the opening IFRS balance sheet, in relation to a reporting date of December 31, 2009, would need to be prepared at a minimum as at which of the following dates?

    a. January 1, 2006
    b. January 1, 2007
    c. January 1, 2008
    d. January 1, 2009

21. IFRS establishes exceptions to the principle that an entity's opening IFRS balance sheet shall comply with each IFRS. Which of the following is **not** a type of transaction that may qualify for one of the exceptions?

    a. Business combinations
    b. Leases
    c. Hedge accounting
    d. Employee benefits

22. There are four situations in which the IASB prohibits retrospective application. Which of the following is one of those situations?

    a. Leases
    b. Estimates
    c. Business combinations
    d. Share-based payment transactions

23. Which of the following statements is **incorrect?**

    a. In regards to derecognition of financial assets and liabilities, in general a first-time adopter shall apply the derecognition requirements in IAS 39 retrospectively for transactions occurring on or after January 1, 2004.

    b. If an entity designated a net position as a hedged item under previous GAAP, it may designate an individual item within that net position as a hedged item under IFRSs, provided that it does so no later than the date of transition to IFRSs

    c. As regards estimates, if more recent evidence that has become available suggests revision of the estimate, IFRS 1 prohibits the treatment of such additional evidence as an adjusting event.

    d. An entity shall not reflect new information regarding estimates in its opening IFRS balance sheet (unless the estimates need adjustment for any differences in accounting policies or there is objective evidence that the estimates were in error).

24. In any financial statements containing historical summaries or comparative information under previous GAAP, IFRS 1 requires an entity to do all of the following *except:*

    a. Label the previous GAAP information prominently as not being prepared under IFRSs

    b. Disclose the nature of the main adjustments that would make it comply with IFRS

    c. Explain how the transition from previous GAAP to IFRSs affected its reported financial position

    d. Quantify the main adjustments required to make it comply with IFRS

25. All of the following statements are correct *except:*

    a. An entity's first IFRS financial statements shall include reconciliations of its equity reported under previous GAAP to its equity under IFRSs for the date of transition to IFRSs.

    b. An entity's first IFRS financial statements shall include reconciliations of its equity reported under previous GAAP to its equity under IFRSs for the end of the latest period presented in the entity's most recent annual financial statements under previous GAAP.

    c. The first set of full IFRS financial statements should present information over the five (or more) years involved on a fully consistent basis.

    d. IAS 34 requires minimum disclosures, which are based on the assumption that users of the interim financial report also have access to the most recent annual financial statements.

Quizzer Questions: Module 2

26. One exception to the more-than-50 percent ownership rule for consolidation is where there is:

   a. An off-balance sheet entity that is categorized as a variable interest entity (VIE)
   b. A limited partnership
   c. A qualified ERISA retirement account
   d. An S corporation

27. The special exemptions in FIN 46R include all of the following *except:*

   a. Special exemption for non-substantive terms, transactions, and arrangements
   b. Special exemption for owners of more than 50 percent of the voting shares
   c. Special exemption for variable interest holders who have difficulty obtaining information
   d. Special exemption for certain entities that are businesses

28. The general rule of FIN 46R is that a primary beneficiary consolidates a VIE if the primary beneficiary has which of the following?

   a. Control over the VIE's core business
   b. Controlling financial interest
   c. Ownership of more than 50 percent of the VIE's equity
   d. Power to control the management of the VIE

29. All off-balance sheet entities are considered to be VIEs. *True or False?*

30. In order for one entity to consolidate an off-balance sheet entity under FIN 46R, there are three requirements that must be satisfied. Those requirements include all of the following *except:*

   a. There must be a VIE.
   b. Entities and/or individuals must have variable interests in the VIE.
   c. An entity or individual must be the primary beneficiary of the VIE.
   d. An entity or individual must own at least 50 percent of the VIE's voting equity.

31. An entity is considered a VIE if, by design, it has one or both of two conditions. One of those conditions is that the total equity investment at risk is not sufficient for it to finance its activities without:

    a. Obtaining additional cash flow from an affiliate
    b. Increasing its revenue to fund financing shortfalls
    c. Obtaining additional subordinated financial support provided by any parties
    d. Reducing its expenses significantly

32. Additional subordinated financial support is referred to as an _____ that will absorb some or all of an entity's expected losses, if they occur.

    a. Additional variable interest
    b. Additional equity investment that is not at risk
    c. Additional receivable
    d. Additional stock sale

33. Which of the following would be an example of an entity that is *not* a VIE?

    a. Entity has a non-recourse loan from a bank with no guarantees
    b. Entity has a recourse loan from a lender with an owner's guarantee
    c. Entity has a non-recourse loan from a bank with an intercompany loan from a related party
    d. Entity has a non-recourse loan with a completion guarantee

34. Company X computes expected losses of $(115,000). X's fair value of equity is $150,000. Which of the following is true based on the results of applying the expected losses method?

    a. X is a VIE because it has expected losses.
    b. X is a VIE because its expected losses of $(115,000) is less than the fair value of its equity of $150,000.
    c. X is not a VIE because the fair value of its equity of $150,000 is greater than the expected losses of ($115,000).
    d. X is not a VIE because it has equity.

35. Company X is a VIE that has the following variable interest holders: Y is a guarantor of X's loan; Z has a loan it made to X that is outstanding; C has a market-value lease with X. Who should perform the test to determine whether X is a VIE?

    a. Y and Z
    b. Y, Z and C
    c. Z and C
    d. C only

36. Which of the following is an example of a variable interest?

    a. Guarantees
    b. Equity investment in a VIE that is not at risk
    c. Most assets
    d. Trade receivables in the normal course of business

37. Which of the following types of lease payments would be a variable interest in a VIE?

    a. No lease payments
    b. Lease payments at above-market value
    c. Lease payments at market value
    d. All lease payments

38. An entity performs the non-recourse financing method to determine if it is a VIE. The entity determines that it does meet the requirements of the test. In this case, the entity is considered to be which of the following?

    a. A VIE
    b. A variable interest
    c. Self-supportive
    d. Dependent

39. When a VIE is reconsidered (retested), the reconsideration should be done at _____ of equity and total assets at the date on which the reconsideration is performed.

    a. Carrying value
    b. Weighted-average value
    c. Fair value
    d. Historical cost value

40. A VIE is reconsidered (retested):

   a. Annually
   b. Quarterly
   c. For each reporting period
   d. Only if a triggering event occurs

41. Which of the following is an example of a variable interest?

   a. Royalty contract that has payments which vary based on an entity's performance
   b. An equity investment in a VIE that is not at risk
   c. Most assets
   d. Accounts payable in the normal course of business

42. In order for an entity to consolidate an off-balance sheet entity under FIN 46R, how many requirements must it meet?

   a. One
   b. Two
   c. Three
   d. Four

43. Which of the following is defined as the variable interest holder that consolidates a VIE?

   a. Issuer
   b. Nonissuer
   c. Majority stockholder
   d. Primary beneficiary

44. A variable interest is a way to provide which of the following to a VIE?

   a. Control
   b. Liability
   c. Stock
   d. Financial support

45. Which of the following types of leases would be a variable interest in a VIE?

   a. Lease with a renewal option at a variable market rate
   b. Lease with an option to acquire at a fixed price
   c. Lease at market value
   d. Lease based on leased assets that are less than 50 percent of the fair value of the VIE's total assets

46. A reporting entity first determines whether it is the primary beneficiary of the VIE at the time when the:

   a. Enterprise obtains a variable interest in the VIE
   b. VIE is initially established
   c. VIE satisfies the expected losses method
   d. Enterprise initially consolidates the VIE

47. A variable interest that is not identified by a contract is referred to as which of the following?

   a. Nonfinancial interest
   b. Explicit interest
   c. Implicit interest
   d. Minority interest

48. The new rules found in ASC Topic 810, as a result of the issuance of FAS 167, are effective for the first annual reporting period that begins after which of the following dates?

   a. January 15, 2009
   b. June 30, 2009
   c. November 15, 2009
   d. December 31, 2009

49. Companies Y, Z and K are unrelated variable interest holders of Company X, a VIE. Y satisfies the power criterion. Z has the obligation to absorb 90 percent of X's losses. K has the right to receive 85 percent of X's benefits from X. Which of the three variable interest holders is the primary beneficiary that consolidates X?

   a. Y is the primary beneficiary because it satisfies the power criterion.
   b. Z is the primary beneficiary because it has the obligation to absorb 90 percent of X's losses.
   c. K is the primary beneficiary because K has the right to receive 85 percent of X's benefits from X.
   d. None of the three variable interest holders is the primary beneficiary.

50. In order for an enterprise to be a primary beneficiary of a VIE, it must have either an obligation to absorb losses or the right to receive benefits from the VIE that;

   a. Could potentially be consolidated
   b. Could potentially be significant to the VIE
   c. Are more than 25 percent of the total for the VIE
   d. Are more than 50 percent of the total for the VIE

51. Company X is a new entity capitalized as follows.

Bank debt	$500,000
Unsecured loan- Company **Y**	300,000
Equity- 100 percent held by Company **Z**	1,200,000
Total	$2,000,000

X purchases real estate for $2 million. X is tested and X is not a VIE. Who is likely to be the primary beneficiary that consolidates X?

a. The bank is the primary beneficiary that consolidates X.
b. Company Y, as the unsecured lender, is the primary beneficiary that consolidates X.
c. Company Z, as the 100 percent equity holder, is the primary beneficiary that consolidates X.
d. None of these entities consolidates X.

52. Assume the same facts as in the previous question except that X is tested and X is a VIE. Who is likely to be the primary beneficiary that consolidates X?

a. The bank is the primary beneficiary that consolidates X.
b. Company Y, as the unsecured lender, is the primary beneficiary that consolidates X.
c. Company Z, as the 100 percent equity holder, is the primary beneficiary that consolidates X.
d. None of these entities consolidate X.

53. Under the tie-breaker rule, the related party that is designated the primary beneficiary is the one that:

a. Is in the same industry as the VIE
b. Absorbs the majority of the VIE's expected losses
c. Is most closely associated with the VIE
d. Has the most power to direct the VIE's activities

54. John is the 100 percent shareholder of X (a lessor VIE) and Y (a lessee). Y leases X's property. The lease is at market value and there is no residual value guarantee, no option to purchase the leased property, and no lease renewal option. Neither John nor Y has guaranteed X's bank loan. How should this transaction **be** accounted for under the FIN 46R (ASC Topic 810) rules?

    a. The lease is not a variable interest and Y should not consolidate X.
    b. John is the primary beneficiary and should consolidate X.
    c. The lease is not a variable interest; Y has an implicit variable interest in X and should consolidate X.
    d. The lease is a variable interest and Y should consolidate X.

55. If the primary beneficiary and the VIE are under common control (e.g., same majority shareholder or owners), the primary beneficiary must initially consolidate the VIE's assets, liabilities and noncontrolling interests at their _____ in the GAAP financial statements of the entity that controls the VIE.

    a. Fair value
    b. Carrying value
    c. Replacement value
    d. Acquisition value

56. In a consolidation of a VIE, the VIE's stockholders' equity should be presented as a:

    a. Part of the consolidated equity
    b. Noncontrolling interest in the stockholders' equity section of the consolidated balance sheet
    c. Deferred credit in the liability section
    d. Deferred credit in the mezzanine section of the balance sheet between liabilities and equity

57. How should a deconsolidation be accounted for under FIN 46R?

    a. A gain or loss should be recognized in the net income attributable to the primary beneficiary.
    b. Any gain or loss is recorded as an adjustment to retained earnings of the primary beneficiary.
    c. No gain or loss is recognized on the transaction.
    d. There should be a reversal of an initially recorded liability.

58. How often should a variable interest holder reconsider whether it is the primary beneficiary of a VIE?

    a. Annually
    b. When there is a triggering event
    c. Continuously
    d. Each time financial statements are issued

59. An entity that holds a variable interest in a VIE, but is not the primary beneficiary, must disclose all of the following *except:*

    a. A tabular comparison of the carrying amounts of assets and liabilities
    b. Carrying amounts of assets in the reporting enterprise's balance sheet that relate to the reporting enterprise's variable interest in the VIE
    c. The reporting enterprise's maximum exposure to loss as a result of its involvement with the VIE
    d. The entity's total initial investment in the VIE

60. An ASU was issued in 2010 deferring the effective date of FAS 167 for which of the following?

    a. Not-for-profit entities
    b. For-profit entities
    c. Certain derivatives
    d. Certain investment funds

Quizzer Questions: Module 3

61. ASC Topic 855 deals with all of the following *except:*

   a. What period should be evaluated in determining events or transactions that should be recognized in the financial statements

   b. Disclosures related to subsequent events that concern income taxes

   c. Circumstances under which an entity should recognize subsequent events in its financial statements

   d. Disclosures required that are related to subsequent events for which guidance is not included in other Codification topics

62. A subsequent event generally occurs:

   a. Before the balance sheet date and before financial statements are issued

   b. After the balance sheet date and after financial statements are issued

   c. After the balance sheet date and before the financial statements are issued

   d. Before the balance sheet date and after the financial statements are issued

63. A Type 2 subsequent event is an event that provides evidence about conditions that:

   a. Existed at the date of the balance sheet

   b. Arose after the balance sheet date

   c. Existed before the balance sheet date but not at the balance sheet date

   d. Could exist at or after the balance sheet date depending on the circumstances

64. Which of the following situations would be considered a recognized subsequent event in accordance with ASC Topic 855?

    a. Litigation is settled related to an event that occurred after the balance sheet date but before the financial statements are issued.

    b. There is a business combination after the balance sheet date but before the financial statements are issued.

    c. A customer for whom receivables are recorded in the amount of $100,000 at the balance sheet date files for bankruptcy before the financial statements are issued.

    d. A building is lost in a fire that occurred after the balance sheet date but before the financial statements are issued.

65. Which of the following is an optional disclosure requirement for an entity that is not an SEC filer under ASC Topic 855?

    a. Pro forma financial data in columnar form on the face of the historical statements

    b. The date through which subsequent events have been evaluated

    c. Whether the date through which subsequent events have been evaluated is the date the financial statements were issued or the date the financial statements were available to be issued

    d. The nature of the subsequent event, including an estimate of its financial effect or a statement that a reasonable estimate could not be made at the time the financial statements were issued

66. Which of the following transactions does FAS 166 (ASC Topic 860) apply to?

    a. Contributions

    b. Subsequent measurement of assets and liabilities

    c. QSPEs

    d. Entire transfer of a financial asset

67. In order for a transfer of a financial asset to be accounted for as a sale, which of the following must occur?

    a. Transferee must not have control over the financial asset.

    b. Transferor surrenders control over the financial asset.

    c. The transferor must be a QSPE.

    d. The asset must be part of a group of transferred assets.

68. If a debtor grants a security interest in certain assets to a lender to serve as collateral, such a transaction is referred to as which of the following?

    a. A transfer of a participating interest with a pledge of collateral
    b. A secured borrowing with pledge of collateral
    c. A secured party with a transfer of financial assets
    d. A transfer of a secured beneficial interest

69. If an entity (servicer) transfers an entire financial asset in a transfer that meets the conditions for a sale, and the servicer enters into a servicing contract to service the transferred asset, how should the servicer account for the transaction?

    a. The servicer should recognize at fair value a servicing asset or liability.
    b. No entry is required as the value of the asset or liability is part of the transferred value.
    c. The transferred value should be prorated between the transferred asset and the servicing asset or liability based on relative carrying value.
    d. At the time of transfer, the amortization method should be used to measure the servicing asset or liability.

70. If a financial asset can contractually be prepaid so that the holder would not recover substantially all of its recorded investment, how should that asset be subsequently measured?

    a. At the original carrying value
    b. At lower of cost or market value
    c. The same way debt securities classified as trading securities are measured
    d. The same way assets that are depreciated on a straight-line basis are measured

71. An entity (transferor) is deciding whether to aggregate disclosures for multiple transfers of financial assets. In making the determination as to whether to aggregate, the entity should consider all of the following *except:*

    a. The types of financial assets transferred
    b. The frequency of the transfers in relation to each other
    c. Risks related to the transferred asset
    d. The nature of the transferor's continuing involvement in the transferred asset

72. Assume a transferor creates an interest-only strip from a loan and transfers the interest-only strip, but not the loan, to a securitization entity. Which of the following is correct?

    a. The interest-only strip is considered an entire financial asset and requires sales accounting.

    b. The interest-only strip meets the definition of a participating interest but not an entire financial asset.

    c. The interest-only strip is not considered an entire financial asset and does not meet the definition of a participating interest.

    d. The interest-only strip is considered an entire financial asset and also a participating interest.

73. Assume that multiple advances are made to one borrower under a single contract, such as a line of credit. The advance is transferred in its entirety and it loses its identity by becoming part of the larger loan balance. The transferor does not retain any interest in the larger balance. How should the advance be accounted for?

    a. As a separate unit of account

    b. As a sale eligible for sale accounting

    c. As a deferred transaction

    d. As a participating interest

74. Which of the following is an objective of the disclosures required by ASC Topic 860?

    a. To provide auditors with a better understanding of the financial statements of an entity

    b. To clarify how revenue and expenses related to transferred assets are reported

    c. To provide more information on the nature of any restrictions that relate to a transferred financial asset

    d. To clarify how often a transferor transfers assets as opposed to other entities within a given industry

75. When the amortization method is used to measure a service asset or liability, the asset or liability must be assessed for which of the following at each reporting period?

    a. Appreciation

    b. Depreciation

    c. Impairment

    d. Decreased obligation

76. Which of the following is the source of authoritative U.S. GAAP?

    a. Accounting Standards Updates (ASUs)
    b. The International Accounting Standards Board (IASB)
    c. Statement of Financial Accounting Standards (FASs)
    d. The FASB Accounting Standards Codification™

77. Changes to the source of authoritative U.S. GAAP are communicated through which of the following?

    a. Accounting Standards Updates (ASUs)
    b. Emerging Issues Task Force (EITFs)
    c. Statement of Financial Accounting Standards (FASs)
    d. International Accounting Standard (IASs)

78. The FASB Accounting Standards Codification is effective for interim and annual periods ending after which of the following dates?

    a. June 3, 2009
    b. July 1, 2009
    c. September 15, 2009
    d. December 31, 2009

79. Which of the following was the first ASU to be issued?

    a. ASU 2008-01
    b. ASU 2009-01
    c. ASU 2009-09
    d. ASU 2010-01

80. The first ASU was issued to amend the Codification for the issuance of which of the following?

    a. FAS 141(R)
    b. FAS 157
    c. FAS 159
    d. FAS 168

81. Under ASC 740, as amended, if an entity pays income taxes attributable to its owners the transaction is accounted for as which of the following?

    a. The transaction is treated as one with the entity and subject to ASC 740.

    b. The transaction is treated as one with the owners and not subject to ASC 740.

    c. The transaction is subject to ASC 740 but limited disclosures apply.

    d. The transaction is subject to ASC 740 and the income tax related to the owners is treated as a shareholder loan.

82. Which of the following is *not* one of the questions that the issuance of ASU 2009-06 attempted to clarify?

    a. Is the income tax paid by the entity attributable to the entity or its owners?

    b. What constitutes a tax position for a pass-through entity or a tax-exempt not-for-profit entity?

    c. Should nonpublic entities be required to provide more disclosures than public entities?

    d. How should accounting for uncertainty in income taxes be applied when a group of related entities comprise both taxable and nontaxable entities?

83. One of the criteria that must be met in order for ASU 2009-12 to apply to an investment is that:

    a. The entity's primary business activity does not involve investing its assets.

    b. Ownership in the entity is not represented by units of investments.

    c. The entity cannot be the primary reporting entity.

    d. The investment does not have a readily determinable fair value.

84. According to ASU 2009-12, if the reporting entity does not know when it will be able to redeem the investment or it is not able to redeem the investment in the near term at net asset value per share (or its equivalent), the fair value measurement of the investment must be categorized as which of the following?

    a. Level 1

    b. Level 2

    c. Level 3

    d. Level 4

85. One of the changes made by ASU 2009-13 is that it eliminates use of the:

   a. Residual method
   b. Relative selling price method
   c. Average selling price method
   d. Estimated selling price method

86. The relative selling price method allocates any discount in the arrangement proportionally to each deliverable on the basis of each deliverable's:

   a. Cost
   b. Cost less overhead
   c. Selling price
   d. Selling price less cost to deliver

87. How is a tangible product that includes both hardware and software that is essential to the tangible product's functionality accounted for according to ASU 2009-14?

   a. The hardware is included as part of the software, which is included under the software revenue guidance.
   b. If the software is essential to the tangible product's functionality, the software is still included within the scope of the software revenue guidance.
   c. Hardware components containing software components are excluded from the software revenue guidance.
   d. The hardware is excluded from the revenue guidance but the software is included.

88. If a parent deconsolidates a subsidiary and there is not a nonreciprocal transfer to owners, the parent should account for the transaction by:

   a. Recognizing a gain or loss in net income
   b. Recognizing a gain or loss in other comprehensive income
   c. Treating the transaction under the nonmonetary transaction rules
   d. Recording any excess on the transaction as part of shareholders' equity

89. Upon deconsolidation of a subsidiary, an entity should measure retained investment in the subsidiary at which of the following?

    a. Cost

    b. Fair value

    c. Selling price

    d. Residual value

90. Under ASU 2010-06, Fair Value Measurements and Disclosures (ASC 820): *Improving Disclosures about Fair Value Measurements,* an entity is required to provide disclosure for each:

    a. Individual asset and liability

    b. Class of assets and liabilities

    c. Significant asset and liability

    d. Line item of assets and liabilities on the balance sheet

TOP ACCOUNTING ISSUES FOR 2011 CPE COURSE   (0777-3)

Module 1: Answer Sheet

NAME _____

COMPANY NAME _____

STREET _____

CITY, STATE, & ZIP CODE _____

BUSINESS PHONE NUMBER _____

E-MAIL ADDRESS _____

DATE OF COMPLETION _____

On the next page, please answer the Multiple Choice questions by indicating the appropriate letter next to the corresponding number. Please answer the True/False questions by marking "T" or "F" next to the corresponding number.

An $48.00 processing fee will be charged for each user submitting Module 1 for grading.

Please remove both pages of the Answer Sheet from this book and return them with your completed Evaluation Form to CCH at the address below. You may also fax your Answer Sheet to CCH at 773-866-3084.

You may also go to **www.cchtestingcenter.com** to complete your Quizzer online.

METHOD OF PAYMENT:

☐ Check Enclosed   ☐ Visa   ☐ Master Card   ☐ AmEx

☐ Discover   ☐ CCH Account* _____

Card No. _____ Exp. Date _____

Signature _____

* Must provide CCH account number for this payment option

EXPRESS GRADING: Please fax my Course results to me by 5:00 p.m. the business day following your receipt of this Answer Sheet. By checking this box I authorize CCH to charge $19.00 for this service.

☐ Express Grading $19.00   Fax No. _____

Mail or fax to:
CCH Continuing Education Department
4025 W. Peterson Ave.
Chicago, IL 60646-6085
1-800-248-3248
Fax: 773-866-3084

CCH
a Wolters Kluwer business

TOP ACCOUNTING ISSUES FOR 2011 CPE COURSE   (0777-3)

Module 1: Answer Sheet

Please answer the Multiple Choice questions by indicating the appropriate letter next to the corresponding number. Please answer the True/False questions by marking "T" or "F" next to the corresponding number.

1. ___	8. ___	14. ___	20. ___
2. ___	9. ___	15. ___	21. ___
3. ___	10. ___	16. ___	22. ___
4. ___	11. ___	17. ___	23. ___
5. ___	12. ___	18. ___	24. ___
6. ___	13. ___	19. ___	25. ___
7. ___			

Please complete the Evaluation Form (located after the Module 3 Answer Sheet) and return it with this Quizzer Answer Sheet to CCH at the address on the previous page. Thank you.

TOP ACCOUNTING ISSUES FOR 2011 CPE COURSE   (0778-3)

Module 2: Answer Sheet

NAME _____

COMPANY NAME _____

STREET _____

CITY, STATE, & ZIP CODE _____

BUSINESS PHONE NUMBER _____

E-MAIL ADDRESS _____

DATE OF COMPLETION _____

On the next page, please answer the Multiple Choice questions by indicating the appropriate letter next to the corresponding number. Please answer the True/False questions by marking "T" or "F" next to the corresponding number.

A $84.00 processing fee will be charged for each user submitting Module 2 for grading.

Please remove both pages of the Answer Sheet from this book and return them with your completed Evaluation Form to CCH at the address below. You may also fax your Answer Sheet to CCH at 773-866-3084.

You may also go to **www.cchtestingcenter.com** to complete your exam online.

METHOD OF PAYMENT:

☐ Check Enclosed   ☐ Visa   ☐ Master Card   ☐ AmEx

☐ Discover   ☐ CCH Account* _____

Card No. _____ Exp. Date _____

Signature _____

* Must provide CCH account number for this payment option

EXPRESS GRADING: Please fax my Course results to me by 5:00 p.m. the business day following your receipt of this Answer Sheet. By checking this box I authorize CCH to charge $19.00 for this service.

☐ Express Grading $19.00   Fax No. _____

Mail or fax to:
CCH Continuing Education Department
4025 W. Peterson Ave.
Chicago, IL 60646-6085
1-800-248-3248
Fax: 773-866-3084

®CCH
a Wolters Kluwer business

TOP ACCOUNTING ISSUES FOR 2011 CPE COURSE   (0778-3)

Module 2: Answer Sheet

Please answer the Multiple Choice questions by indicating the appropriate letter next to the corresponding number. Please answer the True/False questions by marking "T" or "F" next to the corresponding number.

26. ___	35. ___	44. ___	53. ___
27. ___	36. ___	45. ___	54. ___
28. ___	37. ___	46. ___	55. ___
29. ___	38. ___	47. ___	56. ___
30. ___	39. ___	48. ___	57. ___
31. ___	40. ___	49. ___	58. ___
32. ___	41. ___	50. ___	59. ___
33. ___	42. ___	51. ___	60. ___
34. ___	43. ___	52. ___	

Please complete the Evaluation Form (located after the Module 3 Answer Sheet) and return it with this Quizzer Answer Sheet to CCH at the address on the previous page. Thank you.

TOP ACCOUNTING ISSUES FOR 2011 CPE COURSE   (0779-3)

Module 3: Answer Sheet

NAME _____

COMPANY NAME _____

STREET _____

CITY, STATE, & ZIP CODE _____

BUSINESS PHONE NUMBER _____

E-MAIL ADDRESS _____

DATE OF COMPLETION _____

On the next page, please answer the Multiple Choice questions by indicating the appropriate letter next to the corresponding number. Please answer the True/False questions by marking "T" or "F" next to the corresponding number.

A $60.00 processing fee will be charged for each user submitting Module 3 for grading.

Please remove both pages of the Answer Sheet from this book and return them with your completed Evaluation Form to CCH at the address below. You may also fax your Answer Sheet to CCH at 773-866-3084.

You may also go to **www.cchtestingcenter.com** to complete your exam online.

METHOD OF PAYMENT:

☐ Check Enclosed   ☐ Visa   ☐ Master Card   ☐ AmEx

☐ Discover   ☐ CCH Account* _____

Card No. _____ Exp. Date _____

Signature _____

* Must provide CCH account number for this payment option

EXPRESS GRADING: Please fax my Course results to me by 5:00 p.m. the business day following your receipt of this Answer Sheet. By checking this box I authorize CCH to charge $19.00 for this service.

☐ Express Grading $19.00   Fax No. _____

Mail or fax to:
CCH Continuing Education Department
4025 W. Peterson Ave.
Chicago, IL 60646-6085
1-800-248-3248
Fax: 773-866-3084

®CCH
a Wolters Kluwer business

Module 3: Answer Sheet

Please answer the Multiple Choice questions by indicating the appropriate letter next to the corresponding number. Please answer the True/False questions by marking "T" or "F" next to the corresponding number.

61. ___	69. ___	77. ___	84. ___
62. ___	70. ___	78. ___	85. ___
63. ___	71. ___	79. ___	86. ___
64. ___	72. ___	80. ___	87. ___
65. ___	73. ___	81. ___	88. ___
66. ___	74. ___	82. ___	89. ___
67. ___	75. ___	83. ___	90. ___
68. ___	76. ___		

Please complete the Evaluation Form (located after the Module 3 Answer Sheet) and return it with this Quizzer Answer Sheet to CCH at the address on the previous page. Thank you.

TOP ACCOUNTING ISSUES FOR 2011 CPE COURSE   (0970-3)

Evaluation Form

Please take a few moments to fill out and mail or fax this evaluation to CCH so that we can better provide you with the type of self-study programs you want and need. Thank you.

About This Program

1. Please circle the number that best reflects the extent of your agreement with the following statements:

	Strongly Agree				Strongly Disagree
a. The Course objectives were met.	5	4	3	2	1
b. This Course was comprehensive and organized.	5	4	3	2	1
c. The content was current and technically accurate.	5	4	3	2	1
d. This Course was timely and relevant.	5	4	3	2	1
e. The prerequisite requirements were appropriate.	5	4	3	2	1
f. This Course was a valuable learning experience.	5	4	3	2	1
g. The Course completion time was appropriate.	5	4	3	2	1

2. This Course was most valuable to me because of:

    _____ Continuing Education credit   _____ Convenience of format
    _____ Relevance to my practice/   _____ Timeliness of subject matter
    employment   _____ Reputation of author
    _____ Price
    _____ Other (please specify) _____

3. How long did it take to complete this Course? (Please include the total time spent reading or studying reference materials and completing CPE Quizzer).

    Module 1 _____   Module 2 _____   Module 3 _____

4. What do you consider to be the strong points of this Course?

5. What improvements can we make to this Course?

Evaluation Form *cont'd*

General Interests

1. Preferred method of self-study instruction:
   ____ Text ____ Audio ____ Computer-based/Multimedia ____Video

2. What specific topics would you like CCH to develop as self-study CPE programs? ___
   _____
   _____
   _____

3. Please list other topics of interest to you _____
   _____
   _____

About You

1. Your profession:

   ____ Accountant   ____ Auditor
   ____ Controller   ____ CPA
   ____ Enrolled Agent   ____ Risk Manager
   ____ Other (please specify) _____

2. Your employment:

   ____ Self-employed   ____ Public Accounting Firm
   ____ Service Industry   ____ Non-Service Industry
   ____ Banking/Finance   ____ Government
   ____ Education   ____ Other _____

3. Size of firm/corporation:

   ____ 1   ____ 2-5   ____ 6-10   ____ 11-20   ____ 21-50   ____ 51+

4. Your Name _____
   Firm/Company Name _____
   Address _____
   City, State, Zip Code _____
   E-mail Address _____

THANK YOU FOR TAKING THE TIME TO COMPLETE THIS SURVEY!

NOTES

NOTES

NOTES

NOTES